Tarot
of the
Magicians

OSWALD WIRTH

Ⓠ WEISER BOOKS
San Francisco, CA / Newburyport, MA

This published in 2012 by Red Wheel/Weiser, LLC
With offices at:
665 Third Street, Suite 400
San Francisco, CA 94107
www.redwheelweiser.com

First published in English in 1985 by Samuel Weiser, Inc.
First published in Paris in 1927 under the original title:
Le Tarot, des Imagiers du Moyen Age

ISBN: 978-1-57863-531-3

Library of Congress Cataloging-in-Publication Data available upon request
Cover design by Jim Warner
Interior by Kathryn Sky-Peck

Printed in the United States of America
MAL

10 9 8 7 6 5 4 3 2 1

Contents

PART ONE:
The Tarot

PART TWO:
The Symbolism of the Twenty-Two Keys to the
Secret Knowledge of the Middle Ages

PART THREE:
Résumé and Recapitulation

PART FOUR:
The Tarot as Applied to Divination

To the Memory of Stanislas de Guaita

Introduction by Mary K. Greer

A Swiss, an Italian, a Spaniard and a Dutch-Frenchman walked into a bar . . . It sounds like the beginning of a joke, but in the artistic and metaphysical melting pot of *fin de siècle* Paris this was a formula for a creative and volatile, indeed, alchemical mixture as profound in the esoteric world as the symbolist and expressionist movements were in the art and literary world. In 1888, the same year as the birth of England's Hermetic Order of the Golden Dawn, Oswald Wirth joined Stanislas de Guaita, Papus, and Joséphin Péladan in founding the *Ordre Kabbalistique de la Rose-Croix* ("Kabbalistic Order of the Rosy Cross"). The following year Wirth, under the direction of de Guaita, created a landmark Major Arcana Tarot deck that has been reproduced here for the first time since 1889 in a form that you can cut out to make your own deck.

THE MAN AND THE DECK

Joseph Paul Oswald Wirth was born on August 5, 1860 (d. 1943), around 9 a.m. in Brienz, near Bern, Switzerland to Alsatian parents. His father was a painter and Oswald assisted him at his work. Around 1880 he came to Paris, served briefly in the army, tried working as an accountant, joined the Freemasons, and took up the study of hypnotism, magnetic healing and occultism. He soon fell under the sway of the wealthy Italian nobleman, Stanislas de Guaita (1861–1897), who, at 26, was a year younger, and already a well-known poet and author in French esoteric circles. Wirth became de Guaita's close friend and personal secretary, beginning a nearly two year journey that would culminate in the Tarot deck, *Les 22 Arcanes du Tarot Kabbalistique*, originally published by Georges Poirel in an edition of 350 copies.

A hundred years earlier, in 1781, Antoine Court de Gébelin (1719–1784) announced in volume eight of his encyclopedia, *Le Monde Primitif*, that the

Tarot, formerly seen as a card game, came from Egypt and portrayed ancient occult mysteries. Eight years after that, Jean-Baptiste Alliette (1738–1791), under the *nom de plume* Etteilla, published the first specifically occult deck, extensively modified to carry out the Egyptian and creation motifs described by de Gébelin.

De Guaita didn't think much of Etteilla's deck. He felt that the true occult mysteries were already inherent in the traditional French Tarot de Marseille. So, with Wirth as the artist, they designed the *22 Arcana of the Kabbalistic Tarot*, adding esoteric symbolism to the Marseille model. Their deck would be the first to depict the Kabbalistic correspondences and magical philosophy of the great French magician, Éliphas Lévi (Alphonse Louis Constant, 1804–75). Based on a seminal book on the Kabbalah, the *Sepher Yetzirah*, Lévi linked the Hebrew numbers, letters and astrology to the Tarot. Although Lévi had died when de Guaita and Wirth were still youths, many of his unpublished papers were obtained by de Guaita for his extensive esoteric library.

The Wirth Tarot illustrated the 1889 edition of *Le Tarot des Bohémiens* by Papus (Gérard Encausse, 1865–1916), which also contained an essay by Wirth. As jealous animosity developed between them, Papus decided to create his own original Tarot card designs, illustrated by the talented young artist Jean-Gabriel Goulinat (1883-1972), which he used in his 1909 book *Tarot Divinatoire* and in the 1911 reprint of *Le Tarot des Bohémiens*.

Not only were there tensions within the order, but when Oswald Wirth and Stanislas de Guaita infiltrated a rival occult church and published an exposé describing it as a "Temple of Satan," the Kabbalistic Order of the Rosy Cross found itself in the middle of a violent magical conflict that was known as "The War of the Roses." The writer Joris Huysmans, in a novel and an article, charged de Guaita with murdering the Abbé Boullan by occult means. De Guaita challenged him to a duel and Huysmans backed down. There were more duels that included a comedy of errors of misfired guns and collapsed carriages, culminating when Papus and the publisher Jules Bois finally wounded each other with sabers (which didn't stop them from later becoming friends). De Guaita died suddenly in 1897—some said of a drug overdose while others claimed it was the result of a demonic attack.

After de Guaita's death Oswald Wirth took a civil service job in a government library and lived quietly with his widowed sister and his niece. He went on to become a major figure in French Freemasonry, promoting through books and articles an esoteric interpretation of the symbolism of their rituals and of the Tarot as a compendium of Masonic knowledge. Wirth clearly identified himself as the Hermit in the Tarot, which in his deck is supposedly a self-portrait. His occult pseudonym, Diogène Gondeau, alludes to the ascetic Greek philosopher Diogenes, who is usually shown holding up a lamp in his search for "an honest man."

In 1926 Wirth designed a new version of his deck incorporating several changes and including metallic-gold ink and elaborate art nouveau borders containing thinly-disguised glyphs from the early Phoenician alphabet. A year later, he published the book you now hold in your hands, originally titled *Le Tarot des Imagiers du Moyen-Âge* ("Tarot of the Medieval Image-Makers") to share what he had learned in forty years studying the Tarot. But, it wasn't easy getting there.

THE TAROT CHAPEL

Wirth tells us in his preface that he tragically lost the first manuscript of his Tarot opus, but was then given the opportunity for 'uninterrupted meditation . . . stimulated by a Gothic background' at a location 'with one of the finest landscapes in France.' It was there that he was able to complete his second version. It was precisely for the unmatched beauty of the landscape that American heiress, Mary Wallace Shillito, built *Le Château des Avenières* on a hill top in the south of France. Mary Shillito was a devotee of Paris' esoteric, literary and artistic salons who married an engineer, occultist and amateur archeologist of Assyria and Egypt, Assan Farid Dina (1871-1928). Dina was well thought of in metaphysical circles, and together with his wife, they hosted gatherings of prominent occultists including René Guénon, Papus, Paul Chacornac, René Schwaller de Lubicz and Oswald Wirth.

Built in the Gothic style (note Wirth's description above), the Château (now a five-star hotel known for its breathtaking views) contains an even more Gothic chapel, completed in 1917. The walls are covered with enamel and gold mosaics depicting all the images of the Tarot Major Arcana. It is likely that Wirth retreated here to write his book. The chapel art and Dina's own obsession with archaic alphabets must have inspired the revised art nouveau Tarot deck Wirth published in 1926. French writer Alain Bocher speculates that the Tarot mosaics were actually designed by Wirth himself because of the unquestionable similarities. However, there are also images from the deck created by fellow Order member, Papus with the artist Georges Goulinat. But, no matter who copied whom, the chapel makes it clear by the way its images ascend into the vaulted ceiling, that Wirth's own deck, rather than being a psychological or fortune-telling one was created as a moral and initiatory Tarot that describes the apotheosis of human kind.

SACRED SYMBOLS

In his preface, Wirth gives an eloquent description of the power of medieval symbolism that he discovered upon following de Guaita's instructions to restore the purity of the Tarot. "We should learn to appreciate this masterpiece of the Middle Ages; worthy of our admiration to the same extent as are the Gothic cathedrals and philosophic Alchemy." Sacred symbols that "put the esotericism of initiation into picture forms" had more to do with the arts of the stone cutters of the great cathedrals than with the more distant Egyptians. But, both were thought to contain a deep, silent wisdom common to all cultures and kept alive in rituals like those of the Freemasons. These ideas are found in teachings called the Perennial Philosophy, Ancient Wisdom Tradition, the Secret Doctrine or Teachings of the Ages.

Medieval consciousness experienced images as conduits for otherworldly forces to effect the physical world. Statues and paintings were an invocation as well as a remembrance of the forces depicted. In a sense, the Tarot remains as a kind of last gasp of the medieval ideal of a cosmological order that continually reasserts itself in the lives of gods and men. There can be little doubt that in the minds of those who created the deck, it depicted relative positions in society, virtues and values, inevitable forces, and a triumphant end with which everyone could be expected to essentially agree.

Wirth's original title, *Le Tarot des Imagiers du Moyen Age* ("Tarot of the Medieval Image-Makers"), alludes to human kind as constructive workers in the eternal creative work of the Divine. The original word, *imagier*, is incredibly rich as it can be translated as sculptor, artisan, stonecutter, illustrator or symbolist. For Wirth, it referred to the operative craftsmen—architects and builders who made the temples and cathedrals—who would have belonged to a guild that initiated apprentices into the craft secrets that included sacred symbolism. In a broader sense, each one of us partakes of the double nature of artist-artisan, symbolist and builder shaping the rough stone into the perfect cube for a Temple, which is both the perfected self and a world in harmony with all its parts. Achievement of the "Great Work" of union with the Divine is only a first step; it is to be followed by a commitment to remain earth-bound and work toward the betterment of all society.

Most of today's Tarot readers come from a modern perspective that blends Jungian, Neopagan, New Thought, New Age, and earth-centered Eco-Spiritualism with New Physics and a sprinkling of Theosophical concepts in a kind of quasi-pantheistic idea of the immanence of Spirit in all beings and in nature. It is important to understand that Oswald Wirth came from a European world view that had only recently emerged from the rationalist ideals of Enlightenment Humanism found in such advocates of equality, social-responsibility and revolution as Benjamin Franklin and Thomas Paine. The occult Tarot blended this with a more esoteric transcendent deism espoused in Rosicrucianism and Freemasonry and in the practice of theurgic magic. Major influences include Henry Cornelius Agrippa, Paracelsus, Jacob Böhme, Emanuel Swedenborg, Martinez de Pasquale and Louis Claude de Saint-Martin. The idea was to work with Nature but ultimately transcend it. The thread that runs through all this is the Perennial Philosophy with roots in Pythagorean numerology, Neoplatonism and Hermeticism, which was blended with Classical philosophy whose re-emergence had spearheaded the Renaissance. By the seventeenth century a system of correspondences had emerged that included alchemy, astrology and Kabbalah—all suggesting that a direct knowledge of the nature of god (*gnosis*) is possible through a kind of spiritual illumination.

TRANSCENDENTAL MAGIC AND THE ASTRAL LIGHT

Éliphas Lévi stood at the crossroads as the Romantic reaction to the Enlightenment wound down into the spiritual aesthete of the Symbolists. He taught what he called "the Science of Transcendental Magic" in which he sought to reconcile magic and religion. (Two of his books were translated into English by A.E. Waite and a third by Aleister Crowley.) His was a metaphysical idealism, the key of which he proclaimed could be found in a single book: a universal key, "which is the summary of all sciences, which can resolve all problems by its infinite combinations, which speaks by evoking thought, is the inspirer and moderator of all possible conceptions, and the masterpiece perhaps of the human mind." *This book, this "Great Arcanum of Transcendental Magic," is, he tells us, the Tarot.* (The terms Major and Minor Arcana were coined by his follower, Paul Christian.)

The English title of this book, *Tarot of the Magicians*, is found in Chapter Seven's cosmogonic outline: "*The god of Tarot is the Magician*, the father of all things, the eternal generator" who, as Wirth explains, symbolizes creative activity and will, the idea before conception. This idea directly addresses the magic of transcendence that for Lévi and Wirth was accessed through the Astral Light, a sort of etheric electromagnetism (aether, odic fluid, vril, orgone, prana, Qi and *Star Wars*' The Force) that operates uniquely on each plane of consciousness: "It is through this astral light that the signs and wonders of magic are mediated," allowing the molding of energy through will into physical forms.

For both Wirth and Lévi incarnation in the material world serves Spirit by forcing Spirit to free itself from the limitations of an illusion of separateness, both from the Divine and from others. Nature becomes a kind of school in which we are to see through the illusion of separateness that matter imparts. Wirth follows Lévi in seeing the Devil as the force which condenses astral light into a denser animal magnetism—the instinct for physical survival—essential for the life of the body. As a radical force for self-preservation it sees each entity as separate and sees Nature and others for its own benefit—in a way, selfishly damming or short circuiting the free flow of energy. It is a person's direction of this force by a pure will that is the secret to using its qualities for good. This is one of the great lessons that the Tarot teaches.

MAKING THE INVISIBLE VISIBLE

Although the Major Arcana-only Wirth Tarot has never become wildly popular in English-speaking countries, these twenty-two cards continue to intrigue and inspire new expressions (see the list of decks at the end). Perhaps it is because Wirth achieved what few deck designers have done: "a perfect unity of symbolism in which no element is unnecessary." It is this quality that we find in the most iconic decks, from the Renaissance Italian, to the Marseille, to the Rider-Waite and Thoth. A fellow member of the Kabbalistic Order of the Rosy Cross, Sâr Péladan, wrote, "Making the invisible visible: that is the true purpose of art and its only reason for existence. . . . Art is a little piece of God within a painting. . . . If you create a perfect form, a soul will come and inhabit it."

This is true of the Wirth deck, which, like the other iconic decks, seems to endure through time. When the artist, Wirth, worked with the esotericist, de Guaita, depicting Éliphas Lévi's vision of Tarot, he achieved something more than a projection of his own personality. Rather, it is a work edited to achieve not just beauty but faithfulness to an intent that transcends the personal. Wirth drew this deck many times over the years, with slight changes, to illustrate his articles on Masonic Tarot, and as simplified drawings for this book (the illustrations used here were redrawn by Michel Simeon for a modern French edition). They culminated in his 1926 portfolio of gilded art nouveau Tarot plates.

One other change should be noted. The title of the very important Appendix that explains the book's key symbols was rewritten in the 1966 Tchou edition. The 1926 original translates as, "Some Indications on the Symbolism of the *Pantacles* which Accompany the Text." It should read "pantacles" wherever the appendix text previously read "pentacles." This edition of the book has been corrected. A pantacle is *any magical figure* intended to produce results, a mental aid and prompt during magical workings. According to Éliphas Lévi, the pantacle is a complete and perfect synthesis expressed by a single sign, which serves to focus all intellectual force into a glance, a recollection, a touch. It is a starting-point for the efficient projection of will. By contrast, a pentacle (a pentagram within a circle) is the preeminent or archetypal pantacle, representing the Microcosm. Wirth tells us, "At the sign of a pantacle we ought to enter meditation and through ourselves find the all (*pan*), the world of thoughts to which it is related."

FOR TAROT NEWBIES: HOW TO READ THIS BOOK

Tarot newcomers and those interested primarily in reading the cards may get bogged down by the order in which this work is presented. I suggest the following plan:

- Read only the first part of Chapter One on the origins of Tarot (there are some historical errors that are understandable for the time).

- Proceed directly to Part Two on the symbolism of the trumps, referring to the Appendix as needed. (Some familiarity with the myths of Isis/ Osiris and of Ishtar/Gilgamesh helps.)

- Next, study Part Four on the Tarot applied to divination.

- Also helpful is Chapter 11 in Part Three, as it summarizes card interpretations in terms of both good and bad characteristics.

- After this, read the book through from beginning to end. And then read it again a decade or so later.

Those who truly want to experience Oswald Wirth as their teacher and guide will *read this book in the order he intended*. To get the most from the experience, lay out your own cards in the patterns described in Part One using the cards included in the back of this book or another Wirth-influenced or Marseille-style deck. (A list of Wirth-inspired decks can be found at the end of this introduction.) Following his reasoning is like being taken through an intricate and confusing landscape by an experienced guide who points out key elements that will help you make important connections when you later explore on your own.

While his explanations are only one of many Tarot perspectives, they effectively synthesize the great occult and metaphysical ideas that coalesced in France in the late 19th and early 20th centuries. For English-speakers, it can broaden and deepen our parochial Anglo-American Tarot view, shaped primarily by the Hermetic Order of the Golden Dawn and New Thought authors, Paul Foster Case and Eden Gray.

The Meditation Patterns

For Oswald Wirth, the underlying structure of the Tarot is revealed first by viewing the twenty-two arcana in a circle, neatly solving the perennial problem of where the Fool goes. He then divides them into two rows of eleven cards that provide matching pairs, which Wirth next groups into quaternities. Regarding the two rows, the first row (cards 1 through 11) is an active, masculine set expressing what we possess innately. The second row (cards 12 through 21 & 0) is a passive, feminine set that is receptive and susceptible to the cosmic forces that surround us. It helps to think of these two sets as the grammatical active and passive voices. The difference is similar to that between "John throws the ball" and "The ball was thrown at John." We can see this distinction more clearly in the two cards of the Lovers and the Star: The Lovers is about actively making a choice, and the Star is about being at the effect of one's destiny. This dual process forms the bedrock for Wirth's understanding of the Tarot. He firmly believed that anyone who studies these sets will eventually learn all they need to know about the Tarot and about humanity's purpose within the cosmos.

When laid out in two rows, the second row begins with the Hanged Man. For the Hermeticist or alchemist, this card, half-way through, marks the accomplishment of the Great Work—but only within oneself. The rest of the cards show how the Divine works upon the Adept after he or she has completely surrendered to that working.

In both this book and in the short follow-up, *Introduction to the Study of Tarot*, Wirth gives directions for learning directly from the pairs, although the technique is couched in paradox.

- "The main secret is to put the characters together in pairs and listen to their conversation."

- "By their contrast with each other, you can learn to know them best."

- "To make the Tarot speak is our objective, but the arcana only speak to those who have learned to understand them."

- "Words do not suffice for what we see, which is why they are mute. But, out of the need to communicate what is seen in reverie, both the poet and prophet is born."

In order to demonstrate that the cards work at different levels for different purposes, Wirth surveys the cards several times: first, he describes the symbolism that informs any reading of the cards, then a cosmological overview, followed by the path of Initiation, the work of an Hermetic or Alchemical Adept, and finally the allegories of Freemasonry. Some cards have a totally opposite meaning at different levels, for instance the Moon card is about getting lost in deception and illusion at one level, but at another it is about recognizing the symbolic and allegorical truths in old myths, mysteries and superstitions.

DIVINATION

Despite his many-layered approach, Wirth never loses sight of the practicalities of mundane divination. When he first published his deck in 1889 Wirth tells us he was prejudiced against divination. However, many friends asked him for readings, which he could not deny them, and they reported back on the incredible accuracy of what was revealed. After much experience he concluded that, "To divine is to imagine rightly," and that we must educate and discipline the imagination to make divination into a sacred art.

> "Divination is the mother of all our knowledges, all our philosophies and of all our religions. It is worthy of respect and deserves to be taken seriously . . . One must divine in order to understand and acquire the clairvoyance of which the narrow rationalist in his blindness deprives himself. This rationalist runs the risk of assuming the heavy gait of a learned beast."

His spread, which takes the form of a case being tried in court, is as iconic in France as the Celtic Cross Spread is in the English-speaking Tarot world. It provides a perfect opportunity to listen to the cards converse as the prosecuting and defense attorneys argue their case and the judge evaluates their pleas.

Ultimately, for Wirth, the Tarot tells us where we came from, what we are, and where we are going (past, present, future). The purpose is to regain Paradise, but in a Universal Regeneration in which, ultimately, all humans come as close as nature will allow to Divine Perfection. We humans become artists in order to complete a Divine Work that brings order to human chaos. "We become Free Artists, Free Builders, Freemasons, carrying out the plan of the Supreme Architect via the law of life which is that of creative work."

MARY K. GREER
MARCH, 2012

Author's Preface

Indulging as I was in the practice of occultism and before studying its theories deeply, I was, at the beginning of 1887, applying my hypnotic skills on a sick woman who fell asleep under my influence. She was a lucid patient who informed me of the state of her organs and of the effect produced by my fluid. Her tendency to chatter came out in spontaneous revelations, quite unexpected, to which I only paid moderate heed.

One day however, I was struck by my clairvoyant's tone of conviction, which seemed to perceive with more accuracy than usual as she said 'You will receive a letter with a red seal of armorial bearings!' This she exclaimed as if this fact were of particular importance.

'Can you see who the letter will come from?'

'It is written by a young fair-haired man with blue eyes who has heard of you and wishes to make your acquaintance. He will be very useful to you and you will get on extremely well together.'

I asked other questions, but the replies were confused; they merely embarrassed the lady to no purpose. She was floundering and finally said, 'Wait for the letter; I can see it clearly with its red seal. It will reach you in a few days, before the end of next week.'

Intrigued, I looked out for my mail, but the week went by and nothing came, then two more weeks went by and I was tired of waiting. I decided that the sleeping woman had been dreaming, surrendering to the suggestion of her wandering imagination, as was her wont as soon as her vision ceased to relate to herself and to the stages of her cure. In short, lucidity is dependent on the instinct which urges the sick animal to seek its health-restoring grass. In any case it is easier to see clearly within oneself, than to draw true information from the outside. That is to say, vague moving images which receptive imaginations pick up.

Reflections such as these made me forget the letter that I had waited for in vain, to such an extent that the prediction which I have rejected only came to mind when I received a letter with a red armorial seal. Without bothering with the envelope, I hastened to find out the contents, they took me far away from all the mutterings of a sleepwalker.

Stanislas de Guaita was inviting me to come and talk to him. Now, what I knew then of the future author of *Serpent de la Genèse* made me picture him as an erudite man, rich in knowledge accumulated during the course of many years of study. I expected to be received, if not by Doctor Faustus, not yet rejuvenated, at least by a master writer who had passed the half-way mark in his life. You can imagine my surprise when I saw myself joyfully welcomed by a young man of twenty-six years of age: who in no way pontificated. My heart was immediately won. He was young and fair-haired, with blue eyes, and the letter had been sealed with red; no doubt at all . . . this was him, the friend, the protector as promised by the sleeping patient.

The future justified the extraordinary emotion of the clairvoyant when she announced the letter with the red seal, which at that time had not yet been written.[1] My entering into a relationship with S. de G. became for me an event of great importance! He made me his friend, his secretary and his collaborator. His library was at my disposal and benefiting from his conversation, I found in him a teacher of the Kabbala of high metaphysics, as well as the French language; for G. took the trouble to form my style and to refine me from a literary point of view. He made me appreciate well-turned phrases by initiating me into the aesthetics of beautiful French prose. It is to him that I owe my readability.

I am also obliged to him for forming my intellect. When it was his desire to have me as a friend, I was only an elementary handler of fluid, gaining empirical results, but I was weak in logic. Guaita possessed the enlightenment which I lacked. Whereas I had but a smattering of spiritism and vague theosophy, he had assimilated the traditional doctrine of the masters of the science of the occult, of which he said he was a very humble disciple. Starting from Eliphas Lévi he had gone on to the Kabbalists of the Renaissance and to the hermetic philosophers of the Middle Ages, reading and understanding everything with amazing facility. The most obscure texts became clear as soon as he threw the light of his brilliant mind upon them.

Metaphysical problems were like child's play to him, and I was far from being able to follow him, but when I was too far behind he was quick to retrace his steps and in brotherly fashion take me by the hand. He was lenient towards my slow saturnine understanding.

Being caught up as I was in the briars of the earthly forest: I found in Guaita the guide who moved in the heights. Without him how would I have found my way? It was he who inspired the study which I have not ceased to pursue.

Knowing of my skill in drawing, he advised me, right from our first interview in 1887, to restore the 22 arcanas of the Tarot to their hieroglyphic purity and gave me the necessary material by providing me immediately with two Tarots, one French the other Italian, as well as *Dogme et Rituel de la Haute Magie*, the most important work of Eliphas Lévi, in which the Tarot is the object of copious commentary.

Such was the starting point of the present work of which one could say that Stanislas de Guaita is the spiritual father. After I had submitted to him a first Tarot redesigned on the two crude packs which I have compared, this learned occultist gave me his criticism for which he was held answerable at the time of the publication of the *Tarot Kabbalistique*, which appeared in 1889, with 350 copies, with the help of the photogravers of G. Poisel.

This Tarot was valued and appreciated by the occultists. Compared with the card games then in circulation it was very satisfying, but it still had to be perfected. The ideal to be realized demands a perfect unity of symbolism, so that everything fits into the 22 compositions, which must throw light upon each other and must contain no arbitrary detail which is not justified. To lead to this operation one had to grasp the overall idea of it and become acquainted with the concepts which gave it birth.

With the help of Stanislas de Guaita, I set to work to acquire the knowledge of symbolism empowering me to restore the Tarot to the design and colours in accord with the Medieval Spirit. It was a long process, but I had the patience to learn methodically. Whenever I came across them I practised interpreting the symbols even to the point of gaining the reputation of being a specialist in the field. Starting first of all with the constructive symbolism of the Freemasons, I was then led to compare it with that of the Alchemists, who put the esotericism of initiation into picture forms, taken from ancient metallurgy. This esotericism was most carefully adapted to the practice of their arts by the stone cutters of the Middle Ages.[2]

As soon as one is able to make the symbols speak, they surpass all speech in eloquence, for they allow one to find the 'Last Word', that is to say the eternal living thought, of which they are the enigmatic expression. Decipher the hieroglyphics of the deep silent wisdom, common to thinkers of all ages, religions, myths and poetic invention, and you will reveal ideas in harmony and relative to the problems which have always preoccupied the human mind. In a poetic way symbols reveal to us concepts which are too ethereal to lend themselves to the limitation of words. Not everything can be dehydrated into the prose of barristers and rhetoricians. There are some things so subtle that one has to feel and divine them like the adepts of the wise philosophy of the Medieval Symbolists, who will react against the pedantic slavery of words.

It is from these wise and discreet masters that the Tarot comes to us, as a unique monument which instructs the thinker more than all the sententious treatises, for its pictures teach us to discover the modest truth which lies hidden in the depths of our own understanding.

No collection of symbols is comparable to it, revealing as it does, wisdom of a completely unarbitrary kind, for each of us discerns it freely, without being prey to any other suggestion but that of silent pictures.

Containing in a condensed form, otherwise inexplicable thoughts, these pictures have no words, but do not hide the fact that they have to make us fathom their precious wisdom. But does the mentality of the twentieth century lend itself to divination? What would be the lot of the Tarot today if it remained enigmatic, just as it has come to us, without being accompanied by some interpreting text however slight? We are in a hurry and no longer have the leisure time for meditation; to think entirely for oneself takes too long. We need ideas explained clearly to achieve a quick assimilation or immediate rejection.

I did my best to conform to the requirements of the age. My efforts ended in a series of essays which I felt in no hurry to have published in view of their imperfection. In 1922 however, I thought that I ought to draw from my mass of materials a definite manuscript. The editor of *The Green Snake*[3] had made proposals which made me decide finally to produce a work which was bordering on an obsession. The draft copy which I entrusted to the publisher however, did not deserve to see daylight, for it was lost in a rather incomprehensible way. After a long but fruitless wait concerning the result of searches undertaken to find my text, I had to resign myself to starting the work again.

The necessary uninterrupted meditation was found for me in the course of my holidays of 1924/25. Benefiting from a lovely retreat in a delightful spot where the view embraces one of the finest landscapes in France, I hope that my final text reflects the inspiring background and great light of the longest days.

By becoming absorbed in a contemplation stimulated by a Gothic background, I thought that I was in meditative communion with the past, living in the memory which constantly evoked Stanislas de Guaita. I am convinced that the master for whom the veil of mystery was lifted, does not abandon his colleague who is straining to discern the truth.

Like many other theories, that of the Unknown Superior Beings is true, provided that it is understood. Our true initiators often do not reveal themselves to our senses, and sometimes remain as silent as the symbolic compositions of the Tarot, but they keep watch on our efforts at deciphering, and as soon as we have found the first letter, they can mysteriously prompt the second to put us on the path of the third. Guaita certainly helped me, for my thought calls to his so that between us a telepathic connection is established. The relationship between one mind and another is in the nature of things, that has nothing in common with the classic or modernized necromancy in the form of spiritism.

Philosophic occultism is not superstitious although it is based on a study of superstition. It is concerned with indestructible beliefs used to analyse and search for the truth which motivates them; for it would be illogical to admit that humanity is forged with all the patches of false ideas which go with nothing. The smoke which darkens space comes from a fire whose hearth we should discover. The investigators of the obscure occultism assign themselves the task of going back to the source of a belief which by necessity has its 'raison d'être'.

Stanislas de Guaita pursued this investigation with the enthusiasm of an exceptionally gifted neophyte, who discerns quickly and who perceives immediately the theoretical synthesis, realizing the overall significance of the facts which are seen as magical. This marvellous receptivity gives us the worth of books which are the enlightening testament of a tradition which is established from now onwards. Guaita, who has never allowed himself to innovate in occultism, arrived only at interpreting faithfully an orthodoxy, that of the masters of the school to which he was linked. These masters were sacred to him and he did not think of criticizing their assertions, for he could not hold suspect the teaching of those whom he admired without reserve.

At this stage one should point out the most remarkable trait in Guaita's character. His generous spirit led him to admire others. I have heard him praise to the skies Josephine Peladan, Maurice Barrès, Laurent Tailhade, Saint Yves d'Alveydre and a number of other contemporaries whose knowledge or literary talent he appreciated. He gave Eliphas Lévi almost the status of a god and bowed before Fabre d'Olivet with a somewhat mystical respect.

The journalists who saw the author of the *Temple de Satan* as the 'dark Marquis' spending his nights in conjurations with the help of books of spells, made the enlightened author laugh heartily as he was totally opposed to any suspect practices. He was never tempted to carry out the slightest magical act, knowing only too well that whatever can be gained in this way is only dangerous illusion leading to breakdown and madness.

Nevertheless ridiculous rumours are abroad in certain places where it is not accepted that the owner of the 'Clef de la Magie Noire' died of natural causes. They carry their effrontery as far as claiming that the last words of Guaita were 'I die the victim of my own work'. I flatly deny this imaginary story, invented to fit in with the doctrines of charlatans' occult practices. Guaita died in the Chateau d'Alteville towards the end of 1897 without ever having attributed his illness to his studies, which had been undertaken before the onset of his illness. The people who were present during his last moments thought that they heard him murmur. 'I can see! I can see!', while an expression of happy surprise spread over the face of the genial explorer of the occult.

Solar natures in love with an ideal of beauty live the life of the flesh only in part, and then only for a limited time. Like Raphael and Mozart, Guaita was to die young. It was granted to me to live on, but the incomparable friend, the inspiring master, has never died for me. His thought remains as mine; and with him and through him I aspire to initiate myself into the secret things. We collaborate secretly, for he who has gone encourages me to pursue his work, which I deem useful to resume on the basis of the most recent archaeological discoveries. Occultism deserves to be taken seriously, and should not be left to the equivocal dogmatism of disturbed imaginations. In it everything is to be reviewed, weighed up and controlled according to the requirements of an enlightened empiricism.

In this sense I have always done my best, especially when studying the Tarot; as I am conscious of never having ceased to be the secretary of Stanislas de Guaita, who found in me but an inadequate scribe, but strong in his determination in sincerely searching for the truth, and strong too in his cult of gratitude towards the intelligent spirit, whose acts continue, for nothing is lost in this sphere of strength.

May the reader be grateful to Stanislas de Guaita for the ideas which I express, and indulge his pupil who sets them forth here.

—OSWALD WIRTH

Author's Introduction

In occultism a very great importance is attached to the twenty-two arcanas or keys of the Tarot, which all together present in pictures a treatise on high philosophy.

Similar books in which the text can be reduced at the very most to the chapter headings, have nothing to say to the person who has acquired the faculty of making the books speak to him. On the other hand they speak . . . and with marvellous eloquence . . . to those who can question them wisely. Unfortunately we have lost the habit of becoming absorbed in rich and fruitful thought prompted in us simply by the appearance of things. To us the book of nature remains closed with seven seals; its pictures disconcert us, for we understand nothing except the words, whose sound alas bewilders us pitifully.

This has not always been the case. Human language has only recently become philosophical and precise. In early times it did not lend itself to the expression of any abstract idea. The first thinkers were therefore condemned to silence; lacking words, they outlined pictures to relate their dreams to them. Then in order to communicate their ideas to each other, they made for themselves a language incomprehensible to ordinary people, not by inventing new terms, but by drawing the current vocabulary away from its coarse meanings, and giving it a mysterious sense which would be intelligible to the wise. Thus came into existence the system of allegory which all revealers of truth have used.

This language evolved, gradually becoming more precise to provide for the needs of dialectic. Communicative nations acquired the taste of using words, and granted us supremacy in this field, a supremacy which reached its zenith in the ages of scholasticism.

The excess of sterile verbalizing and discussing was bound therefore to cause a reaction, a return to silent meditation based no longer on words and phrases, on definitions and arguments, but simply on the evocative magic of symbols. Tired of pointless quarrels, imaginative thinkers withdrew and turned aside to devote themselves to dreams. The suggestive influence of these dreams was to bring to life poets like the troubadours, artists, like the builders of cathedrals, not forgetting the modern illustrators, whose enigmatic compositions seem to have been inspired in a mysterious way.

Among these, one masterpiece has survived; it is the Tarot, whose pictures of naive appearance proceed from a secret wisdom, as if the refinements of Hermetism, of the Kabbala and other diffused traditions, had taken form in the series of the twenty-two arcanas.

In order to appreciate this strange monument we must study it in a profound way. The present work will facilitate the task of the searcher, who will not recoil when faced with the unavoidable effort involved in a strictly personal piece of work. When interpretations are applied to symbols, which are as windows opening onto the infinite, they can have only an indicative value; they never exhaust the subject. Now the indications are there for whoever can make use of them. Simply to repeat them is of no use if no direct application results from this. To make the Tarot speak is our objective, but the arcanas only speak to those who have learned to understand them. So let us develop our understanding if we wish to interrogate, to some purpose, an android, which far from being a thinking machine like Albert the Great's, teaches us to imagine rightly, with the help of a true alphabet of the imagination.

Is the reader ambitious to discipline his imaginative faculties with a view to acquiring an art once honoured, yet is hesitant now that reason alone claims to guide humanity in the paths of wisdom? Is there a better guide than the symbols of the Tarot to the person who is obsessed by mystery, to the heart anxious to sound the depths of night which at present envelop us?

Combined in such a way as to reveal the secret of their interpretation to perceptive spirits, these symbols lead us to discover the mysteries of a world which is foreign to narrow objective assertions, but one must decipher. How? Through what method?

Being anxious to reply to these questions, the author has dedicated the first part of this book to an exposé on method, the aridity of which may put off impatient readers who could be tempted not to linger long enough to benefit from the results of the method, results condensed in the interpretation given to the symbolism of each of the twenty-two arcanas. Then, lastly instructed in the meaning of the symbols, they will be in a hurry to draw divinatory oracles from the Tarot.

Alas, what poor divination they will practise, those who are in haste. One does not become a diviner by improvization, however gifted one might be with a spontaneous flair for divination, for these gifts do not offer real service except when they have been cultivated. Divination is an art which has its rules like any other art, and if the Tarot is to be the ideal instrument of this art, then this instrument must perforce be handled as an artist would handle it.

The following pages attempt to reach a judicious handling of the Tarot. I hope they will be able to guide those who are curious and worthy of them, in their own efforts to become initiated into the mysteries of human thought. By making known this work through its own right, a work so characteristic of the Middle Ages, may these following pages also pay homage to the unrecognized genius of a so-called 'dark' era, which made the stars of the most sublime idealism shine in the night of the Western World.

PART ONE

The Tarot

CHAPTER 1

The Origins of the Tarot

The oldest game of cards known to us comes from Venice, where it was played as early as the fourteenth century. It is made up of seventy-eight cards, which is equivalent to the sum of the numbers from one to twelve inclusive. This total is divided into two fundamentally distinct categories.

The first category contains twenty-two cards, called 'tarots'. These are symbolic representations, clearly designed with a view to something quite different from the game itself. The players are hampered by them and can do nothing with them, except for the trump cards, which are given a value according to their numerical order, without the players being concerned at all with the subject of the card. One might as well replace them with blank cards, simply marked with a number. But it is even more logical to take out of the pack the so-called 'tarots', as did the Spanish players, keeping only the fifty-six other cards.

This second category is divided into four series or 'colours' of fourteen cards. The distinguishing signs of the series are the Wand, the Cup, the Sword and Money, which correspond to what we, in the game of piquet, call Clubs, Hearts, Spades and Diamonds. Each series has ten numerical cards: Ace, Two, Three, etc., up to Ten, then four persons, King, Queen, Knight and Jack.

All card games played in different countries are, in varying degrees, modifications of the earlier game, which has been kept in its entirety in Italy, French Switzerland, Provence, and in the east of France, as far as Alsace. The name of Tarot is attributed to it by extension, for, strictly speaking, this term only applies to the twenty-two cards which are named thus:

1. The Magician

2. The Priestess (Juno)[4]

3. The Empress

4. The Emperor

5. The Pope

6. The Lover

7. The Chariot

8. Justice

9. The Hermit

10. The Wheel of Fortune

11. Strength

12. The Hanged Man

13. Death

14. Temperance

15. The Devil

16. The Tower

17. The Star

18. The Moon

19. The Sun

20. Judgement

21. The World

…The Fool or Mate

THE ALLEGED BOOK OF THOTH

Until the eighteenth century Tarot was only seen as the remains of a barbarous age, and of no interest whatsoever. No one took any notice of it until 1781, the date of the publication of *Le Monde Primitif* by Court de Gebelin, a work in which appeared, in volume VIII, page 365, the following lines:

If one heard the statement that there still exists today a work of the ancient Egyptians, one of the books saved from the flames which destroyed their superb Libraries, a book which contains their purest doctrine on objects of interest, each one of us would, without doubt, be anxious to know such a precious and extraordinary book. If furthermore it were stated that this book was well known throughout the greatest part of Europe, and that for a number of centuries has been in everyone's hands, then one's surprise would certainly increase. Our surprise would be even greater if we were told that it had never been suspected of being Egyptian, that we have this book without really possessing it, and that no one has ever tried to decipher one sheet of it, and that the fruit of a delightful wisdom is simply looked upon as a collection of extravagant images which in themselves mean nothing at all.

The fact however is only too true: this Egyptian Book, the sole survivor of their magnificent Libraries exists today: it is even so well known that there is no learned man who has not deigned to look into it, no one before us having even guessed at its illustrious origin. This book is the GAME OF TAROTS . . .

Court de Gebelin, quite unprompted, confirms the Egyptian origin of the Tarot. He only needed to discern the symbolic character of the figures until then considered as products of the imagination, to recognize them at once to be hieroglyphics, which one could attribute to the wise scholars of highest antiquity. But this is going too quickly on with our task.

A hypothesis which appeals to the imagination is not put forward without being immediately reconsidered and extended. A wigmaker called Alliette, who under the name of Eteilla, became the high priest of fortune-telling, proclaimed the Tarot to be the oldest book in the world, a work by Hermes-Thoth. He did not stop at that, but believed that he was qualified to revise a document of such importance, but 'this man of imaginative rather than judicious spirit'[5] managed only to falsify a symbolism which had not been studied sufficiently deeply.

Christian in his *Histoire de la Magie* also agrees upon Egypt. This author makes us attend an initiation into the mysteries of Osiris. After this we go into the crypts of the great Pyramid of Memphis, where the initiate undergoes terrifying trials, which lead him to the opening onto a gallery whose double wall has two pilasters, twelve on each side, in twenty-two panels decorated with hieroglyphic paintings. These are the prototypes of the Tarot. The person about to be received walks past these pictures which relate the secret doctrine of the high priests. As he goes along a guardian of the sacred symbols provides explanations which make up the beginner's instruction in initiation.

It is annoying that this gallery should be unknown in the study of Egyptology, which has not brought to light a single trace of this wall-painted book of Hermes of which, when persecuted by the Christians the last of the initiated would have taken a copy, while they were preparing to flee the sanctuary.

According to our present thesis the secret hieroglyphics, once reproduced on portable tablets, were passed on to the gnostics, then to the alchemists, from where we have inherited them.

What one can grant to those who support this connection is that the 'ideas' from which the Tarot takes its inspiration are of great antiquity. These ideas are timeless; they are as old as human thought, but they have been expressed differently, according to the climate of the age. The philosophical system of Alexandria gave them verbal expression, whereas the Tarot was later to present them in the form of symbols. If not by its substance, at least by its form, the Tarot proves itself to be an original work which, in no aspect at all reproduces pre-existing models. Archaeology has not found the slightest trace of what could constitute the remains of an Egyptian Tarot, either gnostic or even of Graeco-Arab alchemy.

The Theraphim

What strikes us particularly in the Tarot is the number 22, which is exactly the number of letters in the Hebrew alphabet. One may therefore, wonder whether it is not to the Jews that we owe our Kabbalistic forms. We know that the priests of Jerusalem used to consult the oracle of 'Urim' and 'Thumin' with the help of the 'Theraphim', that is to say, with representations or hieroglyphics. Eliphas Lévi explains how the consultations took place in the temple, on the golden table of the arch saint, then he adds:

> When the sovereign priesthood came to an end, when all the oracles in the world were silent in the presence of the Word of man, speaking through the mouth of the most cherished and most gentle of wise men, when the ark was lost, the sanctuary profaned and the temple destroyed, then the mysteries of the 'Ephod' and of the 'theraphim', which were no longer traced on the gold and the precious stones, were written, or rather outlined, by a few wise Kabbalists on ivory, on parchment, on silver and gilt leather, then finally on simple cards which were always held suspect by the official Church as containing the dangerous key to its mysteries. Hence came these tarots, whose ancient origin, revealed to the scholar Court de Gebelin through his knowledge of hieroglyphics and of numbers, so strained the doubtful perspicacity and the tenacious investigation of Eteilla.[6]

The information which we possess on the 'Theraphim' is so vague that it is difficult to appear so positive about them. The Kabbala was familiar to the authors of the Tarot, but these philosophical artists could scarcely have belonged to the Semitic race, which, far from encouraging a symbolism in art, has always preferred to link its abstract speculations with the terseness of letters, number and geometric figures. On the other hand, the Aryan mind takes pleasure in the richness of colours and forms: it is, by nature idolatrous and is in love with pictures. From this point of view, Greece could be the homeland of the Tarot, if Italy of the Middle Ages did not give us undeniable proof as to the invention of playing cards.

Positive Data

In the epochs before the invention of wood-engraving, a special industry, that of illustrators or painters of pictures, made by hand very many examples of religious or profane subjects, on parchment or cardboard which delighted the popular customers for these objects. As these buyers liked compositions that were not isolated subjects, but presented as a series, one could offer for sale more and more complicated collections. From the ternary of the godly virtues, from the quaternary of the evangelists, of the elements or of the cardinal virtues, they went on to the septenary of the planets, of the sacraments or of the cardinal sins, without neglecting the allegories relating to the five senses and the nine muses, etc.

The Italians had the idea of putting these pictures all together into a game to amuse and instruct children. So came about the 'naïbi', the innocent cards recommended by moralists such as Morelli, in 1393.

Towards the end of the fourteenth century the first instruction cards led to the invention of playing cards which attributed to Francois Fibbia, who died in 1419. The followers of the Reformation in the town of Bologna did, in fact, grant the right to this lord to place his coat of arms on the Queen of Sticks, and those of his wife, a Bentivoglio, on the Queen of Pennies[7] by virtue of his being the inventor of 'tarocchino'.

The idea of numerical cards (Ace, Two, Three, etc.) seems to have been given to the players by dice, while chess could give them the figures: King, Queen, and Knight, not to mention the Fool and the Tower (House of God) of the Tarot.

But these explanations, tentatively put forward by scholars who were concerned with the origin of the cards, are far from solving the mystery of the origin of the Lombard-Venetian Tarot.

This ancestor of all card games known in Europe is obviously marked by Kabbalistic knowledge, as Papus in his *Tarot des Bohemiens*[8] brought out most clearly. The objects which point out the four sets of fourteen, of the 56 (foreign cards) to the real 22 tarots, are connected with the arts of the occult and correspond to the letters of the divine Tetragram.

 Wand, the staff of augury or magic wand, the sceptre of male domination, the emblem of the male's productive power: the Father.

 Cup, the cup of divination, woman's receptivity, imaginative and physical: the Mother.

 Sword, the blade of the conjuror, which outlines the shape of a cross and so reminds us of the fruitful union of the two principles of male and female, the fusion and the cooperation of opposites. The blade symbolizes, moreover, a penetrating action like that of the Word or of the Son.

Pentacle, the five-sided disc, a sign of support of the will-power, condensing matter of spiritual action; synthesis bringing the ternary to unity, Trinity or Tri-unity.

There is in this choice something else apart from the fortuitous element, and no one can doubt that the inventor of the Tarot, as a game, was conversant with the science of the occult of his time.

But what can one think of the twenty-two trump cards which are of earlier origin than the other cards?

These strange compositions were reproduced in 1392 by Jacquemin Gringonneur 'for the enjoyment of our unfortunate king Charles VI'; but they seem to have been already known by Raymond Lulle, a clever alchemist monk, who lived from 1234 to 1315.

There has been a wish to derive them from the so-called cards of Baldini which are attributed to Mantegna. The two editions which we have of this game only go back to 1470 and 1485, it is true, but one supposes, not without reason, that the engraver of this period was inspired by an older model. Now this unknown model can only be looked for in the Tarot whose Baldini cards are but a systematic extension. The artist, very skilled in his art, but in no way initiated, wanted to correct the Tarot by slanting it in accordance with the demands of his logic and philosophy. In a logical way he tried to classify figures whose incoherence shocked him; this explains this extremely artistic game of fifty subjects grouped in series of tens. The first of these tens designates the hierarchy of social classes: the beggar, valet, artisan, merchant, nobleman, knight, doge, king, emperor and Pope. The nine muses and Apollo make up the second ten. The third is devoted to the sciences which encroach upon the fourth, partly kept for the virtues. Finally the last ten contains the seven planets, as well as the eighth sphere, the first impetus and the first cause.

In this game all the figures of the Tarot are found, slightly modified and adapted according to the ideas of the artist. The latter has, therefore, composed his work in accordance with traditional tarots. If the opposite had been done, one cannot conceive how 22 subjects would have been arbitrarily taken out of a sumptuous collection of 50. Moreover the naivety of the style would guarantee the earlier origin of the Tarot.

The 22 early tarots must, however, be connected with the 'naïbi', those instruction cards not yet used for playing with. An adept of the thirteenth century would have wanted to make a Kabbalistic book with the help of these richly coloured pictures which enjoyed such popularity at that time. Their variety allowed him to choose those which it was possible to link with the ten Sephiroth of the Kabbala, then, by extension, with the 22 letters of the sacred alphabet.

Thus at a place and at a date unknown to us it was possible for the original outline of our Tarot to come into existence.

But is it certain that we are in the presence of the work of an individual? Did a man of genius conceive the Tarot as a whole? This is extremely doubtful, if we are to judge by the changes which the Tarot has undergone during the course of time. The oldest specimens are not the most perfect from the symbolic point of view; they are of a hesitating symbolism, as yet finding its way. It was the successive copyists who finally gave us a Tarot in which every detail has its significance which harmonizes with the whole. One must admit that among the illustrators, some, gifted with a sort of divining sense of symbols, introduced into their reproductions lucky variants which later prevailed; others, carried away by an imagination which did not obey the mysterious directives of tradition, could only distort the original. Although they were continuous, the deviations did not form a school, for a vague but sound instinct brought our most skilled illustrators into the right path of pure symbolism. So, in the Tarot, we receive an anonymous heritage, a work of genius, thanks to the collaboration of various humble people who copied from each other with inspired artlessness, producing, without realizing it, a pure and marvellous work.[9]

The Initiation Value of the Tarot

We can consider as pointless any discussion on the age of the Tarot as soon as we bring in the intrinsic value of this strange document. Relatively modern in its form, but doubtless extremely old in its subject, this collection of symbols has excited all those who have managed to decipher them.

Let us listen to the Abbé Constant who, under the pen name of Eliphas Lévi, published the works from which proceeds, for a very large part, contemporary occultism.[10]

> It is a monumental and unique work—said the Adept (Lévi) when speaking of the Tarot—strong and simple like the architecture of the pyramids, consequently long-lasting like them; it is a book which contains in essence all knowledge and whose infinite combinations can solve all problems; it is a book which, as it speaks makes us think; the inspiring and regulating force of all possible conceptions; the masterpiece, perhaps, of the human mind, and surely one of the finest things which antiquity has left to us; the universal key whose name has been understood and explained only by the enlightened scholar Guillaume Postel[11]; it is a unique text whose first characters alone sent the religious mind of Saint-Marrin[12] into ecstasy and would have restored the power of reason to the sublime and unfortunate Swedenborg.[13]

To these, taken from *Dogme de la Haute Magie*, page 68, one should add the following, taken from *Rituel*, page 355, where it is said, still concerning the Tarot:

It is a real philosophical machine which stops the minds from wandering, all the while leaving us our initiative and freedom; it is mathematics applied to the absolute, the linking of the positive to the ideal; it is a lottery of thoughts, all as rigorously fair, like the numbers; in short, it is perhaps at the same time the most simple and the greatest achievement that the human spirit has ever conceived.

But it is for the reader himself to judge the Tarot, by learning to distinguish in it the marvels which are promised. We are going to proceed methodically, and show how one can make a silent book speak.

CHAPTER 2

Signs Revealing the Secrets of the Tarot

The Wheel

Amongst the Tarot cards there is one which does not bear any number. It is the *Fool* that this peculiarity seems to deprive of any specific rank. One hesitates therefore, when it comes to assigning to this card a place in the pack. Should it precede the *Magician* (Arcana 1), or follow the *World* (Arcana 21)?

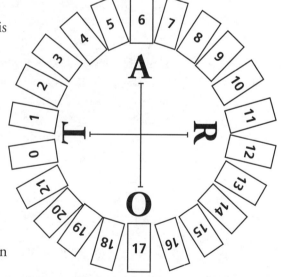

This question does not arise when the tarot is placed as a wheel, as the word ROTA suggests (a word formed from the TARO by Guillaume Postel), since the Fool is thus placed between the beginning and the end, where it symbolizes the irrational and incomprehensible 'Infinite' whence we come and to which we are destined to return.

The placing of the cards in the shape of a wheel is very important, because the circle thus formed is naturally divided into two halves, each being made up of eleven figures. It is practical from the point of view of establishing the links between these to put them into two rows as shown below:

1	2	3	4	5	6	7	8	9	10	11
0	21	20	19	18	17	16	15	14	13	12

The Analogies of Opposites

By comparing the figures which are opposite each other, from one row to the other, it is impossible not to recognize a certain contrast, especially between the arcanas 1 and 0, 7 and 16, 10 and 13, 11 and 12.[14]

It is obvious in fact that the *Magician* (1) could not be anything else but an intelligent and skilful man, knowing precisely what he is doing, whereas the *Fool* is senseless, walking blindly, not knowing where he is going.

The *Chariot* (7) which bears a triumphant rider, rises above the lightning-struck *Tower* (16), from the top of which two persons are falling down; thus the exaltation of success is linked, in the Tarot, with the catastrophic fall, as if to remind us of the Tarpeienne rock near the Capitol.

The *Wheel of Fortune* (10) seems to promise an unexpected piece of luck, as opposed to *Death* (13) which implies the threat of inexorable fate.

Strength (11) opposes creative power to the impotence of the *Hanged Man* (12) whose arms are bound.

Although less striking, the contrast nonetheless exists, so that one may still infer that each half of the Tarot must, as a whole, have its general significance, contrasting with that of the other half.

Jachin and Boaz

How can one determine this general two-fold significance? To start with, we may be tempted to give to the first line a favourable significance, and to the second an unfavourable one; but on looking more closely it would not take us long to put things right. It is less a question of good and evil than a question of activity and passivity.

The first eleven arcanas mark the progress of an essentially active agent, sentient and autonomous. The last eleven, on the contrary, bring into play a passive subject, unaware, sensitive or impulsive, and deprived of initiative. Here again we must not take the word 'passive' solely in a detrimental sense.

Initiation distinguishes two paths called:

Dry, masculine, rational *or* dorian,
　　(Fire and Air),

and humid, feminine, mystical *or* ionian,
　　(Water and Earth)

The first is based on the exalting of the principle of individual initiative, on reason and will-power. It suits the disciplined person who is always in control of himself and only depends on the resources of his own personality without waiting for any help from external influences. It is entirely different as regards the second which takes the opposite course. Far from developing all that one has in oneself and giving according to the full and total growth of one's inner energies, for the mystic it is a question of being ready to receive, cultivating purposefully, a state of mind offering complete receptivity.

This fundamental distinction is reflected in the Tarot whose two halves correspond to the Binary columns, to Man and to Woman; to the Spirit, an inner active fire, and to the Soul, a sensitive surrounding vapour; to the Sulphur and the Mercury of the Alchemists.

The Axis of the Tarot

Each of the two rows of the Tarot is divided into two equal parts by the arcanas 6 and 17, which are preceded and followed by a group of five arcanas. It is thus a question of finding the significance, first of the two middle arcanas 6 and 17 and then of the four groups of five arcanas.

Now in each of the two paths of initiation one can distinguish two phases: preparation and study; and application and putting into practice. Hence the diagram below:

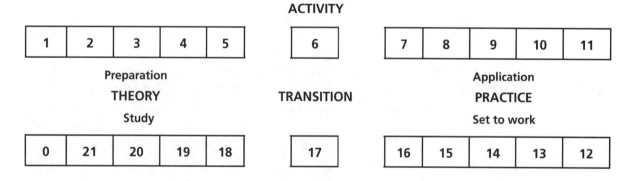

Let us observe that if in the masculine or dorian initiation, theory precedes practice, the opposite is produced in the feminine or ionian initiation, for the passive subject is urged into practical activities before he is given understanding.

In order to reveal a conscious activity (dorian) one must begin by acquiring the knowledge relating to the arcanas 1, 2, 3, 4 and 5. When this instruction is acquired, a moral test, represented by arcana 6 is made, and if passed, one may go on to the practical realization aimed at by cards 7, 8, 9, 10 and 11.

In the field of passivity (ionism), the mystical abandon is immediately put into the forms depicted by the cards 12, 13, 14, 15 and 16; then by means of the outside influences alluded to by card 17, a progressive illustration is achieved through the phases 18, 19, 20, 21 and 0.

We shall not insist at this point on what characterizes the two great paths of initiation, because the reader's attention could not concentrate too much on the four groups of five arcanas which provide the key to the deciphering of the whole of the Tarot. These groups are of extreme importance because of their co-ordination, thanks to which they rule each other as regards the meaning of their analogous arcanas. It therefore follows that when the first group is deciphered, the others become clear by analogy and correct transposition, as we shall demonstrate.

The First Group of Arcanas

The *Priestess* (2) and the *Empress* (3) make a pair with the *Emperor* (4) and the *Pope* (5). This group of four cards is separate from the *Magician* (1) whom fact leads us to envisage in his antagonism with the following arcanas. These in the preparatory or theoretical phase of the dorian initiation places the tetrad in opposition to unity. Now in the question of study and intellectual preparation the unity belongs to the thinking subject. Therefore we can see in the *Magician* (1) the personification of the self, the principle of consciousness which is the starting point of all initiative. It is the simple subject of all knowledge of which the multiple object is symbolized by the four symmetrical arcanas.

These arcanas include two men and two women which are invested with the lay and religious functions.

The sexes can only be concerned with the inductive or deductive knowledge, the inductive being consonant with the female spirit, whereas masculine intellectuality excels above all in deduction. These functions remind one, on the other hand, of the ancient distinction of sciences between the priestly ones, metaphysical or abstract and secular ones, physical or concrete; which brings us to the following interpretations:

> *Priestess* (2): Inductive sacred knowledge, intuitive, metaphysical.
>   Rational faith or Gnosis.
> *Empress* (3): Inductive temporal science, physics, observation of
>   concrete nature.
> *Emperor* (4): Deductive temporal science; mathematics and exact
>   sciences applied to what is concrete.
> *Pope* (5): Deductive sacred knowledge, religious philosophy, ontology,
>   Kabbala, esoterism.

The Revealing Transpositions

Arcana 6 (the *Lover*) marks the transition from the theoretical to the practical, from the preparatory study to its application. Thus it relates cards 5 to 7, so that the *Chariot* (7) alludes to the application of knowledge and of moral qualities of the initiated who is fully instructed, symbolized by the *Pope* (5). An analogous relationship exists between cards 8 and 4, 9 and 3, 10 and 2, 11 and 1. In each case the arcanas of the second group apply, in a practical way, what the corresponding card holds in theory and in potential. The passive row of the Tarot only offers, so to speak, a reversed image of the active row. Thus we might indicate by the following diagram, the relationships to be established between the whole of the 22 arcanas.

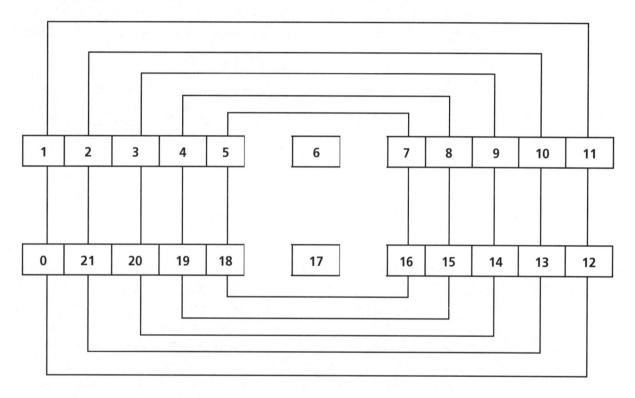

THE SECOND GROUP OF ARCANAS

The transcendental and abstract doctrine proclaimed by the *Pope* (5) from his motionless chair, is applied by the triumphant rider of the *Chariot* (7), who travels the world on a moving throne. Everywhere this intelligent minister adapts the ideal to practical needs. He is at grips with harsh reality which he transforms by the harmonizing of opposites: spirit and matter, egoism and altruism. He is an arbiter, a peacemaker, a wise man who reigns by his knowledge and moral authority.

Mathematical precision (*Emperor* 4) is translated into the moral sphere by *Justice* (8), because 'justice is nothing but mathematics in action, put into practice', as was remarked by Berthault-Gras a follower of Fourier, quoted by Lacuria.[15] The deductive, temporal science shows us how to bring order into the world, to put everything in its place, thus ensuring equilibrium, stability and regular functioning. We can thus relate card 8 to wisdom that conserves and governs.

The inductive temporal science (*Empress* 3) is cultivated by the *Hermit* (9), a 'personification of the scholar, who illucidates progressively with extreme care, the mysteries of nature.

The *Wheel of Fortune* (10) promises success in practical life to the person who knows how to apply the intuitive faculties (*Priestess* 2). One must be a diviner to benefit from the alterations of fate.

Strength (11) depends on the *Magician* (1) who puts into practice his entire programme.

THE THIRD GROUP

The first five arcanas, having, so to speak, returned to their significance, explain cards 0, 21, 20, 19 and 18.

The *Fool* (0), as opposed to the *Magician* (1), is an empty person whose ego, deprived of all initiative, without control, undergoes all external influences.

The *World* (21) representing the Great All, acts on the sensitive and delights him with ecstasy. The ecstatic faculties are, in the passive, what intuition (*Priestess* 2) is in the active.

Judgement (20) opposes spontaneity of inspiration to laborious studies and patience ordered by the *Empress* (3), the personification of inductive temporal sciences.

The *Sun* (19) is the source of the spiritual light which inspired the artist and the poet. This enlightenment of the genius is in opposition to mathematical precision (*Emperor* 4), but nevertheless art obeys stern rules, which consciously or not submit it to the laws of numbers.

In this active order the intellectual synthesis is purely rational (the *Pope* 5); it is imaginative in the passive order. The *Moon* (18) sheds an uncertain light which is often misleading like the mirages of the imagination.

THE LAST GROUP

The *Stars* (17) are those of destiny. They determine the fate of the passive being, who does not choose his path, as the dorian initiate has to do, symbolized by the *Lover* (6), who are called, like young Hercules, to choose between vice and virtue.

An exalted imagination (the *Moon* 18) conceives extraordinary plans the realization of which can only lead to failure, represented by the *Tower* (16), thus alluding to all fanciful enterprises destined to lead to the opposite of triumph (*Chariot* 7).

He who has the gifts of an artist (*Sun* 19) is fit to practise the occult arts. By his incantations he acts on the soul of the world, a mystical agent symbolized by the *Devil* (15). This arcana opposes trouble, the unleashing of irrational instincts, to the normal calm and logic of *Justice* (8).

The inspired one *(Judgement* 20) is not receptive only from the intellectual point of view. He also applies himself to creative works. He attracts to himself the vital fluid of the universe which he becomes able to transmit to others. It is the very fluid which *Temperance* (4) transfers from one vessel to the other. To bathe oneself in the waters of the ocean of this fluid is in fact the opposite of what the *Hermit* (9) does, by retiring into the most strict isolation.

To ecstasy (the *World* 21) is linked the power of evocation which lends new life to what *Death* (13) has mown down. The antagonism of cards 10 and 13 is immediately apparent; they symbolize good luck and terrible fatality.

The *Hanged Man* (12) represents the one who sacrifices himself by renouncement for the benefit of others. The passivity of the *Fool* (0) here takes on a sublime character. It realized the Great Work of which the accomplishment indicates the end of the mystical path, whereas we have seen that the natural or positive path leads to *Strength* (11).

THE ELEVEN COUPLES

At this point we are in possession of all the fundamental data, which is however, far too scant, and which we must gradually complete. With this aim in view let us look at the arcanas which correspond from one line of the Tarot to the other, and develop more fully through contrast, the above-mentioned indications.

I
SUBJECT, STARTING POINT

1. *The Magician* 𐤀	0. *The Fool* 𐤊
Active, positive.	Passive, negative.
Initiative, in control of oneself.	Submission to external influences.
Wisdom, reason.	Impulsiveness, madness.

II
PERCEPTION OF THE UNKNOWN

2. *The Priestess* 𐤁	21. *The World* 𐤕
Intuition, divination.	Ecstasy, clairvoyance.
The spirit of penetrating the unknown.	The unknown revealing itself to the soul.
Hypnotic sciences of hidden things.	Integral sciences of the absolute.

III
ASSIMILATION OF WHAT IS OUTSIDE ONESELF

3. *The Empress* ג
Observation, comprehension,
conception, study. Wisdom, reason behind
the generating of ideas.

20. *Judgement* ר
Inspiration, exaltation. Enthusiasm,
prophecy. Ideas which impose themselves
without being controlled

IV
SPIRITUAL ILLUMINATION

4. *The Emperor* ד
Inner light. The word made flesh.
Concentration of thought and will.
Energy, calculation, deduction, positivism.

19. *The Sun* ק
Universal light. The Eternal Word.
Expansion, illumination which gives genius.
Serenity, fine arts, poetry, idealism.

V
ELABORATION OF A SYNTHESIS

5. *The Pope* ה
Abstract. Speculative reality, metaphysics.
Religion. Spirituality.
Transcendental knowledge. Duty, moral law.

18. *The Moon* צ
Concrete. Sensitive appearance. Illusion of the
senses. Superstition. Materialism. Mistakes,
vulgar prejudices. Whims, fantasies.

VI
DETERMINATION OF ACTS

6. *The Lover* ו
Freedom, choice, test. Doubt.
Anxious battle against the difficulties of life.
Sentiment, affections.

17. *The Star* פ
Predestination, hopefulness.
Surrender to the faith of immortality.
Idealism, aesthetic, love of beauty.

VII
MIND AGAINST MATTER

7. *The Chariot* ז
Domination, triumph. Talent, ability.
The master who commands obedience.
Progress, harmony.

16. *The Tower* ע
Presumption, fall. Infatuation, inability.
The victim of forces in revolt.
Explosion, catastrophe.

Tarot of the Magicians

VIII

ORGANIZATION AND RULING OF FORCES

8. *Justice* 𐤇

Law, order, equilibrium. Stability. Logic.
Placidity, calm, regularity.
Discernment.

15. *The Devil* 𐤎

Randomness, confusion, imbalance, instinct.
Rage, fury, wild disorder.
Blind passion.

IX

THE RELATIONSHIP OF THE INDIVIDUAL WITH HIS SURROUNDINGS

19 *The Hermit* 𐤌

Abstemtion, isolation. Prudence,
discretion. Reservation, avarice. Methodical
and meticulous scholar, a doctor.

14. *Temperance* 𐤍

Participation, communion. Carefreeness,
frankness. Circulation, prodigality. Worker of
miracles; adept of occult medicine.

X

INTERVENTION OF DESTINY

10. *Wheel of Fortune* 𐤉

Luck, ambition, inventions, discoveries.
Life-giving seed.
Maintenance of individual existence.

13. *Death* 𐤌

Fatality, disillusion. Renouncement.
Decomposition, putrefaction.
The end, revival, transformation.

XI

OBJECTIVE, FINAL RESULT

11. *Strength* 𐤊

Strength, power, feasible ideas.
Practical spirit, intelligence ruling matter.
Energy, courage, a person of action who
knows how to overcome difficulties.

12. *The Hanged Man* 𐤋

Impotence, utopia. Dreamer, spirit escaping
from matter and not having a hold on it.
An apostle, a martyr of the lack of
understanding of his contemporaries.

COMPARATIVE TETRADS

The pairs which we have just reviewed bring up certain comparisons which are extremely interesting. Compared in pairs, they bring each time four similar arcanas in joint opposition. The following tetrads deserve our special attention. In each of those tetrads the first arcana is to the second what the third is to the fourth; the first is, moreover, to the third as the second is to the fourth; and again the first is to the fourth as the second is to the third. To make a deeper study of the Tarot, it is important to resolve the series of problems and equations which the presence of these tetrads pose. We have there an intellectual exercise which would be profitable to those who want to apply the Tarot to divination.[16]

The following indications will show how there are grounds for indicating on one hand the synthesizing ideas which relate the four arcanas to each other, and to discern on the other hand the various aspects of the same idea, offered by each of the arcanas in particular.

1 Magician	11 Strength
0 Fool	12 Hanged Man

2 Priestess	10 Wheel of Fortune
21 World	13 Death

3 Empress	9 Hermit
20 Judgement	14 Temperance

4 Emperor	8 Justice
19 Sun	15 Devil

5 Pope	7 Chariot
18 Moon	16 Tower

2 Priestess	5 Pope
21 World	18 Moon

3 Empress	4 Emperor
20 Judgement	19 Sun

7 Chariot	10 Wheel of Fortune
16 Tower	13 Death

8 Justice	9 Hermit
15 Devil	14 Temperance

The principle of individual intelligence:

<table>
<tr><td>In potential.</td><td></td><td>In action.</td></tr>
<tr><td>Giving one the ability to instruct oneself in all matters.</td><td></td><td>Fully instructed and practised in all practical works.</td></tr>
</table>

1. *The Magician* א		11. *Strength* כ
0. *The Fool* ש	X	12. *The Hanged Man* ל

<table>
<tr><td>Inactive, inert, intellectual inability.
Stupidity.
Incomprehension.</td><td></td><td>Hampered, rendered unproductive.
Misunderstood genius. Thoughts too sublime to be rendered intelligible.</td></tr>
</table>

The spirit in the presence of mystery:

<table>
<tr><td>Effort to penetrate it.
Divination, intuition, gnosis, faith.</td><td></td><td>Discernment, discovery.
Stopping at general conjecture.</td></tr>
</table>

2. *The Priestess* ב		10. *The Wheel of Fortune* י
21. *The World* ת	X	13. *Death* מ

<table>
<tr><td>Perceives it fully.
Ecstatic vision.
Integral sciences.</td><td></td><td>Repulses it, denies it.
Disillusion.
Absolute scepticism.</td></tr>
</table>

The spiritual principle, source of thought and life:

<table>
<tr><td>Is drawn into intelligence and held by the growth of ideas. Comprehension, conception.</td><td></td><td>Borne fruit in intelligence constituting the mental sphere. Storage of memory.</td></tr>
</table>

3. *The Empress* ג		9. *The Hermit* א
20. *Judgement* ר	X	14. *Temperance* נ

<table>
<tr><td>Subjugates the intelligence that it fertilizes.
Inspiration, enthusiasm.</td><td></td><td>Circulates and animates a multiplicity of beings.
Universal life.</td></tr>
</table>

The Creative Light:

Fixed to the centre of the personality, principle of voluntary energy, of individual expansion and growth.

4. *The Emperor* ד

19. *The Sun* ק

Shining with its universal source. Opening out of the self, expansion of being. Altruism.

X

Tonalized, harmoniously distributed to insure the normal functioning of the organism and its conservation.

8. *Justice* ח

15. *The Devil* ס

Excessively condensed. Congestion, rut, blind ardour, brutal instinct. Egoism.

The four sources of human convictions:

The philosophical or religious tradition. Enlightened believers.

5. *The Pope* ה

18. *The Moon* צ

Conventional opinions, dominant prejudices. Superstitious slaves of the written word.

X

Independent search for the truth. Free thinkers.

7. *The Chariot* ו

16. *The Tower* ע

Contradiction of opposing doctrines. Anti-religious, sectarian, false free-thinkers.

Various aspects of the truth:

Mystery which requires intuition and asks to be penetrated.

2. *The Priestess* ב

21. *The World* ת

Absolute which only reveals itself in the throes of ecstasy.

X

Dogma whose esotericism requires to be understood. Inner thoughts, enlivening spirit.

5. *The Pope* ה

18. *The Moon* צ

Material signs, forms, envelopes, outer shell of thoughts, dead letter.

Idea in relation to understanding:

Idea is attracted to understanding,
penetrates it and takes root in it.

It develops all its
consequences logically.

3. *The Empress* ג

20. *Judgement* ר

X

4. *The Emperor* ר

19. *The Sun* ק

It takes hold of it spontaneously, producing
the rapture of enthusiasm.

It becomes refined and takes on a potential
or sublime character.

Results of human activities:

Triumph,
success won by merit.

Success obtained
by favour or by luck.

7. *The Chariot* ז

16. *The Tower* ע

X

10. *Wheel of Fortune* י

13. *Death* מ

Failure provoked by illusions
or by mistakes.

Catastrophe inevitable and fatal for which
the victim is not responsible.

Applications of energy:

Balance between income and expenditure.
Normal functioning.

Reduction of expenditure.
Retention, continence.

8. *Justice* ח

15. *The Devil* ם

X

9. *The Hermit* ט

14. *Temperance* נ

Accumulation pushed to the extreme,
then sudden expenditure.
Impetuousness, explosion.

Slackness, languor, indifference,
apathy, coolness.

The reader is asked not to be put off by the dryness of the preceding diagrams, because they offer to his personal initiative a rich field to be explored in depth. To learn to decipher the Tarot it is essential to practise, comparing the arcanas in order to extract all that they can suggest regarding the many similarities and contrasts. A meditative mind will know how to draw from each tetrad the material for a full dissertation. Each person must think for himself. It would be wrong to ease the task of those able to initiate themselves, those who care to study the Tarot seriously.

CHAPTER 3

The Kabbalistic Tarot

THE NUMBER 21

In the preceding chapters the Tarot has only been seen in one of its many aspects. We wanted to consider it first of all as a whole made up of 22 parts, a number which according to its common factors can be divided by 2 and 11.

But we may put to one side the *Fool*, which stands out from the other cards because of its being unnumbered. The Tarot is thus divided into two categories, the first containing one card only, the *Fool*, which seems to counterbalance alone the 21 cards of the second group.

Let us leave the *Fool*, whom we will meet again further on, and lead our investigations onto the series of numbered arcanas. Now 21 has a factor of 3 and 7, we will have to study the cards placed in seven groups of threes and three groups of sevens.

THE LAW OF THE TERNARY

Everything inevitably comes from 'three' which makes but one. Within every act, single in itself, these factors can indeed be distinguished:

1. The active principle, causes or subject of the action.

2. The action of this subject; its verb.

3. The object of this action, its effect or its result.

These three terms are inseparable and rely on each other. Hence this 'tri-unity' which one finds in everything.

One example will make us grasp the importance of this data. The idea of creation implies 1. a creator; 2. the action of creating; and, 3. the thing created. As soon as one of these three elements is removed the two others disappear, for without a creator one can conceive neither the act of creating nor a thing created. On the other hand the creator is only such because he creates; outside the action of creating he does not exist any more than the object created does. In short, without the created the creator creates nothing, so that there is neither creator, nor the act of creating, nor the object created.

In a general way, in the elements of the ternary, the first is above all active, the second is intermediary, active as seen with the following, but passive as seen with the preceding one; whereas the third is strictly passive. The first corresponds to the spirit, the second to the soul and the third to the body.

The same links are found in the Tarot whose arcanas can be grouped thus:

The Seven Ternaries

Active	1	4	7	10	13	16	19	Spirit
Intermediary	2	5	8	11	14	17	20	Soul
Passive	3	6	9	12	15	18	21	Body

The Three Septenaries

Active	1	2	3	4	5	6	7	Spirit
Intermediary	8	9	10	11	12	13	14	Soul
Passive	15	16	17	18	19	20	21	Body

A comparison of these two diagrams shows us that the arcanas 1, 4 and 7 are especially active or spiritual, whereas 8, 11 and 14 are intermediaries or relating to the soul, and 15, 18 and 21 are passive or corporal since their character is asserted both by its position in the arrangement of ternaries and septenaries.

The Theosophic Operations

In occultism numbers have their significance, especially the least complex ones. To determine their nature one proceeds by two operations, known as theosophic addition and reduction.

In the first operation one adds to the number which is being examined all those which precede it in the ordinary numerical series:

$4 = 1 + 2 + 3 + 4 = \mathbf{10}$

$6 = 1 + 2 + 3 + 4 + 5 + 6 = \mathbf{21}$

The second operation brings every number made up of seven back to the simplicity of the first nine numbers.

This result is obtained by adding up (amongst themselves) the figures of a complex number, and by pursuing this method of addition onto the sum obtained as long as it is represented by more than one figure.

$\mathbf{1899} = 1 + 8 + 9 + 9 = \mathbf{27} = 2 + 7 = \mathbf{9}$

When the series of numbers is put to the test of theosophic calculation, we can confirm that the numbers are grouped in threes of which the first is always reducible to the unit.

This table shows that every number is reducible to 1, 3, 6 or 9; it shows us moreover, the importance of the ancient group of 9, the ennead, since the series of numbers is divided into groups of 9, shown by the constant return to the reduced numbers 1, 3, 6 — 1, 6, 3 — 1, 9, 9.

The unit numbers: 4, 7, 10, 13, 16, etc., brings back to unity the ternary which precedes them, so that the series of numbers can be written as follows:

1—2—3

4—5—6

7—8—9

10—11—12

13—14—15

16—17—18

19—20—21 etc.

These glimpses have their importance in connection with the Tarot, whose construction is essentially based on the ancient science of numbers.

Number	Theosophic sum	Reduction
1 2 3	1 3 6	1 3 6
4 5 6	10 15 21	1 6 3
7 8 9	28 36 45	1 9 9
10 11 12	55 66 78	1 3 6
13 14 15	91 105 120	1 6 3
16 17 18	136 153 171	1 9 9
19 20 21	190 210 231	1 3 6
22	253	1

THE SEPHIROTH

According to the Kabbala, numbers, in Hebrew the Sephiroth (plural of Sephirah), reveal the mysteries of creation, explaining how multiplicity springs from the unit. This unit, the cause and mainspring of all things, the centre from which everything emanated and which enfolds everything in its potential, in germ or in its sowing, has received the name of *Kether*, which signifies Crown or Diadem. It is like the *Magician* (1), the source of all activity, and especially of all thought, the Father, the living God who says: 'I am!'

The second Sephirah is called *C'hocmah*, Wisdom, and corresponds to the creative thought, the immediate offspring of the Father, his 'first born', Son, Word, Verb, Logos or Supreme Reason, which the mysterious *Priestess* (2) of the Tarot also symbolizes.

The third Sephirah, *Binah,* Intelligence, Comprehension, is related as well as the *Empress* (3) to the conception and to the generation of ideas, to the Virgin Mary who gives birth to the original images of all things.

This first ternary is of an intellectual order and corresponds to pure thought or to the spirit.

The following ternary, in the moral sphere relates to feeling and to the exercise of the will, that is to say to the soul.

Fourth Sephirah: *C'hesed*, Thanks, Grace, Pity, Kindness or *Gedulah*, Greatness, Magnificence. Active kindness calling beings to existence. Power which gives and spreads life—the *Emperor* (4).

The fifth Sephirah *Geburah*, Rigour, Severity, *Pec'had*, Punishment, Fear or *Din*, Judgement. Will-power which holds in check and governs life given, Duty, Moral Law, the *Pope* (5).

Sixth Sephirah: *Tiphereth,* Beauty. Heart, sensibility, affections which determine the will. The *Lovers* (6).

The third ternary is of a dynamic order: it relates to action, which puts things into practice, and because of this relates to the body.

Seventh Sephirah: *Netsah*, Triumph, Victory, Steadfastness. The co-ordinating principle which governs the world, directs movement and presides over progress: Great Architect of the Universe—the *Chariot* (7).

Eighth Sephirah: *Hod*, Splendour, Glory. The order which nature brings into her work. The unchanging law of things—*Justice* (8).

Ninth Sephirah: *Jesod*, Base, Foundation. The divine plan. Latent energies co-ordinated by what is to come into being. The astral body—the *Hermit* (9).

The triple ternary of the Sephiroth is brought back to the unit by the tenth Sephirah: *Malcut*, Kingdom, Reign, Royalty which synthesizes the actions of thinking, of willing and of acting—spirit, soul and body, in order to bring about the complete being capable of growth. This being is called the Celestial Man or

Adam Kadmon. He possesses no material existence at all, but he unites the divine creative principles which come into play to give birth to Man. Man only takes bodily form on the physical plane, by undergoing individual differentiation, whose wild whirlings is represented by the *Wheel of Fortune* (10).

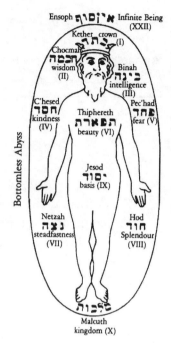

The tenth Sephirah is also called the Queen, the sixth then becoming the King. As for the superior Adam, he is the Mediator 'par excellence' linking the Infinite to the Finite. He is represented through his crown as coming close to the Inconceivable Absolute (*Ensoph* or endless), whereas his feet lightly skim the material world.

THE TRIPLE TERNARIES

The Sephiroth provide the key to the first three ternaries of the Tarot. These nine arcanas make up a whole to which a second group, formed by the following nine arcanas, corresponds.

1	4	7
2	5	8
3	6	9

10	13	16
11	14	17
12	15	18

From one of these triple ternaries to the other the numbers are equivalent in terms of a theosophic sum. In the same way the arcanas represent a perfect analogy of meaning. But if the first ennead relates to the Adam Kadmon, hence to the ideal Man, conforming to the divine plan according to which all human individuality is constructed, then the second alludes to the terrestrial Adam, to Humanity in all its variety, scattered among a multiplicity of individuals, but incorporated in one collective and permanent being, the animator of our transitory organisms, which are to the human whole what each one of our organic cells is to the unity of our individual personality.

The ennead is, moreover, nothing but the tripling of the ternary Spirit, Soul, Body, as the following diagram shows:

1. Spirit of the Spirit	4. Spirit the Soul	7. Spirit of Body
2. Soul of the Spirit	5. Soul of the Soul	8. Soul of the Body
3. Body of the Spirit	6. Body of the Soul	9. Body of the Body

So here is how we will give a parallel interpretation to the arcanas of each of the triple ternaries:

I	
SPIRITUAL LIFE-GIVING CAUSE: SPIRIT OF THE SPIRIT	
1. The Magician א	*10. The Wheel of Fortune* י
The principle of consciousness, the ego, the immaterial core from which thought procedes. Pure Idea, antecedent to all expression.	Fiery matter, principle of individual birth, the spiritual core which stimulates perpetual action.

II	
ACTIVE SPIRITUAL EMANCIPATION: SOUL OF THE SPIRIT	
2. The Priestess ב	*11. Strength* כ
The creative Word, Thought-act from which the Idea is born. Image to be brought into being.	The full development of the individual. His own action.

III	
THE SPIRITUAL PRODUCT CREATED: BODY OF THE SPIRIT	
3. The Empress ג	*12. The Hanged Man* ל
Subjective concept. Thought-object or idea, unexpressed, enclosed in the spirit.	The spiritual sphere of the individual. Mental environment. Ideas made objective, dreams, magnetized and vitalized conceptions.

VI	
THE PSYCHIC LIFE-GIVING CAUSE: SPIRIT OF THE SOUL	
4. The Emperor ד	*13. Death* מ
The principle of life, the centre which gives will-power, experiences feelings and engenders the psychic life.	The renewing principle of individual life. Cause of transformation and exchanges which stimulate vital movement.

V	
PSYCHIC ACTION: SOUL OF THE SOUL	
5. The Pope ה	*14. Temperance* נ
The psychic life, act of feeling and willing.	Universal life which passes from one individual life to another.

VI
PSYCHIC RESULT: BODY OF THE SOUL

6. *The Lovers* ו
Feeling. Will-power shown.
The sphere of the will.
A formulated wish. Desire.

15. *The Devil* ס
Physical vitality.
Vital fluid. The instinct to try.
The impulses of the ego.

VII
ACTIVE CAUSE: SPIRIT OF THE BODY

7. *The Chariot* ז
The generating and
directive principle of
universal movement.

16. *The Tower* ע
The principle of
individual rebellion.
Materializing and incarnating cause.

VIII
MOVEMENT, PSYHIC ACTION: SOUL OF THE BODY

8. *Justice* ח
Organic law of
general functioning.
Act of continuous creation.

17. *The Star* פ
Birth of concrete forms
through which an ideal
of beauty is reflected.

IX
PSYCHIC RESULT: BODY OF THE BODY

9. *The Hermit* ט
Union of active forces.
The immaterial web of the organism.
Astral body.

18. *The Moon* צ
Physical creation.
Organism. Matter.
The senses and their illusion.

THE SYNTHESIZED TERNARY

Earthly Adam, created in the image of the Heavenly Adam is destined to rise from the fall which submitted him to material slavery. This redemption appears to us in the last ternary of the Tarot.

19. *The Sun* ק Spirit, Redeemer, Divine Reason enlightening created man to regenerate and make him divine.

20. *Judgement* ר Soul. The act of Redemption. Holy spirit or divine breath, enriching the intelligence. Eternal life.

21. *The World* ש Body. Redemption accomplished. Reintegration into the divine unity. Matter rendered spiritual, glorious and divine. Reign of God. Holy Jerusalem. Perfection attained.

At this point it is appropriate to put the whole of the seven ternaries into one great unity, depicted by the *Fool*, the symbol of the *Ensoph*, Endless, Infinite, the Unknown, the Mystery of Mysteries. This First Night, Void, Nothingness, Abyss from which everything emerges and returns, seems to be as nothing, although possessing the sole of eternal and constant existence. It is the Being-non-Being which, through its absurd and contradictory aspect, confuses our reasoning power, but it imposes itself upon our reason as being necessary and ineluctable. As a symbol it is given the closed eye, a black disc or the zero, 0, of our numerical system. Concerning our knowledge, we have here the undifferentiated Unity, that which is, although seeming to us as if non-existent. For in fact the absolute state of oneness is beyond the grasp of our perceptions which are enslaved to the law of contrasts. Perceiving, therefore, is synonymous with discernment. But what we can distinguish is infinitesimal compared with what remains fused in the imperceptible Oneness. All our Knowledge will for ever be lost as an atom in the immensity of our ignorance; thus the sphere of the *Fool* must envelop and so to speak drown that of all the other arcanas. [17]

THE THREE SEPTENARIES

Out of the seven ternaries, made up of the first 21 arcanas, the first three are in opposition to the following three, and the last one brings back the whole to the unit. The law of the septenary is thus revealed to us. It is moreover, clarified by Solomon's seal, as the following figure shows, in which the sum of the opposing numbers is always equal to 7 (1 + 6 = 7, 2 + 5 = 7, 3 + 4 = 7).

The two entwined triangles represent the fertile union of the two factors necessary for all birth: Male and Female, Active and Passive,

Tarot of the Magicians

Fire and Water, Spirit and Matter, etc. To this double factor which engenders and conceives are related the first six terms of each of the septenaries of the Tarot, whose seventh term is synthetic, indicating the return to the Unity, at the same time that the result is brought about.

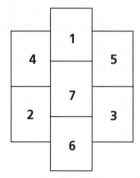 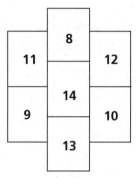 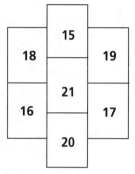

After all that has been said about the ternary, one should not hesitate in the attribution of these three septenaries which correspond to the following trilogies:

Spirit	Soul	Body
Thought	Life	Action
Subject	Verb	Object
Cause	Action	Effect

The first septenary links together the first two ternaries of the Tarot, whose synthesis, represented by the arcana 7, depicts the life-giving Spirit governing the organs. There is no difficulty whatsoever in this point of view if we refer to the earlier explanations.

The second septenary brings about the universal life (14) of the following factors.

Actively:

8. *Justice.* Primordial law of all activity.
9. *The Hermit.* Latent energies accumulated with man's constructive work in view.
10. *Wheel of Fortune.* Life-giving principle which gives its first impulses to individual existence.

Passively:

11. *Strength.* The expansion of the individual.
12. *The Hanged Man.* The individual word translatable into life strength.
13. *Death.* Continual renewing of human existences.

The third septenary initiates us, in a similar way, into the mysteries of eternal substance which is in turn condensed and then etherialized.

Active condensing principles:

15. *The Devil.* Tempting instinct, the source of restrictive egotism, making bodily.
16. *The Tower.* Fall, rebellion, isolation, embodiment.
17. *The Star.* Production of concrete forms.

Principles of etherialization which are passively experienced:

18. *The Moon.* Elaboration of Matter through the fallen spirit.
19. *The Sun.* Marriage of the Spirit with purified matter.
20. *Judgement.* Final spiritualization.

CHAPTER 4

The Astronomical Tarot

THE ZODIAC

It is impossible not to attach the symbolism of certain arcanas of the Tarot to astronomy.

The 18th key, from this point of view is particularly striking. In it one can see a crayfish which corresponds to *Cancer* (crab) the sign of the zodiac which the astrologers designate the home of the Moon. The two dogs remind us of the *Canis Major* (big dog) and the *Canis Minor* (small dog) which mark the dog days, and whose principal stars are Sirius and Procyn, respectively. By their barking, these animals claim the Moon is forced to stay within the ecliptic zone whose boundaries are marked by two towers rising at the two points of the solstice.

The following key, the 19th, shows two characters tenderly embracing. These are *Gemini* (The Twins) as they appear to us in the twelfth century in an illustration of the treatise on Astronomy of King Alphonse X.[18] Our third sign of the zodiac corresponded among the Babylonians to the 'Month of the Bricks'. Now, by a strange coincidence, to say the least, the two children of the arcana 19 are protected by a wall of multicoloured bricks.

It should be noted astrology puts the home of the arcana of the *Sun* in the *Leo* (Lion), and not in *Gemini*. The Tarot takes into account the fact that *Gemini* ends with the longest days, hence at the triumph of light. Moreover, the Sun of the *Gemini* is essentially life-giving, as opposed to that of the Lion which dries up and kills.

The 11th key shows the Lion of the Zodiac tamed by the Virgin of the harvests, who puts an end to excessive heat.

This Virgin is, moreover, represented separately in arcana 3, where she is winged, which suits an *Empress*. This detail is very important, for it suggests the idea of an early Tarot, reproducing astronomical symbolism more faithfully than ours. Moreover, it emphasizes the arbitrary quality of the denominations, clearly attributed to the arcanas in an era when their real significance was lost from sight.

It is again the same Virgin who holds the Scales in arcana 8. The Zodiac constellation which in the Roman era received the name of this instrument had been related, by the Greeks, to the Scorpion, whose claws it depicted. But the new designation seems to have been brought from Chaldea, where the ideas of right and justice have in very ancient times been associated with this region of the sky.[19]

To the five consecutive signs already identified is linked *Aquarius,* who appears to us bearing the features of the spirit of *Temperance* (14).

The other signs are less easy to identify. The monster, Typhon, of the *Wheel of Fortune* (10) however, evokes the figure of *Capricorn,* Suhuruinzu or the Goat Fish of the Babylonians. It symbolizes the darkness and restrictive cold of the winter solstice, and by extension, egoism, ferocity, betrayal.

It is the destructive principle which descends, whereas Hermanubus opposite it rises, reminding us of the dog days, the dilating heat of the summer solstice, devotion, kindness, fidelity. The sphinx armed with the sword corresponds to the autumn equinox (sign of *Libra,* the Scales, arcana 8, equilibrium).

Scorpio, the inauspicious sign which has been held responsible for numerous mythological catastrophes, links up admirably with the 16th key (*The Tower*). One may, moreover, recognize a scorpion in the letter Ayn 𝕪, which the silhou-

ette of the principal figure struck by lightning outlines as he falls.

Sagittarius is especially characterized by the bow and arrow, arms which figure in the Tarot only in arcana 6 (*The Lover*). The Babylonians made a winged centaur of it, with two heads and two tails, of which one is scorpion-like, as the sketch at left shows. This was inspired by the engraved milestone of the twelfth century B.C., kept in the British Museum.

The last three signs present more difficulties.

Could one, moreover, hesitate in connecting the *Ram* to the fifth key of the Tarot? The number 5 corresponds to Quintessence, whose mystery brings back the four-fold Elements to Unity. Now this fifth principle has for its sign the apocalyptic lamb lying on the cross, or the Ram of the Zodiac consecrated to Jupiter Ammon (the hidden god to whom the inner essence of objects is attached). Among the Chaldeans, the heavenly animal which marks the first of the twelve signs was called Lu-lim, sheep's head, because it appeared as the leader of the flock of stars. It was the favourite of Inmishara, the god of agriculture, for one attributed to him the life-giving warmth of the spring sun which revives nature, numbed by winter cold. The ideas of rebirth, or renewal of life and redemption are thus associated right back to early antiquity with the Judaeo-Christian symbol of Easter.

Agnis and Ignis (Lamb and Fire) have, moreover, been compared with the famous Agni of the Vedas (sacred book of the Hindus), the sacred flame which the oldest priestly rites made leap out of the centre of a wooden cross. One should see here an allusion to this Aryan instrument whose bent cross 卍 shown as the swastika, a prehistoric emblem which became familiar to the Christians of the Catacombs.

The Sepher Jezirah attributes the sign of the Ram to the He ה, the fifth letter of the Hebrew alphabet. Here we agree with the kabbalistic treatise, but we disagree concerning all the other attributions.[20]

If the Tarot were inspired by the Sepher Jezirah, the 2nd key would represent the Sun and the 11th the Moon; now these two stars correspond to the arcanas 19 and 18.

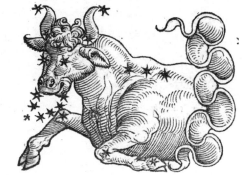

The sign of *Taurus* could have been originally the first in the Zodiac. At least 'alpŭ' or 'alap' means ox in Assyrian, just as Aleph, the first letter of the Semitic alphabet. Now, as this letter corresponds to the *Magician* (1), we thought we could link to this card both *Taurus* and the constellation Orion. This constellation in the sky takes the sign of the Aleph squared א.

Pisces, when together at Andromeda, have only been able to be linked to the 17th key which only shows us, it is true, a young girl naked leaning over a stream of water.

CONSTELLATIONS OUTSIDE THE ZODIAC

Looking at arcana 7, it is difficult not to think of the Chariot of David, the common name for the *Ursa Major*, whose seven principal stars, once called the seven plough oxen, 'Septem triones', have given the north the name of 'Septentrion'.

The 21st key the *World*, represents a young girl naked who is dancing within an encircling garland of leaves. This is the principle of fixity which is moving, only to remain motionless in the whirl of universal life. Astronomically speaking, it is the polar star, the pivot of the revolutions of the stars. The moving garland becomes then the Zodiac, the Wheel of Ezekiel, whose cardinal points are marked by the Kabbalistic quaternary, corresponding to the Evangelists, to the seasons, to the elements, etc.

Angel	*Lion*	*Ox*	*Eagle*
St Matthew	St Mark	St Luke	St John
Winter	Summer	Spring	Autumn
Water	Fire	Earth	Air

Near the pole shine the constellations of the *Ursa Minor* and of *Cepheus*. The king of Ethiopia wears a rimmed turban which is not without analogy with the *Fool*'s headwear. Moreover, he is walking on the Bear, which one could have made into the lynx who is biting the *Fool*'s leg. Moreover, this fits in very well with the dark skin of the Ethiopian.

Black, moreover, fits in with the *Priestess* (2) who corresponds to *Cassiopeia*, represented as veiled and sitting on a canopied throne. In short it is about Isis, black but beautiful, like the spouse in the Song of Songs, and like the wife clothed in Sun, described by the Apocalypse.

Cepheus and *Cassiopeia* have as their daughter *Andromeda*, whom one of the *Pisces* (17) [turned into a sea monster] is threatening. But the African princess is saved by Perseus who can be found in the symbol of the *Hanged Man* (12). Here, and elsewhere, allusion is made to the power of thought. Momentarily powerless in the *Hanged Man*, it acts and triumphs over Lies (Medusa) in the person of Perseus. Let us not forget that this subtle hero received from Pluto the helmet of invisibility, that he shelters moreover behind the buckler of Minerva, which is decorated with the frightening head of Medusa, and thanks to the heel-wings of Mercury, he can fly. What can he symbolize, if it is not the mysterious triumph of thought, which in a telepathic way is powerful as his arms are powerless, condemned to inaction like those of the *Hanged Man*?

The Coachman of the celestial sphere, is none other than the god Pan, the guide of all animals. He carries on his back the goat, Amaltheus, followed by two kids. This ternary corresponds to the *Devil* of arcana 15, flanked by two little devils, male and female. The connection here is strict from the esoteric point of view.

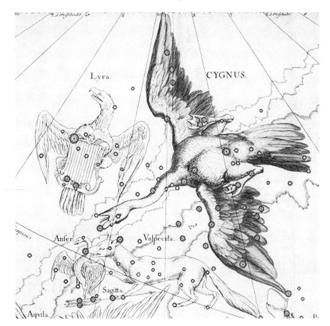

Cygnus, the Swan of the constellations is Leda's. Jupiter, the fire of heaven, took its form in order to mate with a mortal woman by whom he had Castor and Pollux, the Twins of the Zodiac (19). The fertile bird makes us think here of the Dove of the Holy Spirit, the symbol to which arcana 20 has put in its place the Angel of the Judgement, which impregnates the earth with its great breath, in order to make the seeds which are enclosed within the earth hatch out.

Draco, the Dragon, of the Pole, corresponds to the Crocodile which lies in wait for the Fool. A formidable Destroyer, he deserves to be likened to card 13 (*Death*).

The Dragon is what the occultists call the Guardian of the Threshold. The initiated must conquer him in order to get into the garden of the Hesperides and win the famous golden apples. This was accomplished by Hercules, who we may identify with the *Emperor* (4) of the Tarot. The eagle of arcana 4 would then be connected with the constellation of the Vulture.

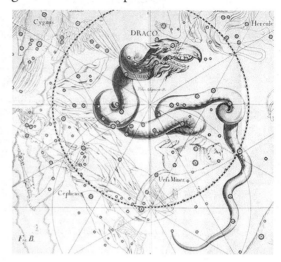

All the arcanas have thus found a place in the sky except for the *Hermit* (9) who can only be likened to the Herdsman. This name reminds us of the seven oxen—*septem triones*—whose leader was also envisaged as a harvester, the husband or father of the Virgin Erigone (3, *Empress*); from the point of view of the Hermit-Herdsman would thus be identical with Saint Joseph.

GENERAL SYMBOLISM OF THE GREEK PLANISPHERE

The Ancients divided the sky into four regions each one dedicated to one of the Elements.

The Spring signs of the Zodiac belong to the Earth: *Aries* (5), *Taurus* (1) and *Gemini* (19), *Orion* (1) and *Lupus* in the south with *Capra* (15) and *Ursa Major* (7) and *Ursa Minor* (21) in the north.

The signs of Summer relate to Fire: *Cancer*[21] (18), *Leo* (11) and *Virgo* (3), then *Canis Major* and *Minor* (18) who also take their part in nature, in the same way as the *Herdsman-Harvester* (9), whose Lion of Ceres has ripened the harvest.

Air is represented by *Aquila*, *Vulture*, *Cygnus* (20), which is at the same time aquatic, and Pegasus, the winged horse which skims the Earth. In the Zodiac this Element has the signs of Autumn, *Libra* (8), *Scorpio* (6) and *Sagittarius* (6).

Water begins at *Capricorn* (14) and *Pisces* (17) complete the signs of Winter. To it one adds also the *Dolphin*, the *Whale* and the *River Eridanus* which leads back to the Earth.

In the centre, participating in all the elements, but especially in Water and Fire, the Dragon of the Pole winds its twisting way. Near to it *Hercules* (4), *Ophichus*, *Cepheus* (0), *Cassiopeia* (21) and *Perseus* (12) participate in more complex natures.

This information and that which precedes it are summed up in two diagrams. One simply indicates the constellations corresponding to each arcana. The other is in the form of a map of the sky made with the help of the 22 keys (see pages 40–41).

Arcanas of the Tarot	Constellations and Signs of the Zodiac
1. א Magician	Orion, Taurus ♉
2. ב Priestess	Cassiopeia, Queen of Ethiopia, wife of Cepheus (Fool)
3. ג Empress	*Virgo,* ♍ daughter of the Herdsman
4. ד Emperor	Hercules, Vantour, Corona Borealis
5. ה Pope	*Aries* ♈
6. ו Lovers	Aquila, Antinous, *Sagittarius* ♐
7. ז Chariot	Ursa Major
8. ח Justice	*Libra* ♎
9. ט Hermit	Herdsman or Harvester
10. י Wheel of Fortune	*Capricorn* ♑
11. כ Strength	*Leo* ♌
12. ל Hanged Man	Perseus
13. מ Death	Dragon of the Pole
14. נ Temperance	*Aquarius* ♒
15. ס Devil	Coachman, Goat
16. ע Tower	Ophichus, *Scorpio* ♏
17. פ Star	Andromeda, *Pisces* ♓
18. צ Moon	Canis Major and Canis Minor, *Cancer* ♋
19. ק Sun	*Gemini* ♊
20. ר Judgement	Swan
21. ת World	Pole Star, the whole of the Sphere
O. ש Fool	Cepheus, Ursa Minor

CHAPTER 5

Notions of Symbolism: Forms and Colours

THE IDEOGRAPHIC TETRAD

As the reader has been able to see, the Tarot is constructed on numbers; now these are closely linked to geometry, loved by Plato who had written on the door of the school: 'No one comes in here, if he is not a geometrist!'

The philosopher certainly did not scorn the science of Euclid; but did he not for preference aim at the methods of Pythagoras, which teach us how to reason through geometric forms? It still remains that the somewhat complex ideography of the Hermetists of the Middle Ages is related to the four following generating signs:

$$\bigcirc \; + \; \triangle \; \square$$

Three of these figures are closed, which makes them correspond to fixed entities, to substances.[22] The cross, on the other hand, is open so that it indicates nothing limited or tangible, but rather a changing of state, an elaboration to be experienced through a living person, or a substance. Thus the cross is never found by itself in the alchemic ideograms, but always linked to one of the three closed signs.[23]

THE CIRCLE

The geometric point without any dimension is a mere nothing which, when extended in all directions, brings about the circle, just as it engenders the line when it moves in one direction. But what does the circle, conceived in this way correspond to, if not to the vacuum of space? It is the zero in our numerical system, which in the Tarot is the number of the Fool. Alchemy has made the sign of Alum-stone 'the principle salt of other salts, of minerals and metals'.[24] This definition evokes the idea of universal substance, rarefied to the point of imperceptibility to make up the inner essence of things, the ethereal and immaterial base of all material things.

When diluted into the unending vacuum of cosmic space, this substance, everywhere identical to itself, is personified in the Chaldean poem of the Creation[25] by Tiamat, the wife of Apsu, the bottomless chasm, the father/mother of all things. The Greeks depicted it in the emblem of the serpent biting its own tail, and known as Ouroboros, whose motto means One is All. It is the chaos out of which all things come, and all returns, only to come out again. Nothingness which is everything, Night preceding the Fiat Lux of Genesis.

Creative initiative is realized graphically by a simple dot made in the centre of the circle ⊙. Immediately chaos ○ is no longer shapeless and empty, for a central fixed point of vibration fills it with light. The coordinating Sun ○, alone fixed and immovable in the middle of what is moving and changing, becomes the pivot of all creation which it draws continuously from Nothingness. The same sign is attributed to Gold because of the inalterable stability of this metal.

In contrast, Silver, a noble metal, brilliant, but changeable, is compared to the Moon of changing aspects and capricious in its journeys through the constellations. But a whole range of ideas is related to the signs of the two great heavenly stars. Here is an outline of them:

⊙	☽
Sun	*Moon*
Male	Female
Activity	Passivity
Agent	Sufferer
Rays of light	Refracted light
Reason	Imagination
Osiris	Isis
Jakin	Bohas
Gold	Silver
Stability	Mobility
Fixity	Mutability

The sign of the Sun ☉ is always identical to itself, whereas the crescent Moon can trace its points facing right, left, upwards or downwards. In the last two aspects its meanings differ radically. With the points upwards ◡ it triumphs over what is beneath it; with the points downwards ◠ it is enslaved by what dominates it.

It is in this way that the Alkaline Salts ♉ represent the primordial substance ○ subject to the Moon ◡, that is to say, infinitely changeable, like the first Matter of the Great Work, which is subject to all the metamorphoses of nature and of art. One is reminded of the alchemic ideogram by the astrological symbol for Taurus ♉, which relates to the fertilized land, capable of producing every variety within the vegetable kingdom. Now the Earth, as we shall see later, is represented by 🜃 a sign easy to compare ♉ with through ▽.

The reversed sign ☊ corresponds to Rock Salt, a fine substance, which has been unalterable, every possible modification having been made in it, from which we have the Moon ◠, which this substance treads under foot.

The Cross

There is no sign more spontaneous than the archaic Tau or Thav of the Phoenicians +. Its Hebrew name means mark, notch, character of writing, or the letter 'par excellence', no doubt because the hand of those who cannot write automatically makes this signature.

This universal sign is made up of two strokes, one horizontal, outstretched lying passive, feminine, the other vertical, upright, standing, active as if to present the action of male energy which pierces and impregnates. Far from being connected with death, the Cross + is therefore, essentially a sign of life, of fertile union and power to carry out action.

Placed above a sign ♁ ⊞ ▽, the Cross indicates an end, perfection attained. In the opposite position ♀ ⊡ △ it denotes work to be fulfilled, latent powers to be used. Inscribed inside the circle ⊕ the Cross animates the substance ○, which is thus given life and is transformed into vital fluid. It is a question of the condensing of life, such as is seen in vegetables, more especially in the verdigris ⊕ of the Alchemists. The vital force is polarized into active and passive uses, to bring about, on one hand Nitre ⦶, an infernal salt, explosive, the source of combustion, but also of active energy, and on the other hand, Sea Salt ⊖, placid, stable, tending always to self renewal in repose and equilibrium. (Flat as opposed to the Perpendicular in Masonic symbolism.)

In all that lives, active and passive combine in varying proportion according to the kingdoms. Fullness of life ⊕ is the attribute of vegetables, thanks to the balance of activity and passivity in them. Their calm life is less active than that of animals, symbolized by Vitriol ⦶. In contrast minerals live passively, as if their souls were only partially active ⊖. One is tempted to say that they do not live, but are lived, in their own way.

The sign of mineral vitality ⊕ is transformed into the ideogram of the *World* when it is surmounted by the Cross ♁. The Hermetists saw in it the emblem of sovereign power (the imperial globe), for marvels are accomplished by the help of the great magic agent, the mysterious strength bound to the Soul of the World.

By laying the sign of sublimate mineral on its side ♁ we obtain that blue vitriol (copper sulphate) ⊕⊢, which is related to the passive and feminine animal fluid, to which masculine active magnetization is opposed, represented by Green Vitriol ⊕. The arrow indicates projection out of oneself, an action performed on other people. The lateral cross, on the other hand, alludes to a fertile union.

If we compare the signs ♁ ⊕ and ♀, we come to the following distinctions:

♁ *Antimony*	{	Intellect, Upward or spiritualizing influence. Spirit freeing itself from matter. Evolution—Redemption	↑
♀ *Verdigris*	{	Vegetable spirit. Physical vitality. Spirit of the flesh, one with matter. Health, balance in life.	+
⊕ *Venus of Bronze*	{	Power of Instinct. Drawing towards the material. Fall of the spirit into matter. Involution.	↓

THE SIGNS OF THE PLANETS

As if nailed to the firmament, the fixed stars keep their distances for ever, whereas other stars wander among them. These are the Planets whom the Ancients likened to the Sun and the Moon, so much so that immense prestige was acquired for the following septenary, conserved even today in the way the days of the week are appointed.

☉	Sun	Gold	Sunday
☽	Moon	Silver	Monday
♂	Mars	Iron	Tuesday
☿	Mercury	Quicksilver	Wednesday
♃	Jupiter	Tin	Thursday
♀	Venus	Copper	Friday
♄	Saturn	Lead	Saturday

The reader already knows three of these signs: ☉, ☽ and ♁. Mars ♂ will offer no difficulty, for Green Vitriol ⊕ corresponds to the martial or aggressive power which is stimulated by the need for action or fighting instinct, personified by the god of war.

In contrast, Blue Vitriol ⊕+ is inspired by Venus ♀, the personification of tenderness and of repose and langour, repairing the destruction caused by Mars.

To this pair of opposites we can add the Sun ☉ and the Moon ☽, which were mentioned on page 49 and the pair Jupiter ♃ and Saturn ♄, planets with ideograms made up of the Cross and Crescent Moon.

But the symbol of change ☽ in ♃ is connected with the horizontal branch of the Cross, which it tends to dominate; in contrast it is hooked under the vertical stroke of the Cross in ♄. One may deduce from this that Jupiter ♃ and ♀ (Venus) relate to an elaboration which is yet to be completed. Whereas Saturn ♄ just as ♁ (Antimony), alludes to a completed work. But since the Crescent is prominent on the two signs, then it is a question of a transforming task in both cases. Moreover these divergencies are shown clearly as follows:

♃ *Jupiter — Tin*

The Cross beneath the Crescent Moon
Potential transforming action in the seed.
Growth.
Youth.
Connection with the horizontal stroke
Materialization.
Construction of the organism.
Generating principle of material life.

As for Mercury ☿ which occupies the centre of the septenary of the Planets its sign is made up of ♀ (Venus) surmounted by the Cross. So it is also vitality ♀ which has undergone involuntary changes as well as the primordial substance ♉ rendered active and fertile. The Mercury of the Alchemists is in fact the universal substratum of life, subject to all modifications.

When the Crescent is replaced by the sign of the Ram of the Zodiac the ideogram obtained is that of Mercury of the Wise Men. This stimulating substance penetrates right into the centre of seeds to make them germinate; it is through its intermediary action that all living beings are animated by the same universal life.

By turning the sign of Mercury upside down ☿ we obtain an ideogram which we only meet in the outline of the Queen of the Skies ♁. Antimony ♁ (the Power of the Intellect) dominates the Crescent ☽ in all that is corruptible and changing, unless it is a question of Rock Salt ♈ crowned by the Cross, that is to say, having reached supreme purification.

♄ *Saturn — Lead*

The Cross above the Crescent Moon
Completed Formation.
Decrepitude.
Old Age.
Suspension on to the vertical stroke
Spiritualization.
Dissolution of the organism.
Transforming principle leading to death.

The study of the septenary of the planets is made easier by the following diagram which brings out the relationships of the planets to each other.

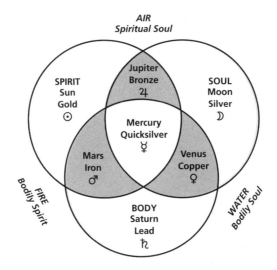

THE TRIANGLE

The Elements of the Hermetists have nothing in common with simple bodies or elements of modern chemistry, for only elemented things come within the sphere of our senses. The elements can only reproduce, recreate, conceive themselves. Their quaternary determines all matter, without their being materializing forces, which put order into chaos by stamping it with their qualities, as in Dry and Humid, Cold and Hot.

Why are they represented by triangles? Probably to remind of flame which rises in a point: △ Fire, or the Goblet ready to receive Water ▽. Air ⊖ could then be likened to Fire △ now made passive by a horizontal stroke and Earth ⊖ considered as Water ▽ similarly thickened, solidified and given weight.

Tarot of the Magicians

Ideograms	▽̶	△	△̶	▽
Elements	*Earth*	*Fire*	*Air*	*Water*
Seasons	Spring	Summer	Autumn	Winter
Kabbalistic Quaternary	Ox	Lion	Eagle	Angel
Signs of the Zodiac	♉	♌	♏	♒
Evangelists	Luke	Mark	John	Matthew
Planets	Saturn	Mars	Jupiter	Venus
Metals	Lead	Iron	Tin	Copper
Signs of Planets	♄	♂	♃	♀
Colours	Black	Red	Blue	Green
Elementary qualities	Cold and dry	Dry and hot	Hot and humid	Humid and cold

The extremely subtle theory of the Elements seems scarcely to have preoccupied the authors of the Tarot; but they were not ignorant of the links which the diagram above shows.

The Cross combines with the Triangle to form the sign of Sulphur ♧ and that of the Great Work when accomplished ♧̶. Sulphur ♧ is the active Fire imprisoned in the core of each being called to life. As long as the Mercury of the Wise Men has not blown on this Fire, life remains latent; it is the breath of Mercury that sustains the vital combustion until all fuel is exhausted (Oil or Sulphur, Humidity).

The Great Work is accomplished when ♧̶ life-giving Water ▽ has undergone the complete series of purifying distillations, when the soul, emerging victorious from its cycle of tests, shows its transcendent powers.

It should be noticed that Water ▽ corresponds in a mysterious way to life-giving essence, which all souls possess, whereas, seen from the same point of view Salt ⊖ represents the total sphere of the personality, constantly enlarged by expansive action of sulphurous or internal energies ♧ and at the same time compressed by the pressure of the surrounding mercurial element.

Such is the brief interpretation of the ternary Sulphur ⚵ Salt ⊖ and Mercury ☿ on which all Hermetism is based.

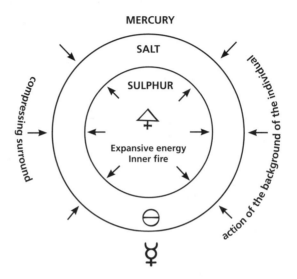

THE SQUARE

When submitted to the coordinating action of the four Elements, the undefined chaotic substance ○ is transformed into matter which is then likely to come into the sphere of our senses □. The opposing pairs of elementary attractions gives shape to what is formless, and maintains a balance, which is an indispensable condition of all manifestation.

The perfect square □ implies an ideal of equilibrium, found in the realm of health and saintliness, such as it is realized by the Adept who has shaped himself in a square form, in impeccable Cubic Stone □, or even better by the Wise man who has found the Philosopher's Stone ⊡. Here as in the ideograms of Saturn, or Antimony, and in the accomplishment of the Great Work, the Cross indicates

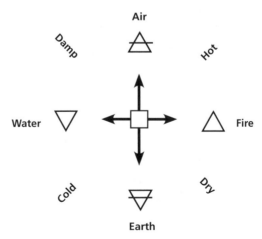

an achievement, that of the individual victorious over material life, so that matter is no longer for him the indispensable support for the manifestation of the spirit, the ballast which holds a soul back in the sphere of bodily action when it is already in the sphere of the skies.

Tartar is in opposition to the Stone of the Wise Man. Already the rectangle, wider than it is high, indicates non-spiritual matter which however would not become base because of the straightness of the angles of the Cross, an indication of its power to be used and put to practical purpose. It is the equivalent of the Unpolished, Uncut Stone, quickly and roughly hewn which the Apprentices have to cut to shape according to future requirements.

The correspondences between the three aspects of the Stone are as follows:

♀	☐	☩
Uncut Stone	**Cubic Stone**	**Philosophers' Stone**
Apprentice	**Companion**	**Master**
J	**B**	**M**
Youth	**Virility**	**Old Age**
Learning	**Practice**	**Teaching**
Birth	**Living**	**Death**
♃	♂	♄

COLOURS

The prism splits up white light into three Primary colours: Red, Blue and Yellow which from this point of view correspond to the ternaries—Mind, Soul, Body or Sulphur, Mercury, Salt. In this pattern of ideas, the secondary colours Violet, Green and Orange are in affinity with the spiritual soul, the Corporal soul or Vitality and the Corporal mind.

In a more general fashion the symbolism of colours can be worked out thus:

White: Synthetic, reminding us of pure snow, becomes synonymous with purity, innocence, candour, loyalty, harmony, reconciliation and peace (white dress of the communicants, of brides, orange blossom, white flag of parliamentarians). It is also the colour of integrity, of honesty, conscience but especially of Being and of Light as opposed to Black. Nothingness is reflected in fact in gloomy Black, the colour of Death, of fatality, despair,

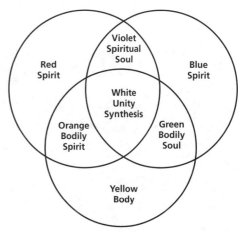

disillusion, but also of depth, seriousness, severity, taciturn application, conspiracy and mystery. Nourishing Earth is black. Every birth is carried out in darkness, in secret, hidden from the indiscreet.

Grey: Ashes, the indestructible remains of what has lived, inertia, indifference, detachment, lack of determination, humility, poverty, sadness, self-effacement.

Red: Blood, the life-giving principle, Activity, Spiritual fire, warmth, love, courage, energy.

Purple: Spirituality, reason, will power, domination.

Blue: The heavenly sky, contemplation, piety, fidelity, faith. Air.

Violet: (combination of red and blue) Intellectuality, discernment, mysticism, teaching, fusion of reason and feeling.

Yellow: (complement of Violet) Rays of light, objectives reached, Body, fixation, stability, harvest, honey, wealth achieved through work.

Orange or Scarlet (complement of Blue) Flame, material fire, vehemence, passion, ferocity, cruel instinct, selfishness, need for action, Mars.

Green: (complement of Red) Vegetation, life-giving fluid, fuel for active fire, Venus, lascivity, languor, laziness.

Indigo: Meditation, experience, knowledge.

Brown: Wood, survival, tradition, superstition, concentration, loneliness, reserve, discretion.

Rose: (flesh colour) Everything that is human or is related to humanity.

Gold: Intellectual perfection, treasures of the mind; incontestable truths, indestructible possessions.

Silver: Moral perfection, treasures of the soul; justified beliefs, nobility of heart, purity of the imagination.

CHAPTER 6

The Tarot and the Hebrew Alphabet

The number 22 incontestably links the Tarot cards with the Semitic alphabet, for this number does not correspond to any other series. Is this a reason for considering the Tarot pictures to be inspired by the form of the letters of the sacred alphabet of the Kabbalists? One could not come to the conclusion that a deliberate system has been followed simply by our referring to a few similarities.

It could, however, be noted that the leaning body of the *Magician* (1) traces an Aleph א with his arms.

The king hurtling down from the top of the *Tower* (16) moreover reminds us of the Ayin ע.

We saw also a Heth ח in the scales of *Justice* (8).

On the other hand some goodwill is needed to see the head, the right arm and the lantern of the *Hermit* (9) in the Teth ט.

The open jaws of the lion tamed by *Strength* (11) makes the outline of the Caph כ turned round. It seems to be going too far to make anything of this.

As for the legs of the *Hanged Man* (12) which reproduce, if you like, the stroke of the Lamed ל, are they really likely to be remembered?

As he bends over his scythe, *Death* (8) at least traces more clearly the outline of the Mem מ.

But as for the arms of *Temperance* (14), do they really aim at sketching a Nun נ?

In that case, the young girl of the *Star* (17) can be seen in the Phé פ.

And why should not the Crayfish of the *Moon* (18) find its outline in the Tsadé צ?

If these connections are justified, they contribute only to show the medieval origin of the Tarot, for they are related to the calligraphic forms of the Square Hebrew and not to those of the oldest Palestinian alphabets. Now the very early forms differ completely from those which have been fixed by the invention of typography.

In order to give the reader an overall picture of the changes which the Hebrew alphabet has undergone, we show below a diagram which indicates the forms which the letters have taken in turn from the ninth century before our era. The oldest alphabetical inscription of known date goes back in fact to Mesa, king-of Moab, who in about 895 B.C. commissioned the engraving of his famous stela, which is now kept in the Louvre.

To the table we have added the name of the letters and the meaning which is attributed to this sign without forgetting the customary transcription in Latin characters.

CARD	HISTORICAL FORMS	HEBREW	NAME	MEANING	LATIN
1		א	Aleph	Ox	A
2	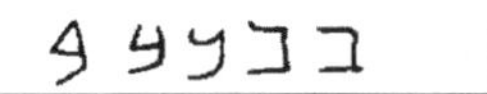	ב	Beth	House	B
3		ג	Gimel	Camel	C
4	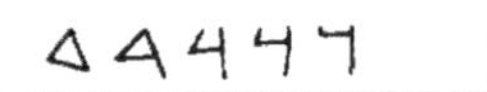	ד	Daleth	Door	D
5	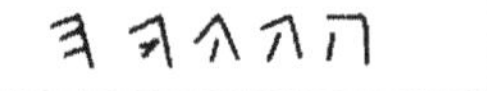	ה	Hé	Window	E
6	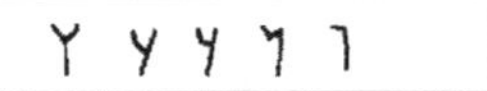	ו	Vau	Hook	V
7	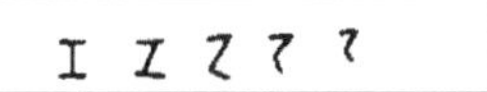	ז	Zain	Arm	Z
8	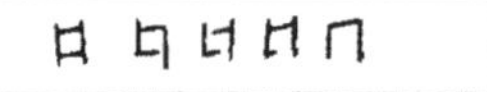	ח	Heth	Hedge	H
9	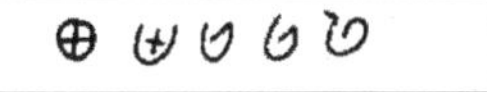	ט	Teth	Mud	Th
10	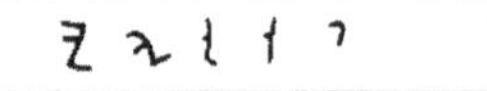	י	Jod	Hand	J
11	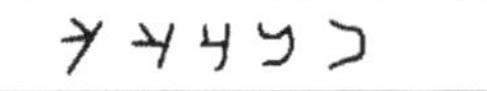	כ	Caph	Palm	K
12	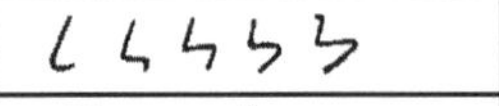	ל	Lamed	Needle	L
13	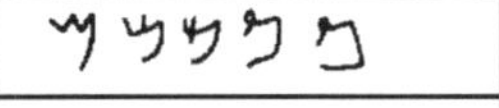	מ	Mem	Water	M
14	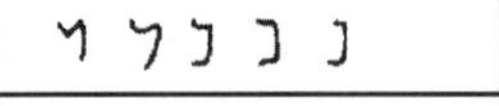	נ	Nun	Fish	N
15	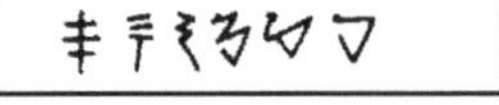	ס	Samek	Post	S
16	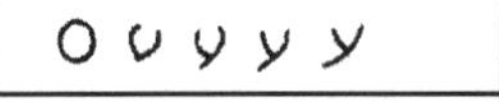	ע	Ayn	Eye	O
17	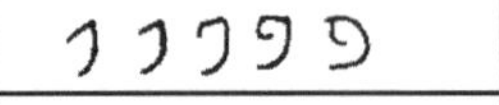	פ	Phé	Mouth	P
18	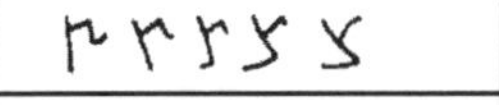	צ	Tsadé	Javelin	Ts
19	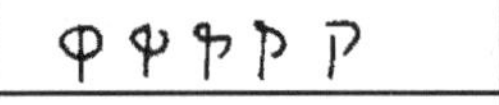	ק	Quof	Monkey	Q
20	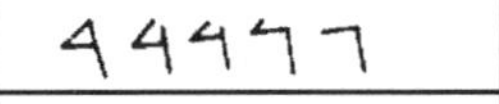	ר	Resch	Head	R
21	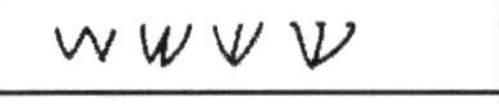	ש	Schin	Tooth	Sch
22	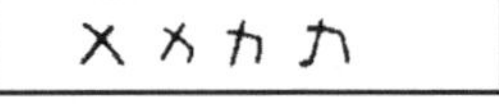	ת	Tau	Cross	T

The Symbolism
of the Twenty-Two Keys to the
Secret Knowledge of the Middle Ages

The Language of Symbolism

With the clarifying explanations of the Tarot as a whole which have been given to him, the reader can start a profitable analytic study of each arcana. For it is a question of explaining (to himself) the symbolism of the details of the twenty-two compositions which offer their enigmas to his powers of discernment. But faced with silent pictures destined to make him think, his task consists in discovering in them the things that are hidden within himself.

But a magic mirror shows nothing to those whose spirit is blind. Without philosophic vision there is no spiritual perception; in this sphere we can only perceive by using our thinking activity and power to evoke. No one can render accessible to us what we cannot see for ourselves, for it is impossible to think, to meditate and above all to study, for anyone else. There is nothing easier than discussing *ad infinitum* a collection of symbols, such as the Tarot, but chatter is just what the authors of all silent books do not intend.

Do not let ourselves indulge in it. Rather than pouring out water freely to the thirsty, we prefer to lead them to the spring where they can draw for themselves at leisure.

Our information—we do not pretend otherwise—is fatally incomplete and arbitrary, for we could only examine it from the angle of our personal vision. The investigator of the Tarot should not therefore be content with what he has found. The result of our exploration is to be found in the marking out of a track, to the right or left of which stretches a wide enticing space for the eager mind to fathom the mysteries. Each of us will become involved in it according to his likings and to what attracts him, at the same time benefiting from our landmarks.

We have established these landmarks as best we can, being careful not to wander, but without claiming to acquaint the reader with the immeasurable territory into which we wanted to penetrate in a straight line. Our itinerary has the advantage of safety, for we have marked it out with the help of all the means we had at our disposal. But it is not enough to follow us passively. We are writing for those truly able to become initiates, whose ambition is to become through their own efforts, initiated into the mysteries, by devoting themselves to the work of the mind, which is indispensable in this respect.

One can learn of worldly things by listening to the words of teachers. It is not the same case with initiation. The real secret remains for ever incommunicable. It is not passed on by word of mouth. To possess it one must succeed in assimilating it in the mind, by discovering it within oneself.

The discovery is made by the use of symbols which become eloquent for the independent thinker, whose thoughts awaken at the unspoken view of things, without waiting for the stimulant of human speech. Ever since knowledge has been inculcated in schools by dint of words, we have unfortunately become unused to thinking. Things mean nothing to us any more, and we just stand stupid when faced with them. We only know how to read what is written in letters of the alphabet and do not manage to discover the meaning of a picture: it is the triumph of the dead letter, victorious over the mind. To learn to think, let us close our manuals and escape from the sound of speech.

Silence teaches the disciple of these ancient wise men who were involved in deciphering the hieroglyphics of natural ideography. For them all forms became expressive, profound views being suggested by the simplest mark. It was in this way that they conceived the philosophic geometry beloved by Plato. The demonstration and the theorem were applied to abstract notions which are related to lines and figures. The dot, the cross, the circle, the triangle, etc. served as themes of meditation which developed the power of thought (in a different way from the light reading which our minds are fed upon under the regime of the printed word).

Without giving up the benefit of our precious encyclopedias, let us get back to pictures in order to rise to the dignity of real human genius, and not learn as parrots do, brought up to recite their lessons with the volubility of a talking machine or of an automat. The Tarot urges us to effort which, freeing our minds from the clutches of borrowed ideas, will allow it to acquire ideas which we will owe only to ourselves.

This effort is required of the reader who wants to take us as his guide. The commentary which we offer is to be controlled and rectified, to be put right and adapted to the vision of the investigator. The attribute of symbolism is that of remaining indefinitely suggestive: each person can see in it what his visual power allows him to see. Through lack of penetration nothing deep is perceived.

Compared with superficial concepts, the motions which have their usual home in the depths of thought, appear fluid and ill defined. We must make our own decision, for only the terms used in banal intellectual conversation have been made exact in their meaning. In as much as it is a method of expression, symbolism repudiates positivism and lay education, it speaks only to the thinkers who are capable of meditating and of studying deeply. It demands furthermore, that the man who reasons should have imagination and should be sensitive to the poetry in life. All the while that one is involved only in thinking in prose, then the symbols remain undeciphered.

Formerly, when one read less, one thought more by talking silently to oneself. The Spirit of the Ancients took pleasure in sitting astride the Pegasus of philosophic dream to rise with the poets into the high realm of ideas. We need to return to this flight into the skies which is so completely different from our habits of earth-bound movements. Contemporary positivism, rigorous in its deductions, must also be helped by a subtle poet (*vates* in Latin) capable of predicting logically, for the complete thinker shows himself to be a 'diviner' who 'divines' what remains mysterious and unintelligible to the common people.

Far from despising prophecy today we should re-establish the practice of it. Even when it is limited to puerile utterances, it opens to the mind doors which are generally closed. So we shall be careful not to discourage those who study the Tarot, especially from the divinatory point of view, for divination is the mother of all our knowledge, all our philosophies and of all our religions. It is worthy of respect and deserves to be taken seriously.

It is our power of reasoning which forbids us to neglect the divinatory interpretations which the twenty-two arcanas of the Tarot suggest to the lovers of cartomancy.

The evocatory power of this collection of pictures is so wide that no notion escapes the numerical classification adopted by the diviner, according to the instrument which he is used to handling. If it is a question of making the Tarot speak, everything that is conceivable must therefore fit into the twenty-two categories, just as for the diviner by geomancy, things fall into sixteen groups, and the astrologer links all his ideas to the seven planets and to the 12 signs of the Zodiac.

This necessary link does not operate without trouble and some disconcerting discoveries. According to the point of view selected the same symbol can give opposing significances. Taken in an optimistic way, it offers a very different meaning from that which is apparent when the omen must be interpreted unfavourably. We ask the reader who is not familiar with the practice of divination not to stop at contradictions which are more apparent than real.

In order to sort out as best we can the chaos of the inexhaustible interpretation, we should point out first of all for each arcana the ideas of the most transcendent kind.

From metaphysics we go on to the moral or psychic sphere where we find virtues, qualities and aptitudes. We finally descend to the most material meanings and end with vices, misfortunes and faults. Setting out from heaven we end in hell.

If seen as a limbering exercise for the mind, divination has the great merit of making the diviner think for himself by obliging him to divine, thus to fathom the darkness to distinguish what lies hidden in it. Not all attempts are successful, but honest effort is praiseworthy and we are dedicated to supporting it in the interest of the progress of the human spirit.

The Magician

How could a juggler have been put at the head of the Tarot, marked with the number One, which is that of the First Cause? In volume VIII of his *Monde Primitif* Court de Gebelin thinks that the choice of this person is essentially a philosophical one. The visible Universe being but magic and marvel, would not his Creator be the Illusionist *par excellence*, the great Conjuror who dazzles us with his juggling? The universal turmoil and whirl prevents us from seeing reality. We are the dupe of appearance produced by forces at work which are unknown to us.

The first cause is therefore a Magician, but as this first cause is reflected in everything that is active, the opening character of the Tarot corresponds, in a general way, to every principle of activity. In the Universe he is God, seen as the great suggestive power of all that is accomplished in the Cosmos; in man he is the seat of individual initiative, the centre of perception, of conscience and of will power. He is the Ego called to make our personality, for the individual has the mission to create himself.

The principle of self creation is shown to us in the features of a slim young man, supple and of great agility. One feels that the Magician cannot stay in repose. He plays with his wand, he monopolizes the attention of the spectators and dazzles them with his continuous juggling and his contortions, as much as by the mobility of his facial expressions. Moreover his eyes shine with intelligence and have long lashes which accentuate their sparkle. The hat which shades them with its broad brim outlines an 8 lying on its side ∞.

This sign, which the mathematicians have made the symbol of infinity is found also in the headress of *Strength* (arcana XI) and in the *Sphynx d'Astarte* as Pruse d'Avennes shows us.[26]

One may compare this horizontal halo with the living sphere made by the living thoughts emanating from the intelligence. We carry around us our mental sky, the domain which the sun of Reason traces, the ecliptic ∞, held within the narrow limits of what is accessible to us.

Blond curly hair like Apollo's frames the smiling but not open face of the Magician, a character full of shrewdness, hardly inclined to betray the depths of his thoughts.

Discreet in his exuberance, this young man moves around behind a rectangular table, of which only three legs are visible. They could be marked with the signs 🜍, 🜔 and ☿ (Sulphur, Salt and Mercury) for they are the three pillars of the objective world, supports to the substance perceived by our prime senses.

On this table, (the realm of phenomena) are placed three objects; a silver cup, a steel sword and a gold skekel, called a 'pantacle'. It is on this disc, where appear five-pointed stars, that the Magician moves with the index finger of his right hand as if to concentrate his personal active emanation of life onto it. But the coin-amulet will not possess all his strength unless the magic wand directs onto this accumulator the charges taken from the surroundings. This explains the gesture of the Magician's left hand which holds this wand in the exact direction of the coin so that the fire of heaven trapped by the blue knob of the mysterious condenser may be projected by the red knob onto the object which is to be occultly magnetized.

The wand completes the quaternary of the Magician's instruments which correspond to the four verbs: To Know (cup), To Dare (sword), To Want (wand or stick), To be Silent (pentacle). The table shows the analogous connections between the Tetrad which rules the minor arcanas of the Tarot, that is to say, the pack of 56 cards connected with the 22 symbolic compositions which this present work is dealing with:

Pentacle	*Sword*	*Cup*	*Wand*
Diamonds	Spades	Hearts	Clubs
Earth	Air	Water	Fire
ה	ו	ה	י
Ox	Eagle	Angel	Lion

In order to possess these mystical instruments, one must have undergone the test of the Elements.

The victory won over Earth awards us the pentacle, that is to say, the vital point of support for all action needed.

By confronting Air with audacity the knight of Truth wins himself the Sword, symbol of the Word which puts to flight the phantoms of Error.

To triumph over Water is to conquer the Holy Grail, the Cup out of which Wisdom drinks.

Tested by Fire, the Initiated obtains at last the emblem of supreme command, the Wand, the king's sceptre for he reigns through his own will merged with the sovereign will.

As if he had undergone similar trials in a Freemasons' lodge, the Magician places his feet at right angles to each other. The direction of his feet outlines a set square with the tulip bud which seems to rise from the ground beneath the steps of the skilled juggler. This flower gives us to understand that the initiation is still in its early stages, for we still find it fully open in front of the *Emperor* (Arcana IV), drooping near *Temperance* (Arcana XIV) but still alive in front of the *Fool* (Arcana XXII). The Magician's costume is multicoloured, but red, as a sign of activity, is dominant. Five buttons fasten his jacket, no doubt alluding to the quintessence of which the body is the covering.

In the movement of the arms and the bend of the body, the character of Arcana 1 outlines the latter Aleph א of early Hebrew. It should be noted that it would have to be compared with the early Aleph ∢ or ∀ if the Tarot were contemporary with the Semitic Alphabet.

Moreover, nothing reproduces more exactly the outline of the Aleph than that of Orion, the giant who pursues the Pleiades to the edge of Taurus (the Bull) in the sky. Among the constellations it is the one that relates the most closely to the Magician. The Magician becomes a cobbler in the Italian Tarot.

DIVINATORY INTERPRETATIONS

Kether, the crown of the tree of the Sephiroth. The beginning of all things: the first cause, the unity-principle, pure spirit, the unique and universal thinking subject, refracting in the ego of every intelligent creature.

Initiative, the centre of action, the spontaneity of intelligence, keenness of discernment and comprehension, presence of mind, self possession, autonomy, a rejection of all impertinent suggestion, freedom from all prejudice.

Dexterity, skill, diplomatic shrewdness. Persuasive speaker, lawyer, cunning, astuteness, agitation. Lack of scruples, opportunist, intriguer, liar, scoundrel, swindler, charlatan, exploiter of ingenuousness in human nature. Influence of Mercury on good as on evil.

II

The Priestess

The personification of the initial cause of all action, the *Magician* (Arcana 1) hustles about and cannot relax, so he is represented as standing, as opposed to the Priestess (Arcana 2) who is seated motionless and calm, impenetrable and priestly. She is the priestess of mystery, Isis, the goddess of deep night and without her help the human spirit could not penetrate the darkness.

Her right hand holds half open the book of secrets which no one can take from her unless the Priestess gives him the keys which she holds in her left hand. Of these keys which open hidden aspects of things (Esotericism) one is gold and is related to the Sun ☉ (Word, Reason) and the other silver, hence having an affinity with the Moon (Imagination, intuitive lucidity). That means that one must unite strict logic and sweet impressionability if one aspires to divine hidden things, the knowledge which Nature hides from a great number of us.

The divination which the Priestess inspires, applies to the discernment of reality which hides behind the veil of what is apparent to our senses. For the intuitive person, favoured by Isis, phenomena are a façade, which, by preventing physiological vision, stimulate the vision of the mind.

On leaving Unity in which all is merged (Arcana 1), we come to the sphere of the Binary or of differentiation, it is the entrance square to the Temple of Solomon, wherein rise the two columns of Jachin and Boaz between which is enthroned the Priestess, in front of a veil with iridescent folds which mask the entry to the sanctuary.

Of the two columns one is red and the other blue. The first corresponds to Fire (vital, devouring warmth, male activity, Sulphur of the Alchemists ☖); the second is related to Air (the breath which feeds life, feminine sensibility, the Mercury of the Wise ☿). All creation stems from this fundamental duality: Father, Mother—Subject, Object—Creator, Creation—God, Nature—Osiris, Isis, etc.

The lofty façade of the Temple symbolizes as a whole, all revelation of phenomena, objectivity in its infinite variety of aspects, which each one of us is allowed to view. As for the curtain which one must lift in order to enter the holy precincts, it is the screen on to which the living images of thought are projected. We perceive them in the shimmering of a material of a thousand nuances, whose folds undulate in the breeze, so that we do not even manage to seize its ever moving embroidered contours.

These images fascinate the visionary who likes to read in the astral light[27] like the Pythons. The true Initiate will not stop at these little distractions on the threshold, which for him are nothing but 'mere trifles at the door'.

The teaching of the Priestess is in fact based on the imagination, as the crescent on top of her headdress shows us. This headdress is encircled by two diadems encrusted with precious stones. The diadem which touches the forehead is alluding to the occult philosophy and to the subtle doctrines of Hermetism; the other, narrower and placed higher is the emblem of Gnosis, faith (of the wise) the fruit of the highest forms of thought.

The Priestess of mystery is clothed in dark blue, but a luminous white stole is crossed over her chest. This forms a cross, of which each branch is marked with a secondary cross. This pattern suggests powers of revelation which make the occult clear, thanks to the light sent out by the conflict of two opposing elements.[28]

Constantly on the lookout for whatever can help him to solve the enigma of things, the human mind benefits from all the flashes of light which streak across the night of mystery. So it happens that we see the Priestess enveloped in a purple coloured mantel with a wide golden border, and lined with green. This last mentioned colour is that of vitality. The conceptions which transfer transcendent truths for our use possess this inner vitality. These are the living ideas of conceptions which haunt the imagination of mortals without managing to take form. They feed our highest aspirations (purple) and initiate religions (golden border) which give way only too quickly to the crude form of our conceptions.

The Priestess is not responsible for the wrong use of her teaching which is addressed, not to the blind believers, but to the thinkers, the craftsmen of a continual religious regeneration. She leans upon the Sphinx who forever asks the three questions: Where do we come from? What are we? Where are we going? Around her, a space of paving stones, alternating black and white, give us to understand that all our perceptions are subject to the law of contrasts—

light is only conceived as opposed to darkness, good would be unknown to us if it were not for evil; we would not be able to appreciate happiness if we had not suffered etc.

The right foot of the Priestess rests on a cushion representing the very small quantity of positive ideas which we can acquire in the realm of mystery. This accessory, which is sometimes neglected, figures on a Tarot published in Paris in 1500.[29] It has its importance for it seems to be borrowed from Cassiopeia, the Queen of Ethiopia of the heavenly sphere, the black but beautiful sovereign, like the Beloved of the Song of Songs, and which corresponds to the arcana 11 of the astronomical Tarot.

The illustrators of the Middle Ages had no scruple about representing a Priestess in spite of orthodoxy. At Besançon it was thought opportune to put Jupiter and Juno in the place of the Pope and the *Priestess* of the Tarot. That gave us two mythological compositions of little interest. Juno however, has the merit of pointing with one hand to the sky, and with the other to the earth as if to say, with the Emerald Table of Hermes Trismegiste: 'As above, so below.' Now the setting up of a visible symbol of the invisible is the starting point of the method of analogy on which the whole of the knowledge of the priestess is based. Two peacocks, the birds of Maya, the goddess of illusion, accompany Juno, who in reality personifies ethereal space, 'Anou' in Chaldean, hence Anna, our Saint Ann, mother of the Virgin. This connection helps to explain the meaning of Arcanas 2 and 3.

DIVINATORY INTERPRETATIONS

C'hocmah, wisdom, creative thought, the word, the second person in the Trinity, Isis, nature, the wife of God and mother of all things. The substance which fills unlimited space; the field of action of the active and intelligent cause; the fruitful opposing forces from which all is born. The differentiation which allows us to perceive, hence to know and to be able.

The Sacred Science whose object is beyond the power of our senses. Divination, intuitive philosophy, knowledge (gnosis) discerning mystery, contemplative faith.

Silence, discretion, reserve, meditation, modesty, patience, resignation, piety, respect for holy things. Deceit, hidden intentions, spite, inertia, laziness, bigotry, intolerance, fanaticism. Passive influence of Saturn.

III

The Empress

Without becoming intelligible to us, the necessary and fundamental unity of things is imposed upon our minds. We cannot conceive what is limitless, infinite, indeterminate except by invoking the image of a night of unfathomable darkness, the realm of Isis, the goddess of mystery, over which the Priestess (2) is sovereign. But our minds strive in vain to plunge into the bottomless abyss of the cosmogonies (Apsou of the Chaldeans); we can only perceive a mental chaos. In the face of this we remain frightened, seized with a religious terror and we are struck dumb. To draw our minds out of the confusion we need the help of the Empress.

This sovereign, dazzling with light represents 'Creative Intelligence', the mother of form, pictures and ideas. She is the immaculate Virgin of the Christians, in whom the Greeks would have recognized their Venus-Urania, born shimmering in light out of the dark waves of the wild Ocean.

As Queen of the sky she moves in the sublime heights of the 'ideal', above all contingency, as is shown by the foot which she places on the crescent with its horns turned upside down. Thus domination is confirmed over the sublunary world, where everything is but mobility, perpetual change and continual transformation. In contrast with this lower realm on which the Moon (18) sheds only a vague and deceptive light, the Empress's sphere corresponds to the higher Waters where Supreme Wisdom[30] resides. There everything is fixed and unmovable, hence perfect: it is the region of the archetype, that is to say of ideal forms or of pure ideas according to which everything is created.

In order to express the immutability of things which are shielded from all change, the Empress is seen in full frontal view, in a pose which is marked by a certain priestly stiffness. A happy serenity none the less lights up her face, framed pleasantly by her soft blond hair; a light crown seems scarcely to weigh upon her head, around which are twelve stars, nine of which can be seen. These numbers remind us of the Zodiac, the celestial space on which the natural growth here below is based, and the gestation period imposed for reproduction.

Just like the Virgo of the Zodiac, the Empress is winged, but her attributes are neither the ear of corn of earthly harvests nor the olive branch exhorting men to peace. The Queen of the sky holds the sceptre of universal and irresistible domination, for the ideal is asserted, the 'idea' commands and determines all production. As her emblem she bears on purple a silver eagle, the emblem of the soul, sublime in the heart of spirituality; as for the full-blown lily on the left of the Empress, this symbolizes the enthralling charm held by gentleness and beauty.

The Empress and Priestess are dressed, one in blue and the other in purple; but the blue of the priestly robe of the great priestess is dark blue to remind us of the depths into which thought is lost, whereas the Empress' mantel is of a luminous sky-blue. Her tunic, on the other hand, is red to express the inner activity from which intelligence or comprehension is born, as opposed to the outer blue clothing, alluding to the receptive placidity which faithfully stores up impressions from outside.

From her inner dark blue the Priestess draws the substance of the idea which she exteriorizes in a spiritual, mystical and diffuse movement; this is represented by her purple mantel enriched by gold. The Empress is draped in sky-blue to seize the living thought, whose rays she captures and makes perceptible. She reveals the occult which the Priestess puts into motion, without giving it body, even spiritually. With **one**, All is in All, merged without any possibility of distinguishing parts; with **two**, Agent and Sufferer are conceived, but the action takes place in the infinite and nothing is perceived: the Occult is only revealed in a mystical way (Priestess). We must get to **three** before light is revealed in the mind. This is as a mirror struck by the imperceptible vibration and through condensation throws a reflection to make itself clear.

Seen as a whole Arcana 3 is related to the sign of Mercury upturned ☿ which alludes to a substance which is both supremely spiritualized and spiritualizing.[31]

The Christian artists were inspired by Alchemy when they placed a crescent beneath the foot of the heavenly Virgin, but they more often than not made the error of drawing the crescent with its horns upturned. Others have followed the correct tradition, as shown in the sixteenth century German engraving at left.

Tarot of the Magicians

Divinatory Interpretations

Binah, intelligence, comprehension, the abstract conception which generates ideas and shapes the Supreme Ideal, thought conceived but not yet expressed.

The sphere of recognizable and understandable objects. Discernment, reflection, study, observation, inductive science. Instruction, knowledge, erudition.

Affability, grace, charm, strength of character, rule through gentleness, civilizing influence. Politeness, generosity. Abundance, wealth, fertility.

Adornment, vanity, frivolity, luxury, prodigality, coquetry, seduction and show of superficial ideas, pose, affection.

IV

The Emperor

Following the Empress fair and full of light, who could rise to no greater heights in the Tarot, comes the gloomy sovereign of hell, for the Emperor is a Pluto imprisoned in the core of things. He personifies life-giving Fire which burns at the expense of the Alchemists' Sulphur, whose sign is a triangle placed on the cross ☖.

Now the Emperor's legs are crossed under a triangle outlined by his head and arms. His throne is a golden cube[32] on which stands out a black eagle, making a strange contrast with that of the Empress's emblem. Here it is no longer a question of the soul having finally reached into heaven, but of the substance of the soul darkened through its incarnation and held captive in the very centre of matter at which it must work in order to regain its freedom. This bird of prey is related also to basic egoism, which gives birth to all individuality.

The Emperor is, in fact, the Worldly Prince; he reigns over the concrete and corporal things, hence the contrast between his lower empire—hence infernal, in the etymological sense of the word, and the heavenly power of the Empress. She rules directly over souls and the pure spirits. On the other hand bodies remain subject to the power of the Emperor who gives them life and rules them after he has created them. He corresponds to the Demiurge of the Platonic philosophers and to the Great Founder of the Freemasons. Living beings take shape and develop on his impulsion: he is their inner god, the principle of fixity, of growth and of action. It is the individual spirit, the objective manifestation of the Universal spirit, One in its creative essence, but shared out in the multiplicity of creatures.

The sovereignty of the Emperor is shared out among all living beings. It is given to them through Mercy (Ch'esed, the fourth Sephirah). His cube-shaped throne is the only one which cannot be overturned, its stability resulting from its geometric shape, attributed by the Alchemists to the Philosopher's Stone. This mysterious stone which is the Wise Men's object of pursuit, is related to the perfection of which individuals are capable. These people must attempt to conform to 'type' within the species, as depicted by the cubic stone of the Freemasons, a rectangular block cut out according to the set-square (*norma* in Latin) so that the ideal envisaged is none other than the completely 'normal' man.

If the Emperor corresponds both in the Macrocosm and in the Microcosm to what is immutable, it is that he is seated on the perfect cube, the starting point which determines all constructive crystallization. In every person he represents the principle of fixity (Archeus ⚏) which becomes active in the seed to construct the organism. This construction proceeds through the agglomerations of elements which were attracted by the first stone to be correctly cut in the living edifice. This stone is the throne of the sovereign of life shared out among all creatures.

The globe of the world which the Emperor holds in his left hand is a sign of universal domination. This globe, moreover, is the symbol, not of the physical universe, but of the Soul of the World, the entity thanks to which all the miracles of Nature and Art are performed. In his right hand the Emperor clasps a massive sceptre which is not without analogy to the club of Hercules. However, we must not see in this a brutal weapon, but the emblem of the highest initiating, or magical, power. The crescent moon inserted near the hand suggests an irresistible domination over all that is unstable, moving, capricious or 'lunatic' according to the term as used in Astrology and in Hermeticism. What is fixed and unmovable exerts a determining action over every disorganized substance whose state remains vague, wavering (lunar).

Let us also take note that the end of the imperial sceptre is in the form of the fleur-de-lys. This emblem is based on the downward facing triangle ▽, which represents Water or Soul. A simple cross surmounting this triangle would form the sign of the Great Work ⚲ (Supreme Glorification of the Soul), but in the fleur-de-lys this cross shape is made more complicated with two foliated scrolls which lead into the horizontal line, while the vertical line is thrust up towards the sky like a plant shoot.

The whole design alludes to a force which comes from the soul both to rise and spread at the same time, as the scrolls show. At work are the highest aspirations which open to give the flower of idealism, to assure it of an irresistible power in the high spheres of human thought.

The Emperor is not a despot who imposes his will in an arbitrary way; there is nothing brutal about his reign: for it is inspired by a great ideal of kindness which is symbolized by the Hermetic ideogram from which the connoisseurs of heraldry have taken their fleur-de-lys. It is regrettable that this emblem has not remained the emblem of the French nation which aims at spreading civilization and setting the example of brotherly feelings in regard to all nations. No other sign expresses better nobility of soul, and true generosity which forms the basis of our national character. Removed as we are from all coarse imperialism, it falls to us to rule through the intelligence and with the heart. Let us be the first to understand everything and to be the most sincere in our affection towards others; in this way we will have the right to set up the fleur-de-lys.

This hierogram whose gold stands out against the sky-blue is related in sense to the lily, the emblem of purity which is the Empress's flower, but it contrasts masculine expansive action with passive, feminine virtue. It falls to the male energy to realize the feminine ideal by purifying the base fire of the seat of ego-ism, the generator of individuality.

Initiation teaches us to descend into ourselves to control the inner fire which, kept alive by art, ceases to smoulder darkly, and gleams with a heavenly brightness after emitting nothing but dull smoke.

The Fleur-de-lys sceptre shows the Emperor drawing inspiration from the sublime aspirations of the Empress, for on earth he is the realizer of the divine 'idea'. This power is legitimate and sacred, although he sets in motion all living forces, however disturbing they may be in their impure origin.

The active energy which constructs all things works like a hidden god, concealed from all glares like Plato's protegés who have become invisible under the helmet of the Sovereign of the Underworld. The crest of this helm of invisibility carries four golden triangles which are related to the work of God, the creator through the quartet of the Elements. If the Emperor reigns supremely over matter, it is that he acts on the birth of all things, because of the marriage of Fire and Water combined with that of Air and the Earth, as shown by the cosmogonic cross figured below.

Fixity which constructs matter, acts upon the matter without coming under the influence of materials which come into play. This must be so in the interest of the constructive work which is accomplished according to a plan which has

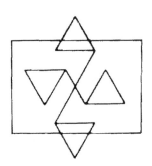

been drawn up. The necessity of putting aside any disturbing intervention forces the Emperor never to give up the protection of his breastplate, which, however, does not make him insensitive, for, at chest height, it bears the images of the Sun and Moon. This shows that Reason and Imagination throw light upon the development of all healthy activity. The spirit which has become individualized in order to act remains accessible to the powerful and divine sun-like rays and to the soft moonlight of pure feelings.

In contrast to the Empress who is shown fullface, the Emperor is shown in profile. His features are strong; his deep-set eye is shaded by a knitted brow which, like his thick beard, is jet black. The imperial necklace is a plait which also adorns Justice (8); it is an emblem in the class of rigour, co-ordination and logical sequence, at the same time as solidity. A link like this is not broken and could not yield: pledges made by the Emperor are enforceable just as are the logical decrees of warranted Justice.

The red which dominates the Emperor's costume is related to stimulating fire which he gives and directs with a view to vitalizing and giving life. This life-giving role justifies the green which appears on the sleeves of the imperial costume. Indeed the colour of the sleeves is suited to his arms which move and provoke the manifestations of life.

At the feet of the giver of vital energy opens the tulip which is first seen in the Magician (1) as a bud. This flower will have passed the stage of blooming when Temperance (14) will prevent it from wilting, so that it will not be dead, even in the path of the Fool (22).

Arcana 4 could not be more adequately represented in the celestial sphere than by Hercules, clothed in the skin of the Nemean Lion, armed with his club and holding the golden apples of the garden of Hesperides. This is the fruit of initiating knowledge; it is won through great struggle and it rewards the hero who accomplishes the twelve labours, or the assiduous initiate of the Great Work.

Now, the Emperor is none other than the Worker who rises to the highest rank, for he knows how to work by carrying out the plan of the Great Architect of the Universe, whose emblem is an eye drawn in the centre of a triangle from which come rays of light.

DIVINITARY INTERPRETATIONS

C'hesed, grace, pity, mercy or Gedulah, greatness, magnificence, the designation of the fourth branch of the tree of the Sephiroth or Kabbalistic numbers[33]; power which gives and spreads life, creative kindness which brings into existence the animating principle, creative light shared out among creatures, and condensed in the centre of each individuality; Archeus, Sulphur of the Alchemists, ♁, life-giving fire imprisoned in the seed, the realizing word incarnate, active fire, the mystic spouse and son of the life-giving substance—Virgin, Empress (3).[34]

Energy, power, sight, will, fixity, concentration, absolute certainty through mathematical deduction, constancy, steadiness, rigour, exactitude, equity, positivism.

Dominating spirit, influencing others without letting oneself be influenced; reckoning by only trusting reason and positive observation; a character unshakable in his resolutions, stubbornness; lack of idealism or intuition; generosity without charm, a powerful protector, or enemy to be feared; tyrant, a despot on the rebound undergoing the influence of the weak; brutal masculinity indirectly subject to feminine tenderness.

V

The Pope

The artists who drew the Tarot liked contrasts. Beside the young blond Magician they placed the dark Priestess seated and shrouded in mystery; then comes the Empress shining in heavenly light and giving a full front view to contrast with the Emperor with his severe profile and dark beard. The frowning expression of this sovereign makes us in turn, appreciate the Pope's face, jovial and full of charm. This pontiff with his bright complexion and full cheeks is, we feel sure, full of indulgence for human failings. He understands all, for nothing escapes the calm look of very light blue eyes, scarcely shaded by his thick white eyebrows. A short white and carefully trimmed beard, moreover, point to the age in which becalmed passions leave the intelligence with all its lucidity to allow it to resolve complex and intricate problems without hesitation.

Indeed, it is the lot of the Pope to reply to the agonizing questions which believers put to him. When he dogmatizes he strengthens beliefs and he formulates religious teaching which is addressed to two categories of the faithful. These are represented by the two characters kneeling before the pontifical chair. One is stretching out his arm and raising his head as if to say: 'I have understood'; the other is leaning his forehead on his joined hands and accepts the dogma humbly, convinced of his own inadequacy in spiritual matters.

The first one is active in the sphere of faith; he is preoccupied with what is credible and does not blindly accept the doctrine taught. He does not dare, however, to break with the general belief and he tries to adapt it to his own enlightenment. In this way a broader faith is established which dogmatic authority would have to take into account and aim at a gradual broadening of the traditional teaching.

Unfortunately those who govern the churches are afraid of the believers who thirst after knowledge. Rather than these, they prefer the submissive and disciplined flock, ready to bow passively without question. Religion suffers because of this, for in this way it is paralysed in its right side, the active and life-giving side represented by one of the two uprights of the chair of the highest teaching. While it is related only to the left upright, teaching falters.

These firm uprights are related to an unshakable tradition, but their green colour wills that this tradition should be living and that by remaining faithful to itself, it should be able to stay in harmony with the life of faith. The symbolism of the binary is clarified for the initiated in the mysteries of the columns Jachin and Boaz of Solomon's temple. Their contrast marks the limits within which the human spirit moves as it is apt that they flank the throne of the Priestess (2). The uprights of the pontifical chair represent in a similar way the two opposite poles in the sphere of faith: an anxious search for religious truth and confident adherence to the beliefs which are held respectable.

Seated between these two columns and speaking to listeners of two different mentalities, the Pope is called to reconcile a quarrel of linked opposites. Keeping the middle way between tradition on the right (rational theology) and the demands of the left (the feelings of pious souls) the Sovereign Pontiff adapts religious knowledge to the needs of humble believers. He also has to make the highest truths accessible to simple people, hence his central position in regard to Four (right and left, high and low); he represents the rose in bloom at the centre of the cross, the flower identical with the Star of the Freemasons which is a Pentagram on which is inscribed the letter G, meaning Gnosis (knowledge, initiating instruction). To conform to the pattern which the Rose-Cross outlines here, the Pope must enter into communion with all those who think and feel in a religious way, in order to

draw towards him the light of the Holy Ghost, for divine goodness shares this light out generously among the minds which search after Truth and the souls who are sensitive to selfless love.

He who formulates the highest teaching makes himself receptive to the diffused light of the surroundings, and by the fact that he concentrates them he is transformed into the shining lighthouse *urbi et orbi*. It is at this point that he enlightens the Church intellectually and morally, in the manner of the Star of the Wise in the centre of the Masonic Temple.

This star instructs those whose task is to confer instruction in initiation. Its soft light does not dazzle like the Sun's or even the Moon's, but a penetrating light emanates from the Star familiar to the Initiated. Its rays do not stop at the surface of things, for it reveals the Esotericism sought by those who abstract the most subtle element from all matter. The Pope is ignorant of nothing in this respect, since his mission is to make known intelligible reality which hides behind the mask of the illusion of the senses. He occupies the fifth rank in the Tarot so as to mark the following progression:

1. *Magician* — the mathematical dot without dimension.
2. *The Priestess* — the one-dimensional line.
3. *The Empress* — surface with two dimensions.
4. *The Emperor* — the three-dimensional solid (cube).
5. *The Pope* — the contents of the form, the conceiveable quintessence, and although imperceptible, the sphere of the fourth dimension.

The number five is, moreover, that of man when seen as the mediator between God and the Universe. By virtue of this the human figure is inscribed in a pentagon, for the head dominates the four limbs, as the spirit rules in the four Elements. Thus is formed the Star of the microcosm which is the symbol of the will.

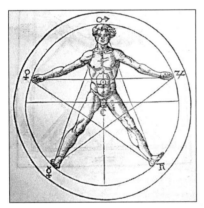

Common magic has illusions about the power of this sign which in itself confers no power at all. The individual will is only powerful in as much as it harmonizes with a more general power. The more noble a force is, the less right one has to use it in an arbitrary way. Everything comes within a hierarchy: the right to command implies responsibilities. If we aim at exercising this right as we please it will be taken from us: the soldier who misuses his command is dismissed or demoted. It is useless to covet magic power: It is conferred automatically on whoever deserves it, whereas the ambitious person may aspire to it in vain. Let us not seek to develop the will by artificial means and try to transform ourselves into 'athletes' of the will. To display strength, one must be the master of it, and know how to control it. To stop oneself from wanting what is inappropriate is the great secret of those who are called to exercise their personal influence at the decisive moment. What they will have accumulated in the way of unused will-power will make their volition in some way dynamic; still they must act according to an order sent from above, for to be obeyed one must oneself obey, since all is contained within the Unity of things.

The Pope is wearing white gloves to show that his hands remain pure, and are never contaminated by contact with earthly affairs. Each glove is marked with a blue cross, the colour of the soul and of faithfulness, for the action of the Sovereign Pontiff is exclusively spiritual, and it works on three levels as is suggested by the three crowns of the papal tiara and the three transverse lines of the pontifical cross.

The tiara weighs heavily upon the Sovereign's head which would be crushed under its weight if he did not have the benefit of superior brain-power as befits this chosen man. Nothing related to religion and faith must escape him; so he could not legitimately wear his first crown, the one that encircles his forehead and shines with the loveliest and most precious stones, if he were ignorant of the smallest detail of the holy mass with its traditional liturgy, its impressive show and its moving ceremonies. But the exterior, the expression and body have no value except through the soul, symbolized by the second crown superimposed on the first. No less rich and slightly wider, it is related to the complete knowledge of the divine law which allows the Pope to judge accurately the actions and feelings of men. As for the last crown, the highest but also the smallest and the simplest, it alludes, in its austerity, less to the ordinary theology than to the discernment of abstract truths which are imposed upon the human spirit and report universal belief which form the basis of a religious doctrine. This leads to the complete Catholicism whose head will be the true Sovereign Pontiff of the whole of the Christian world.

If the supreme authority of the Pope is reflected in the tiara, then the sceptre of his spiritual power is a cross with three transverse lines. Out of the ternary comes a septenary formed by the round ends of the transverse lines and at the rounded top of the cross. Now seven is the number of harmony and also of secondary causes which direct the world: these causes correspond to the planetary influences or to the seven notes of the human scale.

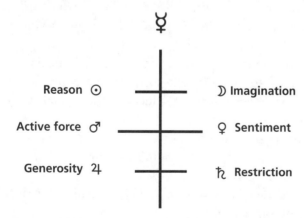

Reason ☉ — ☽ Imagination

Active force ♂ — ♀ Sentiment

Generosity ♃ — ♄ Restriction

It is for the Pope to govern by opposing the innate tendencies of man in order to give them harmony and balance so that not one of them degenerates into vice. When left entirely to ourselves and to the instinctive energies of our nature we fall under the yoke of the seven deadly sins.[35] By helping us to exercise control, spiritual power keeps us in possession of ourselves and makes us participate in the communion of free and virtuous men.[36] The Pontifical cross also reminds us of the Tree of the Sephiroth which has already been discussed.

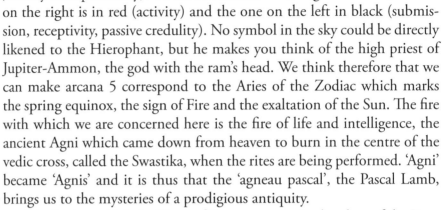
JUPITER.

Like the Priestess, the Pope is clothed in the priestly colours of blue and purple (ideality and spirituality). Of the two faithful kneeling before him, the one on the right is in red (activity) and the one on the left in black (submission, receptivity, passive credulity). No symbol in the sky could be directly likened to the Hierophant, but he makes you think of the high priest of Jupiter-Ammon, the god with the ram's head. We think therefore that we can make arcana 5 correspond to the Aries of the Zodiac which marks the spring equinox, the sign of Fire and the exaltation of the Sun. The fire with which we are concerned here is the fire of life and intelligence, the ancient Agni which came down from heaven to burn in the centre of the vedic cross, called the Swastika, when the rites are being performed. 'Agni' became 'Agnis' and it is thus that the 'agneau pascal', the Pascal Lamb, brings us to the mysteries of a prodigious antiquity.

The Jupiter which the Tarot of Besançon puts in the place of the Pope is the master of the celestial Fire, the giver of life, intellectual and moral as much as physical. It is he who keeps the conscience awake in order to make order, justice, affability, goodwill and kindness reign over the earth. The character of this god is therefore in harmony with arcana 5.

DIVINATORY INTERPRETATIONS

Geburah—rigour, severity, Pec'had, punishment, fear, Din, judgement[37], the will which controls or governs the gift of life. Conscience, duty, moral law, inhibition, restriction, for one must abstain from evil-doing before devoting oneself to doing good.

Priesthood, religious knowledge, metaphysics, Kabbala, teaching, knowing how to (as opposed to being able). Authority, certainty, assurance, absence of doubt, influence or suggestion over the feelings and thoughts of others. Affability, goodwill, kindness, wise generosity.

A director of conscience, the doctor of the soul, moral advice, a sententious character. Absolute authority in his opinions. Function conferring prestige. The influence of Jupiter in good and in evil.

Taken in a detrimental light: immorality, for faults take the place of qualities when an arcana becomes negative.

VI

The Lover

Emerging from adolescence and having just finished his education at the school of the Centaur Chiron initiatory apprenticeship Hercules felt the need to reflect upon the use that he would make, in life, of his powerful faculties which he had so marvellously developed. When he was deep in meditation, two women of rare beauty suddenly appeared to him, each one enticing him to follow her. The first, Virtue, showed him glimpses of a life of struggle, ceaseless efforts, aspiring to find triumph through courage and energy. The other, Sensuality—rather than calling her Vice—urged the young man to enjoy life peacefully by giving himself to its pleasures and by making full use of the advantages it offers to the person who can limit his ambition.

Inspired by this mythological scene, the sixth key of the Tarot shows us a young man standing still at the meeting of two roads, with his arms crossed over his heart, his eyes lowered, uncertain of what direction to take. The Lover hesitates, urged (like Hercules) by an austere queen who only promises moral satisfaction and by a bacchante, the provider of easy pleasures. His choice is not decreed in advance, for he has not the heart of a hero destined to accomplish twelve labours. He is a weak mortal, open to all the temptations and divided in his feelings, as is shown by the alternating red and green costume (colours of blood, energy, courage, and of vegetation—passive vitality, langour, inaction).

Like the Priestess and the Empress, the queen standing on the right (activity) is dressed in red and blue (spirit and soul, spirituality) whereas the bacchante is draped in yellow and green gauze (quality of matter, life-giving sap). As in the costume of the Lover, red and green alternate in the rays of the halo which floats above the three characters. It is an oval of light on which is outlined a Cupid with red and blue wings, ready to release an arrow aimed at the head of the bewildered young man.

So arcana 6 as a whole illustrates the mechanism of the voluntary act of the sentient person portrayed by the Lover who is 'L'Homme de Désir' of Saint-Martin. This personality receives the impressions of the physical world thanks to his sensitivity (the green colour of his costume), then he reacts (red colour, propulsion). Now as it is not a matter of unconscious or automatic acts, called reflex, there is deliberation, choice before the releasing of the action is decided upon.

The decision is awaited by Cupid who above us accumulates the volitional energy which we will be able to have at our disposal. He shoots his arrow with more or less force as soon as we give him the signal, because we are willing it. But if we use our will-power thoughtlessly, without saving it, as arcana 5 teaches us to do, then our volitions will not be powerful.

For our will-power to allow us to compete with Hercules—an ambition which is not forbidden to us—we must involve ourselves, with no going back, in the harsh path of virtue, precisely so that our volitions are not squandered on pursuing pleasure and the little diversions of life. One might judge it wise just to let oneself live by savouring joys which come along without priding oneself on being heroic. This wisdom is not that of the Initiated who identify life with fruitful action, useful (Herculean) work. To live for its own sake is not their ideal for they feel that they are artists and consider that life is given to them with the view to creating a work of art.

As it is a question of the Great Work of humanity to which only the workers of the Spirit can devote themselves, they must have learned how to 'will' and how to 'love'. The Lover is, in this respect, the Initiate whose apprenticeship is completed. If, by crossing his arms he puts himself in the rank of the 'Good Shepherd' known to the Knights of the Rosy Cross, the fact is that he tries to forget himself; he does not allow himself to desire his own personal benefit, but desires only that of others. It is the realization of this moral beauty which corresponds to the sixth Sephirah—Tiphereth—whose emblem is Solomon's Seal, formed by two entwined triangles. In this we must see an allusion to the marriage of the human soul (∇ Water) and the Divine Spirit ($\triangle$ Fire). It is the star of the macrocosm, the sign of supreme magical power, acquired by the individual who, with complete self-abnegation, puts himself in the service of the 'whole.' To love to the point of existing only for others, that is the objective of the Lover.

In the Tarot this character is only a disguised form of active unity (Magician) intended to be represented in three aspects: the Lover brings us back to unity through love, for Man becomes divine by loving as God does.

Let us recall at this point the interpretations which connect the first six arcanas to each other:

1. *The Magician* — the thinking principle; thought seen in its centre of emission, hence as yet only potential.
2. *The Priestess* — thought-act, word (action of thinking from the thinking principle).
3. *The Empress* — thought, result, pure idea, concept in its original essence, unaltered by expression.
4. *The Emperor* — realizer, the principle of will.
5. *The Pope* — volitive radiation, act of willing.
6. *The Lover* — desire, aspiration, formulated will.

If one envisages the different modes of action of the will, the 'Emperor' exerts a compelling command, impetuous and of a harsh nature; the Pope emits a gentle and patient will which is imposed because of the strength of its moderation; as for the Lover, he is content to desire intensely with a feeling of deep affection. Love absorbs his will; he refrains from commanding, and while desiring he 'prays' in the initiating meaning of the word.

To find the astronomical correspondence of arcana 6 it is advisable only to remember Cupid's arrow, the weapon drawn in the sky in the constellation Sagittarius. The Chaldeans made of the archer in the sky a two-headed centaur in which the Greeks wished to recognize Chiron, the teacher of heroes like Hercules, called to find glory through deserving labours.

Certainly Eros who hovers above the Lover is not in harmony with a half-horse half-man with a scorpion's tail. For all that this monstrous collection lends itself to an interpretation applicable to arcana 6 for the human part which bends the bow may correspond to the conscience entrusted to watch over our use of the will-power, while the horse is our organism, the animal with which we are associated. Finally the Scorpion alludes to the propulsions which spur us on with a view to action.

DIVINATORY INTERPRETATIONS

Tiphereth, moral beauty, love, bond uniting all beings, feeling; life sphere undergoing attractions and repulsions, sympathies and antipathies, pure affections, foreign to the sensual attraction.

Aspirations, desires on which depend the beauty of the soul, greetings, wishes; liberty, choice, selection, free will, temptation, trial, doubt, uncertainty, irresolution, hesitation.

Sentimentality, perplexity, indecision, matters held in abeyance, promises, unfulfilled desires.

VII

The Chariot

One may wonder whether the title of a treatise on alchemy which appeared in Amsterdam in 1671 does not reveal the true significance of the seventh key of the Tarot. In this case the Chariot would become the triumphal Chariot of Antimony, the *Currus Triumphalis Antimonii* of Basile Valentin. What is certain is that Antimony is very strongly represented by the master of the Chariot. This young beardless youth, slim, fair like the Magician and the Lover, is wearing a breast-plate and is armed with a sceptre like the Emperor. He incarnates the higher principles of the human personality in order to represent the Intellectual Spirit (☿ Antimony)[38] in which are synthesized the thinking principle (The Magician), the centre of volitive energy (The Emperor) and the centre from which affection radiates (The Lover). But in contrast with the Emperor who in his unmovable, fixed position, is seated on a motionless cube, the triumphant man journeys throughout the world in a vehicle whose form, it is true, remains cubic.

This shape always indicated bodily form. When applied to the moving throne of the active spirituality it suggests the 'idea' of a subtle body of the soul, thanks to which the pure spirit can manifest itself in a dynamic way. It is a question of an ethereal substance playing the role of mediator between the measureable and the imponderable, between the incorporeal and the tangible; it is, if you like, the sidereal or astral body of Paracelsus and the occultists, the *Corps aromal* of Fourier, the *Linga Sharira*, or, no doubt better, the 'Kama rupa' of esoteric Buddhism.

There is nothing less simple than this mysterious entity. First of all one can make out the imperceptible web on which every organism is constructed. It is the phantom-like frame into which matter fits, the scaffolding allowing the body to build itself, but which lives to assure the preservation of all that lives, for without it everything crumbles. The cubic form of the chariot corresponds to this invisible support of all that is visible. Its ethereal nature is confirmed thanks to the winged globe of the Egyptians which decorated the panel of the vehicle. This emblem of the sublimation of matter figures on it above the oriental symbol relating to the mystery of the union of the sexes, as if to say that heaven can only act on the earth by uniting with her in love.

The phantom-like body, the Eidolon of the Greeks, is not in direct contact with material substance, therefore the Chariot does not touch the ground except by the intermediary of its wheels. These have red spokes in token of the whirls of fire which in the vision of Ezekiel support the Chariot throne of the Divinity, the famous Merkabah constantly commented upon by the Kabbalists. These wheels represent the vital heat which is maintained by movement and comes out of matter through friction.

The wheels contrast with the sky-blue canopy which is the image of the firmament separating the relative from the absolute. The amount of sky which our active spirituality can reach is limited; it shelters us and prevents a too ambitious flight of our thoughts, our feelings, and our aspirations. The triumphant charioteer drives his chariot and looks straight ahead of him, without becoming lost in the clouds of a sterile mysticism. Above his head shines the emblem of the Sun ☉ in the centre of stars which correspond to the planets.

The septenary was so constituted that they remind us of the chariot of David, popularly known as the *Ursa Major*, a constellation made up of seven principal stars, from which the Romans made the seven oxen, *Septem Triones*, hence the name Septentrional applied to the region of the north.

From the angles of the Chariot rise the four uprights of the canopy. The front ones are yellow, and the back ones green. Those are the colours dear to the Bacchant of arcana 6. The quartet in which the triumphant driver occupies the centre is thus related to the attractions to which it must not submit. He is defended against them by his red breastplate reinforced by a triple angle shape arranged like a border pattern, held by five golden buttons.

Red expresses activity used in the pursuit of a specified aim (the road to be followed by the chariot); as for the angle pattern, it replaces the insignia on the breastplate of the Master who directs the work in a masonic workshop. This instrument controls the normal shape of the building to be constructed (the set square is called a *norma* in Latin). In order to be integrated in the social life the individual must adapt himself in a rectangular shape to his neighbour. Decorated with the triple angle pattern the Master of the Chariot pursues an ideal of moral perfection which applies to the mind, soul and body. He reconciles warring opinions and leads his enemies to understand each other, puts an end to intellectual discord and so brings about feelings of brotherly goodwill; moreover, he imposes equity even in the smallest actions, being always most careful to deal tactfully with others; in other words he watches over the maintenance of a delightful politeness, the mother of every true civilization.

The five gold nails of the angle pattern refer to the domination of the four elements by quintessence. In it five must lead four into the unity of command so that the master of the Chariot enters into full possession of himself and can direct his vehicle without being distracted by disturbing influences.

But if, in his solar fixity, he is not himself liable to be influenced, his directing action makes itself felt all the more forcibly on whatever is lunar and is hence capricious or changing. Thus the ebb and flow of the emotive tides are at the command of the triumphant driver whose shoulders bear crescent moons placed back to back as if to give to the right arm power over what grows and to the left arm over what wanes.[39]

By knowing how to take into account the fluctuations of the human heart, the Master of the Chariot practises an art of government which wins him the diadem of the Initiated, surmounted by three gold pentagrams. These stars face three directions; those on the right and the left allow him to see the sides of the life-path, for, in order to direct one's way one must not be content with too narrow a view.

The lower pattern of the breastplate protecting the abdomen, in which resides the less noble part of us, contrasts with the three pentagrams shining above his head; this ternary suppresses the lower instincts, drives back the brutal impulses and curbs the silent rebellions of an uncouth atavism.

The expertise of the Initiate demands that all should be controlled in the person invested with the sceptre of wisdom.

This insignia of command is only a simple wand with a group of egg-shaped spheres at the end which seem to emerge from each other, to indicate that the Master of the Chariot presides over the nascent virtues whose seeds all individuals possess. In the hands of those who direct the work of the Masons assembled in the Lodge his sceptre is replaced by the mallet. The President of the Workshop sits under a canopy decorated with stars, like the canopy of the Chariot; in front of him a square altar completes the analogy with the character of arcana 7 whose breastplate is decorated with the corner stone, the distinctive jewel of the 'Venerable'.

But the comparison between the Lodge where constructive work is achieved and the 'Chariot of Progress' finally achieves importance if one considers the two Sphinx tractors as the forces which the columns of Jachin and Boas represent.[40]

Tarot of the Magicians

These are not separate animals, but one single one, a sort of Amphibian with two heads. Such a monster, being able to walk in two directions would become immobile if it were not for the middle part of his body, harnessed to the Chariot. The triumphant driver's merit is that he was able to harness it, for in this way he utilizes energies which left to themselves can only cancel each other out. It is a question of the fixing of the 'Mercury of the Wise' an operation accomplished by Hermes when, placing his wand between two serpents struggling to devour each other, he brought about the formation of the Caduceus. The mission of directing intelligence is to reconcile basic opposing factors. The art of governing is based, like the Great Work, on the capturing and controlling of opposing currents of the universal agent depicted in the *Azoth des Philosophes* by Basile Valentin[41] in the form of a serpent going round the moon and the sun, and whose two extremities are a lion (fixity) and an eagle (mobility), coming together, subdued in their anger.

In arcana 7 the white sphinx symbolizes the good constructive will powers which aspire to the general well-being to be brought about peaceably and smoothly. The black sphinx trembles with impatience and pulls strongly on the left; its efforts risk dragging the chariot into the ditch, but in reality only succeed in stimulating the white sphinx who is obliged to pull harder on its side. Thus the vehicle advances more quickly according to the mechanical law of the parallelogram of force.

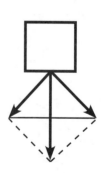

DIVINATORY INTERPRETATIONS

Netzah, triumph, steadfastness—active spirituality, conscious progress, intelligent evolution, constructive principle of the Universe, Great Architect.

Control, absolute domination over oneself, direction, government, full power of intelligence and tact, discernment in reconciliation, peace-bringing and civilizing harmony.

Talent, success thanks to personal merit, legitimate outcome, loyal diplomacy, the ability to benefit from adverse action, ambition, advance, the post of director or head.

In a negative sense: incapacity, lack of talent of tact, diplomacy or spirit of reconciliation; misconduct, bad government.

VIII

Justice

Arcana 7 relates the first two ternaries of the Tarot to the 'unity of the first septenary which corresponds to 'Spirit'; arcana 8 therefore introduces the second which is related to the Soul as the third will relate to the body.[42] Now the first terms of a septenary by necessity play a life-giving role. Just as the Spirit emanates from the First Cause (arcana 1) so does the Soul procede from arcana 8 and the body from arcana 15.

But arcana 8 must also be seen as the second term of the third ternary which makes it passive in regard to the preceding arcana. Now since 7 represents the activating spirituality, the universal activating principle, 8 becomes the life-giving movement, the generator of order and of organization.[43] Justice is thus explained as co-ordinating and organizing chaos.

Without Justice nothing can live since beings only exist by virtue of law to which they are subject. Anarchy is synonymous with nothingness.

In the Tarot, Thémis reminds us of the Empress with her hierarchical attitude, with her portrait presented full-face, with her blond hair, her red tunic and blue mantle, but she is no longer the Queen of the Sky, this star eternally young in her heavenly abode. The woman who holds the scales and the sword seems to have aged and her features have hardened. Now that she has come down into the sphere of action, she has lost her wings. Her throne is massive, solid and stable like the golden cube of the Emperor (arcana 4). It is not a chariot which travels throughout the world, but a great seat fixed to

the ground. The two pilasters which flank it are decorated with half-overlapping discs alternating white and green. By their shape these ornaments remind us of the multiple breasts of Diana of Ephesus, the giver of milk and nourishing sap. By analogy with the columns of Jachin and Boaz of Solomon's temple, the pilasters of the throne of Justice mark the limits of physical life, between them stretches the limited field of life-giving activity. In place of the shell-shape ends of the pilasters one might substitute half-open pomegranates, symbols of fertility as well as of harmonious co-ordination.

The action of Justice-Nature takes place in the double sphere of feeling and vitality, hence the blue and green of the sleeves of Thémis.

In connection with arcana 6 which occupies the middle place in the first set of the Tarot, 4 and 5 are homologous, thus closely connected in meaning.[44]

In fact what would become of the Emperor if it were not for Justice? Law would remain theoretical and potential, if it were not applied in the practical sense in the sphere of the positive; it is the same with abstract mathematics which only becomes meaningful when it is applied. Personifying the principle of numeration, the Emperor would give out mathematics in vain if it were not for Justice who receives and organizes it. Receiving what God gives, Nature functions like the housewife who organizes and administers life, distributing everything in an ordered way following the law of numbers and measures.

As sanction to the close links which bind 4 to 8, a sign common to both decorates the Emperor and Justice: it is the necklace in the form of a plait, the emblem of the simple co-ordination of vital fibres which are linked by a cord which is stronger than a chain whose links are liable to break.

The magistrate's cap which Justice is wearing is marked with the symbol of the Sun ☉, for the spiritual Sun is the great coordinator who assigns his role to every living person and to everything. The number eight is, moreover, that of Sun-Reason, the light of men, as is proved by the Chaldean emblem of Samas, the god of daylight. From a central point emanate four rays, doubled cross-wise, symbolizing light and warmth. Faithful to tradition the Freemasons decorate the

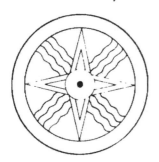 

F, the orator who is responsible for calling one's notice to the law, with a Sun with a cluster of eight rays.

Let us note also that in China the Qua, or trigrams of Fo-Hi under whose influence the world has taken shape, are of the number eight. (See further on in the chapter relating to the Instruments of Divination.)

Let us not forget either that the star formed by a double cross, vertical and oblique ✳ is, in Assyro-Babylonian writing the definite article to divine names.

The star with eight equal rays is, on the other hand, the symbol of Ishtar, the goddess of life, who in certain respects is reflected in Justice, but harmonizes more specifically with the symbolism of arcana 17.

A crown of lance-like iron finials surmounts the cap of Thémis. This is an allusion to the severity of law which is applied with the cold cruelty and the point of a javelin penetrating the flesh.

Moreover, in her right hand the goddess holds a terrible bared sword which is that of fatality, for no violation of the law remains unpunished. Although there is no vengeance, the implacable establishment of any equilibrium which has been broken provokes sooner or later the inevitable reaction of immanent Justice to which arcana 8 is related.

But the instrument of atonement of faults committed is the scale, whose oscillations bring about a balance. Every action, every thought, every desire has an effect upon her beam; as a result there are accumulations which will have their fatal repercussion for good or for ill. The energies at work are stored; those which proceed from a generous kindness enrich the soul, for he who loves makes himself worthy of being loved. Now the feelings of love and sympathy are more precious than material wealth; no one is poorer than the egoist who refuses to give of himself. Let us learn how to give in order to be rich.

So that no-one is asked to give except in the measure of what he has, our destinies are weighed in the balance. Joys and pains are distributed fairly, in the sense that they are proportionate, for we can only appreciate by reason of contrast; so that to be happy one has to have suffered. Let us weigh carefully what we feel and we will see that everything in life is accurately balanced.

It is like this even in the workings of vital forces which are subject to alternating exaltation and depression. To illustrate this physiological law an ancient belief, which inspired Raphael in the decoration of the stanza of the Vatican, puts into the picture two Satyrs, one male, the other female playing on a see-saw near a basket, the holy basket which the initiated of Eleusis carried. This is an allusion to the rhythm of life and to the necessity of conforming to it in using one's energy to the full. Every phase of active excitement must be balanced by a compensatory passivity. It is to our advantage to prepare ourselves for an effort by resting, and to preclude brain work by sleep or inner contemplation.

To become excited by artificial means is an error which Nature punishes (arcana 8) by imbalance which tends to become permanent.

Astronomically speaking Justice is Astraes, the Virgo of the Zodiac who holds the Scales of the autumn equinox. The columns of her throne represent, in this respect, the two solstices. Astrologers make of the Scales a sign of air which they place as a daily home to Venus. The activity of the day restricts the goddess to the calm and methodical work of life, so much so that she seems remote from the passions of the lover besotted with the handsome Adonis.

DIVINATORY INTERPRETATIONS

Hod, splendour, glory, divinity manifested by order and harmony of nature, the conserving power of things. Law, equilibrium, life stability, logical and necessary procedure of ideas, of feelings and of actions. Fatality flowing from all that is accomplished, Immanent Justice, ineluctable consequences of all action.

Logic, sureness of judgement, impartiality, independence of mind, honesty, integrity, regularity, discipline, respect for hierarchy, submission to propriety and custom. Decree, decision, resolution, steadfast purpose, rules of conduct.

Method, exactitude, motion, work. An administrator, a manager, a judge, a man of law or an agent entrusted with the maintenance of order. A man of dialectic, quibbling and full of casuistry. Routine, conservative nature, fear of innovations. A subordinate knowing how to obey, but incapable of initiative.

IX

The Hermit

The Master of the Chariot (arcana 7) is a young man impatient to bring about progress who is curbed by Justice (arcana 8) who favours order and is hostile to revolutions.

The Hermit reconciles this antagonism by avoiding precipitation as much as he does immobility. He is an experienced old man who knows the past from which he gains his inspiration to prepare the future. His walk is careful, for armed with a bamboo cane with seven mystic knots, he sounds the earth on which he advances slowly, but continuously. If on his path he meets the serpent of selfish desires, he does not try to imitate the winged woman of the Apocalypse who puts her foot on the reptile's head—an allusion to the mysticism which is ambitious to conquer all animality. The wise man prefers to cast a spell over the animal so that it twines itself round his stick as round the stick of Esculapius. It is in fact a question of vital currents which the miracle-maker picks up with a view to practising the medicine of the Initiated.

The Hermit does not tap upon the earth blindly, for a discreet glow throws light upon his firm and untiring path. Indeed his right hand holds up a lantern which is partially veiled by a piece of our philosopher's wide cloak. He is afraid of dazzling his eyes which are too weak to bear the brilliant light of his lantern.

In this way he only lets his own personal knowledge shine in as much as it is useful in guiding him. He is modest and has no illusions about his own knowledge, which he knows to be infinitesimal in comparison with his ignorance. Therefore, giving up overproud intellectual ambitions, he is content to receive humbly the ideas which are indispensable for him in the accomplishment of his earthly task.

His mission is not to fix beliefs by formulating dogma, for the Hermit is not the Hierophant (arcana 5); he does not address the crowds, nor let himself be approached, except by the seekers of truth who dare to penetrate into his solitude. Once assured that they are capable of understanding him, he trusts them, for the wise man does not cast pearls before swine.

The light which the Hermit has at his disposal is not limited to throwing light upon the surface: it penetrates, searches out and reveals the inner quality of things. In order to recognize a true man Diogenes had to use a lantern similar to the Hermit's in the Tarot.

This character's cloak is dark outside, almost brown (austerity), but its lining is blue as pertaining to clothing of ethereal nature and endowed with the insulating properties attributed to the famous mantle of Apollonius. The Freemasons know that one must be 'under cover' in order to work to some purpose and Alchemy requires that the carrying out of the Great Work should be pursued within the hermetically-sealed test tube. Without insulation nothing can be concentrated, and without initial concentration no magic action could be carried out. The energies which have been silently and patiently accumulated, sheltered from any disturbing infiltrations, will throw out an irresistible force when the time duly arrives. Everything that is bound to take bodily shape is worked out in secret in the dark womb where the secret work of mysterious conspirators is pursued.

The Hermit conspires in the shelter of an austere psychic atmosphere which cuts him off from all worldly frivolity. In his retreat he works out his concepts by intensifying his will-power; he holds this in check by magnetizing his fine aspirations with all the disinterested love of which he is capable. In this way this dreamer can prepare formidable events, for being unknown to his contemporaries, he becomes the actual maker of the future. Detached as he is from immediate contingencies, with no self interest he weaves the subtle web of what is to take place. As Secret Master he works invisibly to condition what is soon to be brought forth. As a transforming agent he has no cares for immediate effects and is attached only to the productive energies of the future creations.

To flee from the society of men in order to live in the intimacy of his own thoughts, is to enter into a mystic union with the Ideal depicted in the Tarot by the woman of arcanas 3 and 8 (Empress and Justice) to whom the Hermit becomes the husband. The old man of arcana 9 is related thus to Saint Joseph the carpenter, to whom the Vedas give the name of TWASHTRI. According to Emile Burnouf he is the personification of plastic strength spread throughout the Universe, manifested particularly in living people.[45] One may see in him the mysterious artisan of the invisible scaffolding without which no vital construction could be made. In Jesod the immaterial foundation of objective beings, the strong creative energies, are synthesized when they are applied to a definite realization. Before taking form everything pre-exists as an abstract concept, as an intention, as a drawn-up plan and as a living picture, animated by a dynamism which brings about its reality.

Arcana 9 is related to mystery of real but occult generation in which only the spirit and the soul participate. The Hermit is the master who works on the drawing board, where he draws up the exact plan of the intended construction.

The figure which commonly appears on this drawing board is a square with lengthened sides, containing nine divisions in which the first nine numbers, used by the adepts in the magic square, can be put. When set out in this way the odd numbers form a very significant cross, while the even numbers are relegated to the angles as if they had to relate to the quartet of the Elements. Without attempting any explanations which would take us too far afield, let us simply point out that the life-giving core of the strong being is represented by 5 (quintessence), the number flanked by 3 (formative ideality) and by 7 (the directive Spirit) whereas it is overlooked by number 1 (Pure Spirit) and is supported by 9 (the Synthesis of realizing powers).

When seen in the normal numerical order the Kabbalistic Ennead forms a Rhombus in which 9 occupies the lower point, thus depicting the trunk of the tree of the Sephiroth, the basis or support of the whole.

The character of the Celestial Sphere which best corresponds to the Hermit is *Boötes*, the Wagoner, the keeper of the Seven Oxen, *Septem triones*, the old name given to the septenary of the Ursa Major or the Chariot of David. In fact he is a harvester who raises his sickle over a sheath, in which the modern astronomers see the hair of Berenice. When the Virgin of the zodiac descends, Boötes bends over and seems to follow her; so he has been made her husband, or better still the father of the Virginal Erigone who presides over harvests. Hence the affinity already stated between arcanas 3 and 9 is confirmed.

The Tarot of Bologna replaces the Hermit by a winged Patriarch who walks with difficulty, bent over two crutches. From his belt hangs a purse which contains the heritage of the past. He is moving away from a column which marks one of the poles of universal movement, that from which living men move as they evolve. This old man who progresses but slowly, in spite of his wings, makes us think of Saturn, the god of Time, seen as the eternal continuation always on the move to conquer the future which he imperceptibly unfolds from the past. In this connection let us note that Charles VI's pack makes the Hermit hold not a lantern but an hourglass.

Divinatory Interpretations

Jesod, basis. The potential living being, the potential strength within the seed. The living plan existing before its materialization. The invisible weft of the organism that is to be constructed, the prototype putting the stamp of the species onto individuals. The Astral body of the occultists.

Tradition. Experience. Unperishable patrimony of the past. Profound knowledge. Prudence. Circumspection. Meditation. Silence. Discretion. Reserve. Isolation. Continence. Chastity. Celibacy. Austerity.

The wise man detached from the world, dead to wicked passions and ambitions. Profound, meditating spirit, adverse to all frivolity. Experienced doctor of the mind, soul and body. An Initiate practising Universal Medicine. The Hermetic philosopher possessing the secret of the Stone of the Wise. Initiator. Master capable of directing the work of others and of discerning what is in embryo in the sphere of human development. Midwife.

The character of Saturn, serious, taciturn, sullen, distrustful. Timorous nature, meticulous, heavy. Sadness, misanthropy, scepticism, discouragement, avarice, poverty.

X

The Wheel of Fortune

The first chapter of the book of Ezekiel describes a vision upon which innumerable Kabbalists have made unending comments. When the heavens had opened the prophet saw in them strange animals grouped in fours, and near to them four wheels of fire, each being double. The tenth key of the Tarot, whose symbolism has been affirmed by Eliphas Lévi, was inspired by the sacred text where it shows us a wheel with two concentric rims, the image of the double whirl which generates the life of each individual.[46]

This life is engendered like an electric current as soon as a whirl, checked in its movement, takes the opposite direction to the girating movement around it. The individual is the result of the force opposing everything of which he is in fact a part. He only becomes the central point by rebelling against universality. His life proceeds from a vaster life which he strives to preserve. He only manages this to a limited extent, hence the brevity of individual existence to which the Wheel of Fortune alludes. This is also the wheel of the Future or of Destiny.

A starting handle sets this fateful wheel in motion, rapid at first, but slowing down till its stop marks death. After the precipitation of the strong rhythm of youth comes the calm regularity of maturity then the decline into old age which ends in a fatal and complete standstill.

The Wheel of Becoming moves on the sombre ocean of chaotic life supported by the masts of two boats side by side, of which one is red, the other green. Their shape reminds us of the crescent Isis, the great creator, the mother of all beings.

From each boat springs forth a snake; one is male, the other female. They correspond to the two types of vital currents, positive or negative, and become propulsion (red) and sensitivity (green).

The movement of the Wheel of Fortune draws with it as it rises a Hermanubis holding the caduceus of Mercury. As it comes down a Typhonic monster armed with a trident is drawn with it. Thus on one side are symbolized all the beneficial and constructive energies which favour the growth of the individual and stimulate vital development, and on the other hand we have the collection of destructive agents which the living person must resist.

The two opposing factors represent summer, whose warmth is favourable to life, and winter, which restricts the radiation of life. The character with the dog's head corresponds to the canicular constellations of which *Sirius* is the chief star. Its opposite takes us to Capricorn, fish-goat, amphibious, hence a miry, chaotic monster as the earth-green colour of its body indicates. If the face and smoky clothes of the winter devil are of dark red, it is because a hidden force burns within him: the fire of selfish passion, for he is the spirit of chaotic matter, Hyle, to which he tends to lead everything that is organized, co-ordinated and subject to rule. But cold which condenses and materializes is not to be taken only in a derogatory sense. Without it, there would be no incarnation of the Word, nor redemption. Capricorn has therefore not been considered evil by the Christians of the Catacombs who have associated it with the trident of Neptune on the wall of one of the crypts of the Ardéatine. They obviously saw in it the symbol of fallen man, but regenerated through the power of the water of baptism.

Hermanubis, whose body is blue, therefore ethereal, corresponds to the Azoth of the Wise, an ethereal substance which penetrates all things, to excite, support and revitalize if need be, the movement of life. This sort of mysterious fluid is, at the same time, the vehicle of a directive Intelligence[47], the great Mercury, the messenger of the co-ordinating gods of Chaos.

The life-bestowing divinities number seven; they have their counterpart in the planetary influences of astrology which reflect on all that exists. Hence the differently coloured seven spheres which are crossed by the seven spokes of the Wheel of Becoming.

Above this, on a motionless platform a Sphinx is firmly placed. It represents the principle of equilibrium and fixity which assures the transitory stability of individual forms. Like Justice (arcana 8), it is armed with a sword, for it is for him to cut through and decide by intervening in the conflict of condensing or expanding forces, selfish in a restricting way or over-generous in their outward-going desires. It is the Archeus of the Hermetists, the fixed and determining core of individuality, in the centre of which burns Sulphur ☿. This principle of unity has power over elementary attractions which it synthesizes and converts into vital energy. This explains the four colours of the Sphinx which correspond to the elements: red head, Fire; blue wings, Air; chest and front legs green, Water; back part, black, Earth. The Sphinx is, moreover, human in its face and woman's breasts, an eagle in its wings, a lion in its claws and a bull in the main part of its body. In it can be found the animals of Ezekiel's vision which have become the symbols of the four Evangelists: Man or Angel, Saint Matthew; Bull or Ox, Saint Luke; Lion, Saint Mark; Eagle, Saint John.

In connection with Capricorn-Typhon and Dog-Hermanubis which correspond astronomically to the solstices, the Sphinx occupies the place of Libra (the Scales) in the zodiac which Justice is holding (arcana 8). It is in contrast to the snakes which transform the supporting beam of the Wheel of Fortune into Mercury's wand. Just like Aries whom they substitute, the reptiles symbolize the awakening of life in spring. They emerge from the Ocean of chaos depicted by the region in the sky where Pisces and Cetus (the Whale) swim, not far from the mouth of the river of Eridan. As is stated in Genesis, the Spirit of Elohim hovers thus above the dark waters as the impenetrable master of the turning of the cosmic wheel.

Severe, placid and forever enigmatic, the eternal Sphinx remains master of his secret which is the great Arcana, the creative Word, hidden from created beings, the initial Yod of the divine tetragram.

DIVINATORY INTERPRETATIONS

Malcut, kingdom. The sphere of the sovereignty of the will. The principle of individuality. Involution, seed, sowing, sperm, fertilizing energy. Yod, Jachin's column.

Initiative, sagacity, presence of mind, spontaneity, aptitude for inventions. Divination of a practical type. Success due to opportunities seized at the right moment.

Luck, fortuitous discoveries which enrich or lead to success. Favourable destiny which brings about success outside any real personal merit. Advantages seized by chance. An envied but unstable situation. 'Ups and downs' of fortune. Inconstancy. Minor good fortune in geomancy. Transitory benefits.

XI

Strength

Supreme energy which no brutality can resist is represented in the Tarot by the aspect of a blond and graceful queen who without any apparent effort tames a furious lion whose jaws she is holding apart. This conception of strength, seen as a cardinal virtue, is remote from the banal representations of a Hercules leaning upon his club and clothed in the spoils of the lion of Nemeá. It is not physical strength, nor muscular, which arcana 11 is extolling. It is concerned with the exercise of feminine strength, much more irresistible in its gentleness and subtlety than any outburst of anger and brute force. The wild animal, the incarnation of uncontrolled and passionate violence, is represented by this voracious Leo of the zodiac. Its annual return marks the epoch at which the Sun when burning, dries up and kills vegetation. It is conquered by Virgo (Empress, arcana 3) whose harvests it has ripened.

It is not an evil animal in spite of its ferociousness. Left to itself, it hoards, devours and destroys with a selfish fury; it is not like this if it is tamed, for, being very like the black Sphinx of the Chariot (arcana 7) it renders great services to whoever can master it.

There is, therefore, no reason to kill the animal, even within our own personality, as the ascetics do. The Wise man respects all energies even when dangerous, for he is of the opinion that they exist to be caught and wisely used.

Guilgames, the Chaldean hero, is careful not to suffocate the lion which he presses against his head after stunning it with the aid of a weapon made of a skin bag filled with sand. This Initiate scorns nothing inferior; he considers to be sacred even the least noble instincts, for they are the stimulant necessary for every action. Strong mastery over life requires that the forces which tend to evil should be changed into useful energies. What is vile must not be destroyed, but ennobled through change, like lead which one must learn how to elevate to the dignity of gold.

This rule is applicable in all spheres. It is useless to expect from the mass of people virtue, disinterest, the austere accomplishment of duty. Egotism in all forms remains the Prince of this base world; the Wise man makes his decision and takes the Devil into account to force it, in spite of itself, to take part in the Great Work. Such is the teaching of arcana 11.

The feminine Magician who thus puts the masculine or dorian programme into practice is called Intelligence. She is the Charmer to whom we owe the conquests of learning and the progress of civilization; but the marvels which she brings about secretly are more admirable than those which are obviously confirmed. She is active in each organism. Without her the unconscious cells could not compete for the common good. She is reflected in the soul of every collectivity, for life is individual only in a relative way; the person seen as the most simple is in fact complex. Every life, whether it is that of an isolated individual or that of a nation, is based on the association of diverging factors unaware of each other's existence. These require, however, to be reconciled in the interest of higher things. This indispensable reconciliation is everywhere the work of the mysterious power represented in the Tarot by Strength. Were it not for the irresistible intervention of the royal tamer, in which are united the Empress (arcana 3) and Justice (arcana 8), the unleashed selfish interests would oppose all collective life. If the organism resists the discords of the elements which make it up, it is because it possesses an organic soul in which resides a strength superior to that of mean grabbing. When the citizens think only of themselves, the nation is in danger, if it resists the force of individual appetites, it is the miracle of national spirit symbolized in the Tarot by the Woman victorious over the rapacious Animal.

The queen who is calmly mastering rebellious energies is clothed in the colours of the Priestess (arcana 2): a blue dress and red mantle, for her action is mysterious like that of Nature-Isis. But the blue of strength is the light sky-blue of the Empress (arcana 3). Green appears on her sleeves as on those of Justice (arcana 8) while still combining with yellow. For the lion-tamer is inspired by the highest ideal (arcana 3) and directs vitality (green) by the interspersal of coagulated light (yellow), conforming to the laws of universal order (arcana 8). It should be noticed that 3 + 8 = 11, a number which leads to 2 by theosophic reduction.

The number eleven appears, moreover, as of capital importance in Initiation, especially in its multiples 22, 33, 77 and just as when it is broken down into 5 and 6; these numbers remind us of the pentagram and the Seal of Solomon, that is to say of the Stars of the Microcosm and the Macrocosm. The union of these two stars makes up the pantacle of magic Strength, exercised by the human spirit (Pentagram), now becomes the centre of action of the universal Soul (Hexagram).

Our mastery is affirmed in the limited sphere of the Microcosm, which is held within the Macrocosm, from which we emanate (arcana 1) and at whose service our efforts are expended (arcana 11).

Like that of the Magician (arcana 1), the headdress of Strength takes on the shape of an eight on its side ∞, the sign expressing flowing movement, adapted by mathematicians as a symbol of the infinite.

The return to this sign at the end of an active row of the first eleven arcanas[48] assigns the Infinite both as the source and the end of conscious, willed and dorian activity.

The Magician's hat is simpler than Strength's, having neither crown nor coloured plumage, for spiritual power (crown) is only acquired by exercising it, and practical knowledge is not innate. The Magician has the capacity to achieve all, but he has instructed and disciplined himself in the course of his career as an Initiate in the masculine or dorian sphere. Arcana 11 in this respect, marks the ideal which it is possible to attain. The wise man can have at his disposal an immense strength if he thinks wisely and if his own will is identified with the Supreme Will.

With gentleness he will tame violence; no brutality will resist him, provided that he knows how to use the magic power to which every true Initiate must aspire. Let us tame the lion of dominating passions and selfish instincts within ourselves if we aspire to really great Strength superior to all others.

DIVINATORY INTERPRETATIONS

Psychic energy. Power of the body's spirit which dominates and co-ordinates the impulses in conflict in the heart of the organism. Reason and feeling combined to master instinct. The individual word. The expansion of the Thought-will emitted by the individual. Triumph of intelligence over brutality. Human wisdom and knowledge subjugating the blind forces of Nature.

Virtue, courage, calm, intrepidity. Moral force imposing itself upon brute force and selfish passions.

Complete mastery of one's self. Strong mind. Energetic and active nature. Work. Intelligent activity. Tamer.

Lively character, quick-tempered, hotheaded. Impatience, anger, temerity. Martian influence. Boasting; exhibitionism. Insensitivity, roughness, coarseness, cruelty, fury.

XII

The Hanged Man

Active Initiation, called masculine or dorian is related in the Tarot to the first eleven arcanas. It is based on the growth and unfolding of the energies which the individual draws from within himself. It starts at 1 to end at 11. The would-be Initiate, stimulated by a noble and legitimate personal ambition, if he proves himself worthy, has finally at his disposal the supreme magic power. He then realizes the ideal of the Magus, the absolute master of himself and because of this is the master of anything that comes under his ascendancy. One is tempted to think that it is impossible to go any further, yet the Tarot does not stop at arcana 11, but at 12 it touches upon a completely different sphere, which is that of Passive or Mystic Initiation, known also as feminine or ionian. From now on the personality gives up the exaltation of its natural energies, far from behaving as if at the centre of autonomous action, it is effaced in order to undergo in a docile fashion, outside influences. The Magus has faith in himself, in his intelligence and in his will-power; he feels that he is sovereign and aspires to the conquest of his kingdom. The Mystic, on the other hand, is convinced that he is nothing but an empty shell, powerless in itself. His passive renunciation puts him at the service of whatever acts upon him. He hands himself over with a foot and arms bound. Like the Hanged Man who in the Tarot, seems to be the same character as the Magician. In arcana 12 in fact the slim blond man of arcana 1 reappears; but what a contrast between the Magician, over-skilful with his fingers, and the tortured man, free only in his right leg which he bends behind the left to form a cross above the upturned triangle outlined by his arms and head.

The whole representation thus reminds me of the alchemic sign of the Accomplishment of the Great Work ♉, the inverse of the ideogram of Sulphur ♉, to which the outline of the Emperor (arcana 4) is related. The contradiction clearly shown is that of Fire and of Water, or inner or 'infernal' (in the literal sense of the word) Fire, and of sublimated or celestial Water. Sulphuric heat is the Archeus of the individual, the principle of his exaltation and of his sovereignty (Dorism). Water when exteriorized represents the purified life substance in which the virtues from above are refracted. The Hanged Man is inactive and powerless where his body is concerned, for his soul is freed in order to envelop the physical organism in a subtle atmosphere in which the purest spiritual rays are refracted. The Emperor is enclosed and concentrated within himself; he has been absorbed into the centre of his own individuality, practising the descent into oneself of the Initiated. The 'retreat into oneself' leads to the realization of the Great Work along the 'dry path' of Dorism △, whereas the 'coming out of oneself' makes its way there along the damp path of Ionism. ▽

He does not tread the earth on which mortals find their support, for properly speaking, he is not an earthly being, for material reality escapes him; he lives in the dream of his ideality, supported by a mysterious gallows made of two trees stripped of their branches, joined by a piece of dead wood. This crossbeam is yellow, to indicate that its substance is condensed light, or otherwise though fixed or worked out to a system. This is the doctrine which the Hanged Man has made his own, to which he adheres to the point of being hanged from it with his whole person. It concerns a very high religious conception, too sublime for the mass of mortals to attain, an ideal, moreover, too high to be realized in the practical sense. It is the religion of the élite souls, a tradition superior to the teaching of Churches and of confessions which accommodate themselves to human weakness.

The Hanged Man is bound, not as an instinctive or blind believer, but as a wise man who has discerned the vanity of individual ambitions and has understood the wealth of the heroic sacrifice which aspires towards total oblivion of self. Concerning common mysticism this neglect of self is extended even to the exclusion of all care for individual salvation, for pure devotion discounts any benefit in the form of reward. Moreover, it is not the conquest of heaven that the Hanged Man aspires to, his head being turned towards the Earth. It is saying that his preoccupations are earthly and he is devoted to the good of others, to the redemption of poor humans, the victims of their own ignorance and selfish passions.

The two trees between which the Hanged Man swings correspond to the columns of Jachin and Boaz which stand to the right and left of every Initiated person. They depict the sun of emotional aspirations which tend to shield man from crude materialism. Their blue bark turning gradually to green indicates from the start a serene contemplation, faithful devotion to religious practices, then a progressive vitalization aiming at freeing the moral and truly living side of religion from the practice of religious services.

The warm sap which has made the two trees grow gives a purple colour to the scars left by the branches that have been cut off.[49] If active spirituality (purple) is manifest in twelves, then it is because it animates the universality of the religious sphere, facing the sun which moves through the twelve signs of the zodiac. There is nothing narrow about the Hanged Man's religion; it goes beyond private confessions to reach integral Catholicism, such as results from pure religious feeling common to all epochs and all nations.

Red and white alternate on the Hanged Man's tunic, like the red and green in the Lover's clothing (arcana 6). The activity of red seems to contradict the passive nature of the character who, however, could not be passive in every respect, for he needs to be active in order to reject harmful influences and seek good ones. As for white it is related to the purity of the soul and imagination, indispensable for the conception of just ideas and the growth of generous feelings. On the flares of the tunic two crescent shapes, one red and the other white are in contradiction. They remind us of the similar crescents which protect the shoulders of the Triumphant Charioteer (arcana 7). Here, however, they command not the arms but the legs, that is to say in some way the aerial limbs of the Hanged Man. In fact this person does not walk, since he is hooked up by his left ankle and beats the air with his right leg.

In these conditions the red and waning Moon on the left relates to the humility felt by the mystic, whose self-denial is active, and the white waxing Moon on the right relates to the intuitive faculties whose task is to gather in the impressions of the imagination without changing them, then to interpret them correctly.

Of the buttons on the tunic two are red and four white. This detail is not insignificant, for two refers to the Priestess, thus to the active faith in the mystic, whereas four indicates the Emperor, the master of will-power, which must be pure and disinterested in feminine or Ionian initiation, since the Initiated gives up will-power through himself and above all for himself: he only wants what is willed by the mysterious power which he serves. Where the Magus claims to command, the Mystic aspires only to obey.

This confident abandon is revealed by his serene, carefree appearance, hence the calm and smiling face of the Hanged Man, a strange sufferer, whose bound arms are holding a bag from which fall gold and silver coins. These are the spiritual treasures accumulated by the Initiate who has enriched himself intellectually. Holding to nothing, he scatters liberally the gold of the just ideas which he has been able to formulate and the gold of precious knowledge which he has striven to acquire (⊙ Gold, Spirit, Reason). He is no less liberal with his affection, with his kind feelings and his good will, symbolized by the silver coins scattered on his left (☽ Silver, Soul, Sensitivity).

The mythological hero who is most clearly related to our arcana 12 seems to be Perseus, for the son of Jupiter, the heavenly life-giver, and of Danaus, the soul imprisoned in the brass tower is a personification of active thought. This thought is taken afar to conquer lies and calumny. Medusa whose head Perseus cut off, represents error and ill-will which paralyses the spirit, hence the petrifying power attributed to the glance of the terrible Gorgon. His conqueror had to borrow the mirror-like shield of his sister Minerva, Plato's helmet of invisibility, the work of Vulcan, and the winged sandals of Mercury. Thus armed, he was able to travel far off to carry out an action of an occult or telepathic kind, without being seen. After triumphing over frightening and perfidious stupidity, he frees Andromeda, the soul chained to the rock of matter, the black reef rising above the foam of the wild waves of the terrifying ocean of elementary life.

The person who accomplishes all those noble deeds scarcely seems to correspond to the motionless Hanged Man; but one must not be deceived by the apparent inactivity of the hanging man of arcana 12. If he is bodily powerless, he has at his disposal an occult or spiritual power. Though not moving with his muscles, he exerts an irresistible psychic influence, thanks to the subtle influence which emanates from him; his thought, his aspirations and his feelings are felt from afar, as are the interventions of Perseus.

DIVINATORY INTERPRETATIONS

The soul freed from the enclosing body. Mysticism. Priest. The man entering into contact with God. Collaboration with the Great Work of universal change from evil into good. The individual freeing himself from instinctive selfishness to rise to the divine. Redeeming sacrifice. Activity of the soul. Remote intervention. Telepathy.

Moral perfection, Self denial. Complete forgetfulness of self. Devotion. Absolute disinterestedness. Voluntary sacrifice. To benefit a higher cause. Patriotism.

Priest, prophet, seer. Utopian, dreamer lost in the clouds and deprived of common sense. An enthusiast filled with illusions. The artist conceiving beauty, but incapable of translating it into a work of art. Unworkable plans. Liberal but sterile desires. Unrequited love.

XIII
Death

The pictures of the Tarot bear their designation in letters: Magician, Priestess, Empress, etc. Only arcana 13 remains intentionally silent as if the illustrators of the Middle Ages had been loathe to name the skeleton reaper whose harvest is of human heads. Would they have refused to see Death only as the universal destroyer of perishable forms? Considering life as the only existing thing, it seems that they fear neither Death nor Nothingness. What 'is' changes its aspect but is never destroyed: everything persists by being changed indefinitely by the action of the great transformer to whom individual beings owe their origin. By decomposing forms that have worn out and are incapable of fulfilling the job for which they were destined, this agent intervenes as a rejuvenator since he sets free energies which are destined to enter into new combinations of life. We owe our transitory existence to what we call Death. It allowed us to be born and can lead us to rebirth.

There is a precise connection in the Tarot between the first terms of the second ternary and the fifth, represented by arcanas 4 and 13.[50] Now 4 (Emperor) represents the Sulphur of the Alchemists 🜍, that is to say inner Fire, the active principle of individual life. This Fire burns at the expense of reserves which are drawn[51] from the gradual slowing down of its heat and its final extinction into what we call Death (arcana 13). This, in reality, extinguishes nothing, but sets free the energies overwhelmed by the weight of Matter's increasing inertia. Far from killing, Death revives by dissociating what can no longer live. If it were not for the intervention of Death everything would wilt, so that life finally would not be distinguishable from the common image of Death. So it is quite right that arcana 13 should relate to the active generator of Universal Life, permanent life, of which Temperance (arcana 14) symbolizes the moving dynamism, whereas the Devil (arcana 15) shows its static accumulation. The profane must die to be reborn to the superior life which initiation confers. If he does not die in his state of imperfection, then all progress in initiation is denied him.

'To know how to die' is therefore the great secret of the Initiated, for, by dying he frees himself from what is inferior to rise through sublimation. The true wise man therefore strives constantly to live better. That does not imply any practice of a sterile asceticism on his part, but if he wants to achieve an intellectual autonomy, must he not break with the prejudices which are dear to him and so die to his usual way of thinking? To be born to freedom of thought one must free

oneself by being dead to all that is contrary to the strict impartiality of judgement. This voluntary death is demanded of the Freemason so that he can say that he is 'born free' as he strikes the door of the Temple. The symbolism, unfortunately, remains a dead letter, the recipient for the most part, not having the least idea of what his passage through the funeral cave, called the Room of Reflexion, signifies.

In Alchemy, the subject destined to provide the matter of the Philosopher's Stone, in the other words the profane admitted to initiation, is also condemned to death. Imprisoned in a hermetically sealed container, hence isolated from all outside living influence, the subject dies and putrefies. It is at this point that the colour black appears, symbolized by Saturn's crow which is a good augur at the beginning of operations of the Great Work. 'If you do not see this blackness in the first instance predominant over all other colours, then you must have failed in the work and must begin again!' In accordance with all the Hermetic philosophers, Nicholas Flamel urges the would-be Initiate to withdraw from the world and to forget his frivolities in order to enter the path of progressive changes within oneself which lead to true initiation.

This initiation includes two successive deaths. The first implies an incubation similar to that undergone by the chick (in the egg), whose shell he finally breaks. The mystic must withdraw into himself in the darkness of the 'Philosophers' Egg' with a view to conquering light and liberty. One must die in a dark prison in order to be reborn to a life of independence and light.

The new life achieved is not an existence of triumphant rest: it imposes continuous tasks, rich and glorious, the reward of which is the second death. Not content with freeing himself from his coarsest surroundings, the initiate dies this time more profoundly than at the beginning of his initiation, for he dies to himself, to his own personality, to his radical self. His renunciation, however, is not

Tarot of the Magicians

that of the ascetic, who has become indifferent to his own and to the fate of others. How would the Initiate, having died twice, despise human lives, when he only came back to life in order to live for them? If he has become one with the Great Being who becomes particularized in us, it is in order to share his infinite love. What distinguishes the ideal Wise man is that he can love with ardour until self is completely forgotten. He who achieves this generous disinterestedness has at his disposal immense power and possesses the Philosopher's Stone; a double death of initiation alone has been able to lead him to the zenith.

Contrary to common practice, the Reaper of the Tarot is cutting to the left. Thanks to this anomaly the skeleton outlines a Hebrew Mem מ. The handle of the scythe is red, for death has fire which devours dried up strength; the straw in which the vital sap no longer circulates. It is to be noted that the skeleton's bones are not white, but flesh pink, the characteristic hint of all that is human, sensitive and feeling. Would not decomposing Fatality then have all the cruelty that one lends her? The scythe which restores the bodies to the earth greedy to assimilate them, seems to spare heads, hands and feet. The faces keep their expression as if they were still alive. The one on the right bears a royal crown, the symbol of the regality of the intelligence and will, which no one gives up at death. The features of the face on the left have lost none of their feminine charm, for affections do not die, and the soul continues to love beyond the tomb. The hands which rise out of the earth, ready for action announce that the work could not be interrupted, and the feet appearing among the green shoots offer their services to advance ideas already in progress. The disappearance of the individuals brings no loss or prejudice to the task they were accomplishing: nothing ceases, everything continues!

Shiva takes from Vishnu the life given by Brahma, not to destroy it, but with a view to rejuvenating it. In the same way as Saturn prunes the tree of life in order to intensify the strength of the sap, so a rejuvenating spirit tailors humanity in the interest of its continuance and fertility. In the grimacing Reaper, the Initiate recognizes the indispensable agent of Progress; so he feels no fear at his approach. In order to live as an Initiate, let us consent to die. Death is the supreme Liberator. The wise man makes his way towards the tomb without regretting the past; he accepts serene old age, happy to benefit from the release from the bonds which hold the spirit prisoner within matter. The calming of passions gives to the intellect a more complete freedom which is able to express itself in kindly lucidity and even in prophetic clairvoyance. The privileges of Domination over self are, moreover, reserved for the old man who has been able to stay young in heart, for the power of the Master is based on sympathy. He has no longer any other strength but that of affection; but he knows how to love with self-denial. Vibrating with all the energy of his soul, he has at his disposal the 'Strong Strength of all Strengths', and is the possessor of the real Philosopher's Stone, capable of accomplishing the miracles of the 'Unique Object'. Happy is he who comes under no inferior

attraction, but who nonetheless burns with an intense and generous warmth of heart! He has died in order to enter a higher and finer life. If he is a Christian the Pascal rebirth has taken place within him; if he is a Freemason, he can call himself 'Son of Putrefaction' in all truth after decomposing in the tomb of Hiram and leaving there anything which hampers his spiritual flight.

Nothing in the sky is related to death. The Dragon of the Pole, however, figures as the enemy of life, or at least of forms which have but transitory life. He is the insatiable devourer of all that has lived; in him everything that must return to chaos is destroyed before it can take on a new aspect. Hercules (arcana 4) met this monster in the garden of Hesperides where he defended the golden apples. But the terrifying reptile only deters the profane those unworthy of approaching the treasure of initiation: it recoils before the Initiate who has died and come back to life.

DIVINATORY INTERPRETATION

The transforming principle which renews all things. Ineluctable necessity. The fatal progress of evolution. Eternal movement which is opposed to all stopping, to all definite fixation, thus to everything that would be truly dead. The Spirit of Progress (The Holy Spirit of the Gnostics). The consoling Paracletes which sets the spirit free from the yoke of matter. Liberation, Spiritualization. Dematerialization. Shiva.

Disillusion. Intellectual penetration, Perception of reality despoiled of all sensory surrounding. Complete lucidity of judgement. Integral initiation. Death in the initiating sense, Detachment. Asceticism. Inflexibility. Incorruptibility. Power to transmute, capable of regenerating a corrupted sphere. Control.

Necessary end. Fatality. Failure whose victim is not responsible. Radical transformation. Renewal. Heritage. Influence of the dead. Atavism. Necromancy. Spiritism.

Melancholy, mourning, sadness, old age, decrepitude, decomposition, corruption, dissolution.

XIV

Temperance

If initiation teaches us to die it is not in order to recommend annihilation. In all certainty, what does not exist is Nothingness! To aspire to this corresponds to the most false ideal that can be conceived, for nothing is destroyed, everything is transformed. Far from suppressing life, death provides for its eternal rejuvenation. It decomposes the 'container' in order to liberate the 'contained' that one can envisage as a liquid unceasingly poured from one perishable vessel into another without one drop being wasted.

Key 14 of the Tarot shows us this vital fluid poured from a silver urn into a gold one by Temperance who becomes the angel of universal Life. The jars of precious metal do not correspond to crude bodily containers; they allude to the double psychic atmosphere whose natural organism is only the earthly ballast. Of these concentric containers the one, the nearer (gold, conscience, reason) is solar active; it directs the individual in an immediate way and supports its energy of the will. The other stretches beyond the first; it is lunar and sensitive (silver). Its domain is more mysterious; it is that of sentimentality, of vague impressions, of the imagination and of the unconscious on a superior level. This ethereal sphere picks up vibrations of life common to the individuals of the same species, a permanent life which is the reservoir from which we draw the vitality which we individualize. What is concentrated in the silver urn flows into the gold where condensation is completed with the view to maintaining psychic life.

The mystery of the two urns dominated the whole of therapeutic thaumaturgy, whose miracles are performed with the aid of the universal fluid. Beginners in the art of healing have for most of the time an urn overspilling with gold for their use. So they transfer to others their own fluid and practise healing magnetism by commanding the currents of life. If the silver urn is not revealed to them then they remain as apprentice healers incapable of sustained action which is more broadly efficacious. The true miracle which is within the reach of every pure soul, fundamentally generous, depends on the extent of our realm of feeling. With our whole being let us sympathize with the sufferings of others, then exteriorize our affection so as to make for ourselves an environment of love, as vast as possible. We will thus benefit from a refracting and life-giving milieu, favourable to the picking up of the lightest waves of vibration by means of which the true medicine of the Saints and Wise man is practised.

The Spirit of Temperance is bisexual; The Devil (15) too is bisexual, whereas Death is without sex. If this is the case then the complete fifth ternary (13, 14 and 15) relates to collective life which is not individualized, to the universal fluid without sex, although susceptible to sexual polarizations.

Like the Empress (3) Justice (8) and the Angel of Judgement, Temperance is blond; she is related, moreover, to these three characters by the colour of her clothes; a red underdress, a blue mantle with green lining. Red denotes inner spirituality, blue, lively serenity and green, tendencies towards vitalization.

The Spirit of Temperance is winged like the Empress (3), for it is analogous with the Queen of the Sky; but it is not confined like her to the heights of an inaccessible ideal and prefers to stoop to the level of the living who owe it to her to live both physically and spiritually. Temperance limits itself, however, to supporting life without bringing about its birth like the Magician (1) does. The angelic cupbearer of the vital fluid revives the flower that is about to wilt; it waters it or condenses the morning dew on it to allow it to resist the heat of the day. In its quartet of cardinal virtues, Strength displays devouring activity which would consume the vital Humidity of the Hermetists if it were not for the refreshing intervention of Temperance. This character restores new sap to the vegetable overpowered by the ripening heat of Leo to which Aquarius stands in opposition; that is to say the Angel of St Matthew or Man associated with the Bull, the Lion and the Eagle in the Vision of Ezekiel.

Aquarius fulfils the role of Indra, the god of fertilizing rains who, among the Chaldean gods corresponds to Ea, master of the Celestial Ocean where supreme Wisdom is found. This Wisdom is shared out among humans by means of the water which falls from above. Hence the sacred character of lustral water, and its role in initiating purifications. Christians were inspired by the ancient mysteries when they compelled the candidate for baptism to plunge into the waters of baptism in order to emerge washed clean of all mortal sin and be regenerated. This means to be born again to Christian life, after dying, through submersion, to the pagan life.

In Alchemy the subject, blackened as much as he wishes, hence dead and putrefied[52], then undergoes ablution. This operation uses the constant waters formed through condensation of vapours which emanate from the corpse by means of a moderate fire outside which is, in turn, allowed to flare up and die down. From this repeated action of making water results the cleansing of the subject who turns from black to grey, then finally to white.

Now whiteness marks the success of the first part of the Great Work. The Initiate only succeeds by purifying his soul of all that normally disturbs it. If, after an effective renouncing of himself, he frees himself from all equivocal desire, then he can approach an ideal of purity of intentions which makes the miraculous action possible.

The art of healing with the help of mysterious forces is based essentially on the purity of the healer's soul. So let him make himself holy by self-denial and devotion to others, and then he will quite naturally perform real miracles: but to this end he must become detached from himself even to the point of indifference, and undergo trial by water which wipes out all evil passion in the heart of man.

One may recognize the Archangel Raphael in the Spirit of Temperance who bears the mark of the sun on his forehead, already seen on the headdress of Justice, and under this sign the Angel of Judgement will be seen (20). This ideogram is always an indication of discernment either when applied to the co-ordinating power of constructive energies (8), to the just and fair sharing out of vital forces (14) or to the enlightened action of the regenerating Spirit which gives breath where it wills (20).

Let us not forget that arcana 14 synthesizes the second septenary of the Tarot, in which it occupies the central place. Now since the three septenaries, each one in its entirety, are related to the Spirit, the Soul and the Body, the second is life-giving; its synthesizing term (14), therefore alludes to the mysteries of the universal Soul, the mysteries which one must penetrate in order to practise the High Medicine of the Initiated.

When the arcanas of the Tarot are arranged in two rows, the Hermit (9) which personifies Prudence becomes the companion-in-line to Temperance (14). Temperance translates into the passive sphere what the lonely philosopher shows in the active. As a man of experience and study, our man stands aloof from suggestions which the mass of people undergo. Without hurrying, he seeks the truth, limiting the field of his explorations, careful to keep within the narrow field of human knowledge. For Temperance his reserve is seen as moderation, a negative virtue which spurns extravagance and exaggerations. Moreover, it is a question of practical life rather than abstract speculation. The Initiate who has bathed in the fluid which the solitary Angel pours out is no longer troubled by the fever which shakes ordinary men. Being dead to evil ambitions, to selfish passions, indifferent to the hardships which threaten him, he lives calmly in the sweet serenity of a gentle wisdom, indulgent towards the weaknesses of others.

DIVINATORY INTERPRETATIONS

Universal Life; its unceasing movements, its motion within living people. The animating fluid which restores spent energy. The repairing and restoring agent of whatever wears out and ages. The curing energy of Nature. Healing thaumaturgy based on the tapping and controlling of vital currents. The transfusion of life-giving strength, healing magnetism, occult or mystic medicine. Transmutation of a vital order. Psychic Alchemy. Regeneration. Mysteries of water and fire. Miracles. The fountain of Youth.

Philosophical carefreeness, serenity of spirit which rises above human misfortunes. Indifference to the pettiness of life. Even temper, peace-giving calm, health, good circulation, regularity of exchanges, conditions favourable to the prolonging of life, disinterestedness, impassiveness, resignation.

Ease in adapting oneself, suppleness, docility. Sensitivity to outside influences. Receptive impressionability. Coldness, apathy, mobility, changing and unstable nature. Rest, holidays, alternances, change, 'happy-go-lucky' attitude, abandon, flow, lack of reserve. Passivity, laziness, lack of foresight, hasty expenses, prodigality.

XV

The Devil

S een in its essence which is common to all living things, universal life circulates unceasingly, always identical to itself, flowing indifferently from one recipient into another. If nothing had come to trouble the regularity of this peaceful flow, then life would have remained conforming to one's 'ideal' of paradise; but the Snake intervened, and under its influence every living being wanted to hoard the common property in order to condense life around itself for its own individual benefit. Thus came about the revolt against the universal order of things. Individual whirls were born in the heart of the general swirl, now stirred and troubled by the radical selfishness which the Devil personifies. This Adversary (Satan in Hebrew) is the Prince of the material World[53] which without him could not exist for he is at the base of all differentiation between one individual and another. It is he who pushes the atom to set itself up at the expense of the substance which is uniformly ethereal. He is the one who differentiates, the enemy of unity. He sets the worlds against the World and living people against each other. Having incited them to wish to be like God, he then indicates the instinct which relates everything to themselves, as if they were the centre around which everything must gravitate.

The Devil appears to us in the Tarot like Baphomet of the Templars, with a goat's head and legs, a woman's breasts and arms. This monstrous idol derives from the Goat of Mendes and of the bisexual Great Pan of the Gnostics. Like the Greek Sphinx, it draws together within itself the four Elements, of whom the Devil is the principal life-giver. Its black legs correspond to the Earth and to the spirits of the dark depths which the Gnomes of the Middle Ages represent and the Anounnaki,[54] feared by the Chaldeans. The Undines, spirits of the water are recalled by the green scales which cover the monster's thighs whose blue wings are related to the Sylphs, powerful spirits of Air. As for the red head, it symbolizes the furnace where the Salamanders, the spirits of Fire find pleasure.

The Occultists are convinced of the existence of Spirits of the Elements. Magic teaches one to subjugate them, without hiding the dangers in the relationships which can be established between them and man. The least that one can say is that they are demanding servants in regard to the person who tames them, reducing at the same time to the worse servitude the would-be Magus who is ambitious to submit them to the power of his fallacious conjurations.

Being careful to control himself in a moderate way by repressing his baser desires, the wise man leaves the mastery of the invisible to the witches and the falsely Initiated to the pretentious occultists who rig themselves out in titles which betray their childish vanity. Let us curb only our bodies and not enter into any contract with any diabolical promiser of petty profits. Let us allow the Gnomes to guard jealously the buried treasures, and let us go back to the study of the earth in order to discover metal strata. Let us not trust the Salamanders to mind over our cooking, nor the Undines to water our garden, and if we wait for propitious wind before we embark, let us not sneeze too much to whistle at the Sylphs as was formerly the custom of sailors.

Disinterestedness is essential in thaumaturgy, for if Nature lets herself be divined it is the simple souls who for preference enter into communion with her, openly and without malice. She loves to make the 'poor in spirit' benefit from her secrets, they who are totally incapable of imagining a knowledgeable theory based on the results they obtain. Far from attributing a personal power to themselves the modest healers consider themselves to be very humble instruments in the services of superior forces. They practise priesthood and are distinguished by their feeling of loving piety. Let them set up the multicoloured plumes of the Red Indian Witch Doctor or the dress and paraphernalia of the African mascot bearer, these children of Nature, who have been taught only by her, if they are honest and sincere, are the respectable colleagues of the worthy Adept who refuses to be associated with charlatans.

The serious Adept is not ignorant of the fact that the Devil is the great magic agent, thanks to whom miracles are performed unless they are of the purely spiritual kind; for as long as pure spirit acts directly upon spirit, the Devil does not have to intervene. But as soon as the body enters into it, nothing can be done without the Devil. We owe to him our material existence, for if the desire to be and the self preservation instinct which came from him, had not dominated us from birth, then we would not have been able to hang on to life with the exclusive egoism which is characteristic of early childhood.

Tarot of the Magicians

The Devil well and truly possesses us when we come into the world and this must be so. But this possession is not lasting for we are destined to free ourselves little by little from the tyranny of our innate instincts. All the while we are bound to our animal organism it is impossible for us to make an abstraction of the spirit which rules over the body. Just as the knight cares for his mount, we must take the animal into account who, beneath us, claims its rights. The Devil is not as black as he is painted: he is our ineluctable associate in life in this base world. Let us learn how to treat him fairly, not as a systematic and irreconcilable enemy, but as an inferior whose services are precious.

Let us not forget that it is the Devil who makes us live in the material sense. He provides for us to meet the needs of this life of perpetual struggle, hence the impulsive actions which are not bad in themselves, but among which harmony must be maintained if we do not wish to fall under the yoke of cardinal sins which share out among each other what one can call the ministerial departments of the infernal government.[55] Let us be moderate in all things and we will fight all conflicts which alone become diabolical. Let us curb our pride so that it appears in the form of dignity, in this noble pride which inspires horror of all baseness. Let us tame our anger to transform it into courage and active energy. Let us not fall into sloth, but give ourselves the rest necessary to repair spent energy. Let us not fear to rest as a precaution with an eye to future effort. Artists and poets can be lazy to some profit. Let us avoid greed: it is degrading to live only to eat, but to live in good health, let us select our food and appreciate its qualities of taste. Let us reject envy which makes us suffer because of what others possess, but let us oppose, in the general interest, secret hoardings and the vices of the powerful. Let us not fall into avarice, but let us be careful and practise economy without spurning the honest love of gain as the efficacious motive for work. As for licentiousness in which the domination of the Devil is most powerful, we must put in its place the religious respect of the great mystery of the union of the sexes. Let us cease to profane what is holy.

If the exercise of magic power imposes chastity, then it is because the propagating instinct plays a leading role in the workings of occult influences. The male who desires the female is exalted to emit electricity from his body enabling him to perform his action as soon as favourable conditions are found. The woman, sure of herself who plays the coquette with her lover, may succumb at the moment when she least expects it. She is then the victim of natural spell to which she left herself open by playing with a treacherous force. Overwhelmed by a mysterious inebriation, she has lost control momentarily, and the act which she had decided against has taken place. Seducers practise an elementary magic as efficacious as it is instinctive. They have the talent to make the Devil intervene without a book of spells, and outside all conscious invocation. Instinct is enough as in a number of other acts in daily life, in which similar reactions are produced

Have a firm will and you will act on the Devil without the slightest difficulty; the white pentagram which adorns Baphomet's forehead bids you to do so. Everything in Nature has a hierarchy in which unconscious forces submit to the direction of what is superior. But is it dangerous to attribute to oneself a ficticious superiority in order to exercise unjustified control: the Evil one is not deceived by this and he takes it upon himself to mystify cruelly those presumptuous people who have a very high opinion of themselves. For obedience he requires that the pentagram should be of perfect whiteness, in other words, that the will should be pure, untainted by egoism, and that the orders given should be legitimate. In the last analysis it is the Devil who is at the service of God and does not let himself be used wrongly or mistakenly. If he provokes trouble, it is never of a lasting nature: his disorder is within order, and comes back to order, for the Devil is subject to the universal law of which Justice 8 assures the application; now 8 dominates 15 when the 22 arcanas are set out in two rows. (See page 13.)

Nothing makes this better understood than the triple pentagram which is the plan of the principal character of arcana 15 (3 x 5 = 15). Intelligent

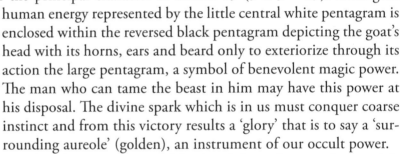

human energy represented by the little central white pentagram is enclosed within the reversed black pentagram depicting the goat's head with its horns, ears and beard only to exteriorize through its action the large pentagram, a symbol of benevolent magic power. The man who can tame the beast in him may have this power at his disposal. The divine spark which is in us must conquer coarse instinct and from this victory results a 'glory' that is to say a 'surrounding aureole' (golden), an instrument of our occult power.

The vibratory tension of this 'aura' depends upon the strength of the infernal fire which burns in us (red head of Baphomet, black pentagram of the diagram). Without a diabolical ardour we remain cold and important: we need to have 'le diable au corps' in order to influence others and in this way act outside of ourselves. This action is exerted by the limbs of the great fluid ghost and more especially by his arms which are not tattooed in vain with the words: COAGULA, SOLVE.

The magical process consists in effect in coagulating the Astral Light, that is to say, the phosphorescent atmosphere which envelopes the planet, thanks to the action of its central fire. Living creatures swarm in the heart of this diffuse light which illumines their instinct. By borrowing the left arm of Baphomet, we can draw towards us the surrounding and invisibly vaporized vitality and condense it into mist which is more or less opaque in its fluorescence. It is 'coagulation' which operates to the advantages of the phallus as is indicated by the Hindu symbol of the union of the sexes, which the Devil raises in his left hand.

Tarot of the Magicians

The coagulated fluid 'charges' the operator like an electric battery; but no effect is produced as long as there is no 'discharge' otherwise known as 'solution'. At this point intervenes the right arm bearer of the burning torch of Baphomet; this image of fierce flames is to be feared. To avoid the explosion which upsets and throws one into a panic, dazes and risks unleashing madness, one must pick up the current which the gradual flow of accumulated fluid causes. A skilled magnetism utilizes this current by an intelligent application of the formula, *Coagula, Solve*.

He uses alternatively the little red devil and the little green devil which are attached by a rope to the gold ring fixed to the cubic altar on which Baphomet stands.

The little satyr and the young female faun represent the positive and negative polarizations of the universal and neuter fluid or more exactly Androgyne, as the sign of hermaphroditism ☿[56] which characterizes the sexuality of the Great Pan. Pan takes a double part as either a son or daughter who both form the sign of esotericism by bending the last two fingers of the hand they stretch out. The little devil on the right thus raises his left hand, brushing the right thigh of Satan to draw out of him some positive fluid which he transmits to the devil on the left by means of the cord which binds them. This green female faun (the colour of Venus) touches with her right hand the left paternal hoof in order to restore the excess fluid. This contact sets up the circuit of the magic slavery whose agents are on one hand pride and male excitement in all its forms and on the other feminine lascivity.

The pedestal of the temple idol is not like the throne of the Emperor (arcana 4), a perfect cube of pure gold. Its flattened shape reminds one of the Alchemists' sign of Tartar ♃ , a substance which deserves to be put to use like the rough stone of the Freemasons, although it is only inconsistent dross. The colour blue indicates aerial matter resulting from the tension between two similar but opposing dynamisms, represented by the base and the platform of the pedestal. The red of the three steps at the bottom and their exact counterpart at the top denotes fiery action, as if the lower polarization provoked by the central fire summoned an equivalent accumulation of static electricity. The altar of the witches' sabbath is constructed according to the laws of the occult, and it would be of profit to us to be instructed in them more deeply.

The horns and the forked hooves of the sorcerers' goat are golden, for what comes from the Devil is precious. From the she-goat Amalthea, Jupiter's wet nurse, came the famous 'horn of abundance' which provided the nymphs with all they desired. He who would possess a devil's horn would likewise draw from it all that he wished. Moreover, what are the properties of the milk drawn from the teats of Baphomet's wife? Tradition does not tell us; but the goat of Jupiter who, accompanied by her two young ones, appears in the sky on the back of the

Herdsman (*Boötes*), corresponds exactly to the ternary of arcana 15. The celestial herdsman holds the whip and the reins which allow him to lead animals; he is Pan, the protector of the living who are subject to the life of the instincts.

The fifth letter of the Hebrew alphabet is Samek whose form is circular in the usual Hebrew calligraphy ◘.[57] Some have thought they recognized in it the Ouroboros, the Cosmogonic Serpent who bites his own tail; others have thought of the tempter, the cause of Adam's fall. These comparisons would not be at all justified if the Tarot were not as old as the alphabet's characters. The early Samek is in effect, a triple cross, like the one the Pope in arcana 5 is holding. If one wanted to exploit the irony of the symbolism one could suggest that it is the fear of the Devil alone that confers on the sceptre its executive power on the government of the Church. Let us conclude in a general way that no one rules on earth without making an alliance with the 'Prince of this World'.

DIVINATORY INTERPRETATIONS

The Soul of the World seen as the reservoir of the vitality of all living beings. The astral light of the occultists. Vital electricity in its static state in its double polarization, active and passive. Occult forces connected with animal life. Instinct, unconscious, subconscious, impulsion.

Magic arts, sorcery, hoodoo, fascination, practice of human magnetism. Suggestion, influence exerted occultly. Action on the unconscious state of others. Domination of the masses. Incantations, disturbing eloquence. Rousing of appetites, of coarse instincts and base passions. Demagogy, revolution, upheaval, denial.

Trouble, lack of balance, disorder. Over-excitement, panic. But, concupiscence, lubricity, hysteria. Intrigues, machinations, use of illicit means. Perversion. Misuse, greed, lack of moderation in all forms.

XVI

The Tower

The Tower in arcana 16 is the first building that we
meet in the Tarot, where similar constructions are
only shown in the Moon 18. Now 16, 17 and 18
make up the sixth ternary, which corresponds to the body of
earthly Adam, that is to say to the organism which is constructed out of human individuality, or to the organism of
humanity seen as a whole. We have in 16 the first term of
the ternary what one may call the 'corporizing spirit' and in
18 the last term of the same triad, the result of corporization
when it has been carried out. Nothing is corporized without
the presence of condensation, firstly ethereal or fluid, under
the restrictive or particularizing influence that it is agreed
we attribute to the Devil. So the Devil becomes the spiritual
father of the smallest atom, no less than of the immeasurable
cosmic system, for at the root of both one and the other there
is conceived a wild whirlwind around a centre of attraction
which is perforce selfish and grabbing. In small things as in
big, everything becomes concrete by the help of an obscure
instinct towards individualization which appears as a rebellion against the universal order of things; hence the legend of
Lucifer and that of original sin, which are to be seen again, for
God is not the old Apsou of the Chaldeans, the bottomless
pit, the Infinite asleep in his infinity from which he refuses to
emerge in order to create. We have given up this ideal divinity, which is, however, metaphysically speaking consistent within itself, to adore the first Cause,
which proceeds by a method of differentiation and does not take umbrage at
the insubordination of matter which is indispensable for the realization of her

plan. Let us not introduce into the necessary unity an illogical dualism. Everything remains as One and our unique God alone assumes the final responsibility for what is. It is forbidden to blaspheme against his creation which is good and perfect in its ideal from which ensues its realization; the Great Work is in the process of being accomplished, and could not be judged all the while it is incomplete. The beauty of a building is not obvious until the scaffolding which allowed its construction has been taken away. We cannot admire our imperfect world and do it justice except by conceiving the perfection to which it aspires.

Since everything is constructed let us ask the builders the secrets of their art. They will lead us up to two columns standing before the Temple which they build to the glory of the Great Architect of the Universe. The first of these columns, that on the right, bears a Hebrew name whose initial letter is Jod, and which means: he establishes, he founds. This pillar is consecrated to the inner fire which animates living beings to make them act through themselves, by taking all the initiative, beginning with the initiative to exist. So it is the individualized creative power which is represented in the phallic form on the buildings which the ancients love to build high.[58]

Arcana 16 presents us with the picture of a similar tower in the Lightning-struck Tower, a typical designation, for it is less a temple, a house of God, than a sacred building of a body mistakenly identified with God.

This identification is the consequence of original sin which clouds the spirit descended into matter for it to elaborate this matter. The Fall is the natural consequence of incarnation, which is not necessarily the result of a primordial fault. The sin of Adam is relative and only exists in relation to blind humanity which whines on seeing itself condemned to work without understanding that they make themselves divine by associating themselves willingly with the eternal work of creation.

But their transitory blindness conforms to the divine plan. In the interest of transmutatory work to which we are bound, we must forget God in order to identify ourselves with matter. God makes this command when we are made flesh; he does not want us to be distracted from our initial task by nostalgia for Heaven. At the beginning child is but pure animal. He builds up his organism by being preoccupied by nothing but himself with the most absolute and unconscious egoism. His body grows in the spirit which animated the builders of the Tower of Babel, a ramshackle building of which arcana 16 presents a symbolically correct image.[59]

The bricks that it is built of are of an overall flesh colour to indicate that it is a question of a living construction endowed with sensitivity. On a large scale it is human society, and on a small scale it is the individual body of each one of us, that is to say a collection of cells born of each other to unite as organs, like the stones of a building which might be capable of creating themselves and fitting together in obedience to mysterious attractions. The materials which form a

Tarot of the Magicians

border round the openings of the Tower are bright red, as if activity had to require the most resistance and solidity. There are four of these openings: one door and three windows of which two let in light in the middle storey of the mind's abode, and the third, the upper chamber, with the ground floor being sufficiently well lighted by the door which stays open.

This lower part, easily accessible corresponds to commonly held ideas which are passively confirmed. From the first storey the view is extensive and observation out of the left window becomes a conscious act: it is knowledge which is made up of the accumulation of the fruits of experience. Through the right window enters the light of reasoning which co-ordinates the ideas acquired and draws a philosophy from them. But it is possible to go higher to reach the sanctuary which is lit by only one window, that of faith or of abstract speculation, seeking for a synthesis.

This is not all. At the very top of the Tower is a crenulated terrace, from which one can view the sky. A double architrave made up of two layers, first of green stones then of red bricks, supports the crown of the Temple. The dull green alludes to the mystic sentimentality, and red to warmth and generosity which lead to the beatific vision and to transcendental contemplation.

There is a risk in rising too high; we are warned of this by the thunderbolt from the Sun which takes the top off the Tower. The Sun here is a symbol of Reason which governs men and is opposed to their extravagant ideas. When we pursue a fanciful enterprise, the catastrophe is fatal. It is instigated by our own fault, but completed by the action of light which illumines intelligence. What is unreasonable condemns itself to collapse. So much the worse for the ambitious man who takes so much trouble to rise very high, not suspecting that heights attract lightning.

The two characters in arcana 16 receive the punishment befitting their presumption; they are thrown headlong together with parts which have come away from the Tower. The first is a king who remains crowned in his fall; he represents the immortal spirit for whom the Tower was built. The silhouette which he outlines as he falls reminds us of the Ayn, the sixteenth letter of the sacred alphabet; but here the remark already made in connection with the Samek is more obvious. The early Ayn was a circle from which is derived, by a series of changes revealed by the study of Hebrew inscriptions, the present character of square-shaped Hebrew.[60]

The Master of the Tower is wearing a costume whose colours clash, to which it is difficult to give a significance. Blue is predominant in it, as a sign of ideality; it is put next to the red which implies activity on the right arm, and with green kept in the region of the heart, sensitive in feminine charm. If finally the left leg is yellow in contrast to the right which is blue, this can indicate a step shared between piety, fidelity (blue) and envy, coveting of material possessions (yellow).

The second character is dressed in red, for he is the Architect of the Tower, the constructor of the body which dies with him; so on the nape of the neck he receives a mortal blow. This maker of the organism is identified with his work which is transitory; but if he disappears he is none the less acting according to a lasting tradition for each individual creates himself, not as he pleases, but according to the lasting plan of the species. The species persists thanks to the strong architecture which is peculiar to it. When a seed develops progressive organization takes place, inspired first of all by the general type of the species, then by the particularities of the race, of the ancestral style, and finally by the individual character. In this corporeal way we are constructed by a creative agent, the architecture of our bodily tower of flesh which is put to the service of our spiritual kingdom.

It remains to mention the multicoloured spheres which the explosion of the Tower seems to have projected into its environment. They are the energies accumulated by life, condensations which red indicates as being sulphurous or fiery, green as being passively vitalized in the mercurial order, and yellow as being dead like straw or even empty seashells.

These phantom-like forms whose active life has departed are the ruins which survive as witnesses of the past. We are besieged by these larvae which we can animate if we set ourselves to the task like the foolish men who let themselves be extortioned.

Woe to the vain occultist who imagines himself to be served by invisible entities! His uncertain servants live at his expense and have a hold on him in the same proportion as he has a hold on them. He belongs to them in the same way as they belong to him. There are therefore, two alienations on his part: he has alienated himself in the true sense of the word and moreover leaves himself open to losing his reason, the catastrophe which threatens him in arcana 16.

The inauspicious meaning of the Tower has its link in the sky in Scorpio, the constellation which precipitates the fall of the Sun towards the southern regions and in mythology plays the part of a treacherous poisoner. This poisonous animal

is no less the support of Ophiucus, the Serpent-Bearer, the handler of the healing fluid since he is lifting the serpent of Aesculapius who refuses to crawl in the earthly mud. This is an allusion to the great magic agent, that is to say, to the vital fluid which is sublimated by its detachment from the selfish grasp of the living. When we act to help others with our bodily dynamism, we are practising ancient holy medicine. We are rising above the Scorpio of Instinct, the Scorpio who generates all animal energy.

Seen as a whole, arcana 16 is related to the principle which determines all materialization and to the tendency towards materialization. This tendency is inclined to thicken the forms which serve as a vehicle to the spirit. So authoritarian dogmas are born, opaque crusts which imprison and disfigure living truth. Hence also human rapacity, the source of all despotisms, which are on a small or large scale, perhaps with regard to this intensive exploitation of the earth and of human energies on which this present age of ours prides itself. How can one not understand the systematic reproach of all moderation that leads us towards a terrifying social cataclysm? May our pride be humiliated before the Wisdom of the Tarot!

The Tower is replaced in certain Tarots by Hell, represented as a monster with a pig's snout who is devouring the damned whom the Devil is attracting by beating a summons.

DIVINATORY INTERPRETATIONS

Materialization. Condensing attraction, radical egoism in action. Restrictive hoarding. Spirit imprisoned in matter. Vital construction from which the whole organism results.

Pride, presumption, pursuit of fancies. Materialism which attaches itself to coarse appearances, greed to acquire, mania for material wealth. Megalomania, excessive enlarging of what one possesses. Insatiable ambitions and appetites. Excessive conquests. Unreasonable exploitation. Excess and misuse leading to rebellion and upheavals. Narrow dogmatism, the source of disbelief. False alchemy eager for common gold. Merited failure of all senseless enterprise. Punishment resulting from excess. Illness, disorganization, filth, hardening, putrefaction of all that was supple and living. Ruin of empires established and maintained by brute force. The collapse of intolerant Churches that proclaim themselves infallible. The error of the presumptuous person who undertakes things beyond his capacity and who does not know when to stop.

When this arcana ceases to be unfavourable, it puts one on guard against what it threatens. Salutary fears, reserve, timidity which preserves one from ill-considered risks; simplicity of mind remote from errors of learning, common sense, the wisdom of Sancho Panza.

XVII

The Star

In our thirst for individual existence and autonomy, we have cut ourselves off from the universal life of the Great Being of whom we continue to be part. We live in him, but not the life that is particular to him, since we are content with our narrow life, limited to the sphere of our sensations. What those sensations reveal is infinitesimal compared with the unfathomable and unknown which surrounds us. We are plunged in a dark night, but when we cast our glances towards the sky, we see the Stars shining brightly.

These lights above encourage us and make us feel that we are not abandoned, since what the gods originally called 'the shining ones', watch over us. They direct us with the aim of our fulfilling our destiny, for we have a task in our limited life, no one being created without his destiny being traced in its broad outlines, without its aim being assigned to the earthly traveller. A mysterious route map marks the essential stages of our pilgrimage, as if the court of justice of the Anounnaki[61] had made a decree on our account by fixing our destiny.

If we followed our programme faithfully, life would be what it should be for us. We complicate it by our intractability which awards us the hardships of which we complain; life is not cruel in principle, but its aim is not our pleasure: it has its task and asks us to accomplish ours. She is a gentle and lovely goddess like the naked girl in arcana 17 who, kneeling at the edge of a pond pours into it the contents of a golden urn, from which flows a burning liquid to give life to the stagnant water. To this vessel held in the right hand corresponds another which the left hand is tipping up to pour out onto the arid earth a fresh and fertilizing water. This second receptacle is silver; like the first it is inexhaustible. The constant watering supports the vegetation, represented more exactly by a branch of acacia and a rose in bloom.

The mimosa of the desert, acacia resists desiccation; its persistent green colour indicates a life which refuses to be extinguished, hence its character with the emblem of hope in immortality. In the legend of Hiram this plant reveals the tomb of the Master, the keeper of lost tradition. In order to assimilate this secret, the adept must make the deceased Wisdom relive in himself. To this effect he must imitate Isis who travels throughout the world in search of the remains of her husband's body. These precious remains are gathered by the thinker who knows how to discern the truth hidden under a pile of superstitions which the past has bequeathed to us. The spiritual corpse of a god who once enlightened the world, survives, shared out among the ignorant crowds, in the form of enduring beliefs in spite of their contradiction to accepted orthodoxies. Far from spurning these disfigured remains of a lost knowledge, the Initiate collects them together carefully in order to set up in its entirety the body of the dead doctrine. Once it is re-established in its synthesis, this doctrine becomes capable of being revived, like Hiram or Osiris. But without the acacia to reveal phenomena to us, how could we know where to search in the soil?

The discreet verdure which, in the East, decorates the abandoned tombs contrasts with the rose which blooms joyously in our gardens. As the symbol of all that embellishes earthly life, this flower of love and beauty is reflected in the pond, the reservoir of the vital fluids. Psyche's butterfly landed on the corolla with the suave perfume of delicate feelings, which is lit up by a refined intelligence which has managed to free itself from all coarseness. The rose of arcana 17 is that of the knights of the spirit, a flower which will be placed on the cross with the wood provided by the acacia. Then faith will cease to be blind, religious feeling and philosophical meditations will harmonize to the satisfaction of the souls which are anxious to believe with discrimination.[62]

But the dawn of comprehension which is reserved for the Initiated does not yet dispel the darkness of human intellectuality, although we can see the stars of our night sky pale before the brilliance of one of them, Lucifer, the Light-bearer, otherwise known as Venus or the star of the morning. This heavenly body is the great star of arcana 17 which sends forth green lights between its eight golden rays. The colour of Venus thus matched the octagon of Ishtar, the goddess *par excellence* of the Chaldeans. These people made the stars divine, so that in their primitive writing the ideogram ✳ is read as 'god'. This sign was maintained by the Assyrians as a definite article to the divine names that its precedes; but the star with eight rays remained the sacred emblem of Ishtar, a popular divinity, the recipient of the most fervent devotion of mortals. How could it have been otherwise, since humans believed that they owed their life to the tender and generous Ishtar? An enchantress, she inspires souls with the desire to take bodily form. Her charms lead us to become flesh in order to enjoy the charms of earthly life, by agreeing to face the trials which she imposes, for Ishtar demands of her followers the courage to live; she wants them to approach courageously

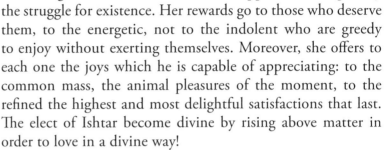

the struggle for existence. Her rewards go to those who deserve them, to the energetic, not to the indolent who are greedy to enjoy without exerting themselves. Moreover, she offers to each one the joys which he is capable of appreciating: to the common mass, the animal pleasures of the moment, to the refined the highest and most delightful satisfactions that last. The elect of Ishtar become divine by rising above matter in order to love in a divine way!

Let us note that Ishtar is double: a warrior in the morning and languorous in the evening. An early riser, she awakens the sleeping, shakes off their torpor and incites us into a Lucifer-like rebellion against the tyranny of ruling dogmas.[63] At dusk the star of Ishtar reappears in the red light of sunset. Her light then is of a soft peaceful whiteness. The tired man looks at it with gratitude; it seems to him that the goddess is summoning him to deserved rest, to expressions of tenderness and serene meditation. Is she not the revealer of the beauty of things? At this hour the poets no longer see in her the impetuous lover, frightening with the violence of her passions, this Ishtar whose advances are rejected by the wise Gilgamesh; no, the goddess has become Siduri, the chaste guardian of a closed paradise which overlooks the western sea; the sea breeze fondles its trees which bear no other fruit but precious ones.[64] The young maid in arcana 17, she, too, seems to be an incarnation of the great feminine divinity whom our distant ancestors have adored. She is the personification of earthly life in what is winning and charming about it; she is kind Nature, merciful and beautiful, the mother who is eternally young, who becomes the lover of the living.

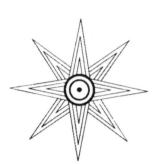

This earthly life, which we love more than anything in spite of the material slavery to which it binds us, leaves us plunged in a darkness which would be complete if it were not for the stars in the firmament. The stars symbolize the obscure light from which the humble in their spiritual aspirations benefit. The children of nature turn towards the ideal with a spontaneous piety which comforts them in their aim of accomplishing their earthly task. Sanctifying what pertains to life, they make this life divine. Would that we could appreciate the sound beauty of their religious conception, truer in its simplicity than our ambitious systems, complicated by disturbing metaphysics.

The stars of arcana 17 number eight which leads us to arcana 8 (Justice), in other words to the Intelligence which co-ordinates natural actions and reactions. But at this point eight leads back to the unity of the great star, a mere modest septenary of stars, of which four arranged in a square are yellow, and the three others blue. The whole is related to the influences which our personality undergoes on the part of these celestial bodies; but the illustrators of the Middle Ages were not embarrassed by our present day classical notions of astrology. The septenary which they make subordinate to Venus is not necessarily that of the planets which our Horoscope holds to. Venus is exalted in the part of the sky where Pisces is the neighbour of Andromeda and the 'square of Pegasus'. The stars fixed in this square, joined to the shining ternary of Andromeda therefore make up an Ishtar-like septenary deserving to be considered here.

When an abstraction has been made by the interpretations of pedantic astrologers, let us find our inspiration only in the immediate suggestions of symbolism and in the first place see only two stars: the larger and the smaller. The latter shines in the centre of the collection, under the large star and exactly above the head of the naked girl. In her we may see Eve, personifying man made flesh. This small and nearby star represents the star peculiar to each personality, for we have each one of us our star which is the receptacle through which the influences of the stars filter in order to be concentrated in us.

This personal star is blue like the two other bigger ones, placed a little higher on the right and the left. They are the condensers of the influences which are exerted on the soul which they illumine mysteriously, the blue star on the right gathering what is addressed to the conscience and to Reason (Sun) and the one on the left gathers in the intuitions of feeling and imagination (Moon).

The yellow stars share out amongst each other the inclination attributed to Mercury, Mars, Jupiter and Saturn; but the predominance of Venus also remains marked in arcana 17, as in palmistry, where the Mount of Venus is much more important in volume than the others.

As the Pisces of the zodiac swim in the celestial ocean of Ea (the Chaldean goddess of supreme Wisdom) these inhabitants of the starry spaces are in proportion so much less foreign to arcana 17 than Andromeda is close to them. Now this princess, the daughter of Cepheus and Cassiopeia, was chained naked to the wave-beaten rock where a sea monster would have devoured her if it had not been for the intervention of Perseus. It is a question of the living soul bound to matter, hence the young Eve of the Tarot whose mother, queen of Ethiopia according to mythology, is in reality productive Nature, depicted as the Priestess (arcana 2). Her father the black king who rules over the unfathomable abyss of the Infinite, becomes the Fool whose domain escapes human reason. Perseus who marries Andromeda, corresponds to the spiritual soul (NESHAMAH) whose union with the life of the corporal soul (NEPHESH HAIAH) lifts her away across the airs of spirituality.

Arcana 17 occupies the middle of the second row of the Tarot, where it marks, just like arcana 6, which is superimposed upon it, the passage between one phase of initiation into another. Now the Lover in the active sphere passes from theory to practice; the mystic's soul is guided by the Stars and reaches discrimination after he has entered in a practical sense into a relationship with the non-ego. From 12 to 16 forgetfulness of self is not simply recommended or taught but imposed in its practical realization. Having reached 17 the adept no longer has to choose resolutely between two routes, like the young Hercules of arcana 6, for he is predestined; for him the stars trace a destiny against which he does not think of rebelling, since he gives himself up docilely to the heavenly influences which must lead him to the mystic enlightenment. This is the reward for works accomplished according to the promptings of the heart, and not the result of a methodical study such as is imposed upon the dorian Initiate whose acts are inspired by a knowledge gained earlier. The Magician (1) instructs himself theoretically (2, 3, 4, 5), then submits to moral trial (6) before applying his knowledge (7, 8, 9, 10) to reach the fullness of his power (11). In opposition to Dorism, based on the conscious possession of self and the integral development of the personality, Ionism proceeds from complete self denial. The Hanged Man (12) extends sacrifice even to the annihilation of individual initiative (13) in order to commune with what is outside himself (14, 15, 16); so he reaches 17, which depicts the receptive state of the children of Nature, the simplicity of heart and spirit outside of which no one is admitted into the Kingdom of God. The Mystic enlightenment whose stages are marked by 18, 19, 20, 21, throws light upon this holy innocence which is untroubled by any proud knowledge. The sky will instruct the naked girl because she is untouched by any human teaching.

The mysteries of arcana 17 are those of sleep and night. When we sleep our spiritual soul escapes from the resting body, now left simply to the automatic functioning of its organs.

In the course of the night what are the occupations of the liberated self? Do we not live, in two parts, as flesh and thus periodically set free from the bonds of the flesh? Is there a more vital need than that of sleep? We cannot live without sleeping. We divide ourselves into two existences, of which one is unknown to us. Every morning we return from a journey and we know nothing of its adventures except at most what we learn in the form of dreams; these happen when our brain registers images, witnesses of our unconscious nightly activity. We pay no attention to these reminiscences which reveal, at least, how emotions are provoked by functional disturbances. What a patient had dreamed once used to guide the doctor in his diagnosis; in the temples of Aesculapius where the supplicants came to sleep, the god loved to show in a dream to those involved the remedy suitable for curing them. Nowadays the sleeping patients show themselves to be more especially lucid as to the medical cares which are necessary to them. Sleep is therefore a source of information which must not be neglected. Through it the curtain of mystery is drawn aside, to allow us a few furtive glimpses giving shape to the too vague presentiments which make us guess at another world. Dreams have been the first initiators of humanity.

What happens when, closing our eyes at night to what surrounds us, we set off for the unknown? Let us compare ourselves with the diver who, when his task is over comes up to the surface where he takes off his diving suit. What a contrast between the bottom of the water where the diver's view carries only over a very small distance and the vast luminous horizon which he discovers before him as soon as he breathes the fresh air! But let us suppose that all memory of above is wiped out for the diver who has returned to his difficult work in the depths of the waters. In this way we can visualize plunging into darkness in the state of being awake compared with the light-filled emancipation which sleep affords us. Our spirit does not become numbed like our body; while the body is at rest our intelligence remains active. As a result night brings counsel because of the clairvoyance achieved by the sleeper who is freed from his enclosing shell through which his earthly activity takes place. When we fall asleep preoccupied by a decision which has to be made or a burning problem to be solved, we sometimes happen to find ourselves when we awake with a firm resolution in mind; this has been made or is now seen as an obvious answer to a question which harassed us the night before. Everything is explained by the intervention of our little blue star which was able to question her larger sister stars.

DIVINATORY INTERPRETATIONS

The consoling woman who lifts and comforts the man who is overwhelmed by the struggles of existence. Eve to whom the Redeemer is promised. Life shared out among creatures. Soul binding matter to spirit. Nature in activity. Night and its mysteries. Sleep and its revelations. Immortality. Destiny, predestination. The ideal which life strives to realize. Objective beauty. Aesthetics. The cult of the beautiful. Religion of life, sanctifying what is related to it. Ishtar.

Hope, liveliness, good humour, courage bearing joyfully the vicissitudes of life. The idealization of reality. Poetry, fine arts, music, sensitivity, refinement, tenderness, compassion. Adaptation to necessities. Easy-going character.

Innocence, candour, naïvety, ignorance. Youth. Charm, seduction, attraction. Epicurism, sensuality, daydreams, abandon, negligence. Confidence, resignation, fatalism.

Astrology, astral influences, occult protection, intuition, premonitions, presentiments, Indiscreet curiosity. Pandora's box.

XVIII

The Moon

In order to display the splendours of the sky, the Night plunges the earth into darkness, for the things above are not revealed to our sight except to the detriment of those below. However we aspire to relate the celestial to the terrestrial by a simultaneous contemplation, which is made possible when the Moon spreads her pale light. This body which is close to the stars without subduing their brightness completely, only half lights up the objects bathed in her uncertain and borrowed light. The Moon does not allow us to distinguish colours; everything her rays strike upon she tinges with a silvery grey or with vague bluish shades, leaving the opaque darkness of the shadows of night to continue.

By observing the effects of the moonlight, how can we not think of the imagination whose way of illuminating is revealed in a similar way in our intellect? The imaginative visionary sees things in a false light. Fascinated by Hecate he turns away from the poetic shining of the stars to concentrate his attention on the contrasts of the deceptive chiaroscuro of the moon. In metaphysics he forges erroneous theories, based on unreal contrasts, optical illusions of the mind: out of good and evil, out of Being and non-Being he makes objective entities and falls into the trap of a dualism which is fatal to the healthy appreciation of reality. The dupe of apparent contrasts, he imagines matter to be dense, solid, heavy and indestructible, whereas in the last analysis it is reduced to the infinitesimal whirling of a weightless, ethereal substance. The chief errors of the human mind derive from the imagination which cannot stop itself from making the subjective objective. Now as this feminine faculty is awakened in the face of masculine reasoning, we imagine first of all, then we try to reason afterwards, free then to strive to build logically with doubtful representations. The result is not brilliant.

We must, however, achieve full light by exploring at our own risk and peril the immense space which the Moon lights up only in part and very imperfectly. The field which is offered to us is uneven land where stumbles are inevitable. Let us expect frequent falls, by being wary of traps and hidden snares.

Luckily others have gone before us in this dangerous exploration. Their steps have traced a path where drops of blood are seen. This painful track leads to a goal for him who perseveres in spite of obstacles and threats.

The rash man who set out skirts first of all a marsh where frogs croak. Their uproar attracts the traveller who is curious to look at the reflections of the moon; he advances into a soil which is becoming more and more wet until his feet sink in. Fearing that he will be sucked under he recoils to get onto a mound from where he can safely admire the play of light on the surface of the stagnant water.

Allusion is made here to the products of the imagination. Its attraction risks stopping our progress by holding us back in the mire of inconsistent conceptions; thus it is right to enjoy the charm of fictions by taking care to stay on firm ground. What the poets imagine is suggested to them by a mysterious reality, for however powerful the fantasy may be it is impossible to create it out of nothing. Nothing is radically factitious, a very subtle first matter like that of the Alchemists, being brought into play by the inventive mind. Myths, fables, popular stories proceed from truths which are too deep to be put into direct language. The thinker takes delight in them if he can discern the esoterism behind the façade of naïve and coarse appearances. To reject superstitions in the way that 'clever people' do is a weakness, for credulity is never completely blind: an instinctive lucidity holds him to powerful truths which however are too diffuse for the men of reason to grasp.

Far from turning away in disdain from the marsh of instinctive faith, the wise man tries to penetrate the mystery of it. Even in dull daylight he would perceive nothing of what is stirring in the depths of the troubled water, but by the light of the Moon he can distinguish an enormous crayfish emerging motionless from the foul water. This crustacian devours everything that is rotten. Thanks to him the marsh does not give off any foul vapour, for he keeps guard on that. It would be fatal to let dead beliefs continue, leading to reprehensible practice: the fierce crab sets things in order there. If it walks backwards, that is because its domain is the past, and not the future from which it flees. What it eats forms a thick carapace, but only a temporary one, for the animal rejects it when it becomes too heavy. If only it could teach ponderous beliefs to become renewed when they have finished their time!

The crayfish in the Tarot is red, not because it is cooked, but on the contrary, by reason of the inner fire which makes it display an incessant activity in order to fulfil its mission of making things salubrious.

At this point it is fitting to recall the analogy of the opposites which, in the double row of the Tarot, superimpose arcana 5 onto arcana 18. The Hierophant receives beliefs in order to synthesize them in the form of positive dogmas, whereas the crayfish (18) acts by negative selection, devouring all that is decomposing and cannot stand upright in face of believers' good sense. The crustacian respects what has the right to live, but it is not a schoolkeeper and does not set itself up as a teacher.

In the crayfish astrologers recognize Cancer, the home of the Moon. When, in its annual cycle the Sun reaches this division in the zodiac it begins to decline as if it has suddenly changed from its high ambitions. By analogy the period of Cancer favours serious reflections on and examination of one's conscience, and the conversion of the sinner as if in the muddy waters of the soul a purifying crab was moving about. In the place of this animal the Egyptians put their zodiacal scarab, a symbol of moral and psychic regeneration.[65]

Near the marsh where Cancer rules, two dogs guard the route which is, astronomically speaking, that of the Sun. They are the barking animals of the

Canicula, the *Canis Major* and the *Canis Minor* of the celestial sphere. They bark at the Moon to prevent it from crossing the boundary of the tropics for this capricious star constantly wanders away from the line of ecliptic which is outlined by the unchanging journey of the Sun.

The Canes (Dogs) become placed in charge of the defence of the forbidden regions where the imagination wanders. Their howling increases at the approach of the bold person who has turned aside from the marsh to continue his interrupted pilgrimage. They watch over what is permissible relating as much to faith and feelings as in matters of social or political institutions. The little white dog on the left yaps furiously at the impious who refuse to believe what is accepted as being true. He stands up on his hind legs, for he feels that he is in the service of spiritual interests. The big black dog on the right remains lying down by reason of his positivism which keeps him attached to the earth. Anxious to preserve good order and the intangible rights of propriety, he howls at the revolutionaries with subversive plans. The person with a firm step walks disdainfully between the two dogs, fills them with fear and is not bitten by them.

But here are two massive fortresses, two square towers, different in form from the round tower of arcana 16. The flesh-coloured walls form living buildings and

Tarot of the Magicians

their golden crown, placed on a red foundation, likens them to intelligent beings capable of acting with discrimination. They are bodies, or better still public bodies placed as sentries to warn the foolish man of the dangers that threaten him if, once past the dogs, he aspires to rushing into the treacherous steppe to which the Moon draws him.

From the tower on the right, which is lit up, come the reasonable warnings about the sad destiny of Hecate's victims, liable to lose their mental balance, their reason, their physical and moral health, even their life.

The dark bodyguard on the left is no more reassuring: it echoes with mystic murmurings on the impiety of giving in to tempting curiosity. Let us remain ignorant, rather than jeopardize the salvation of our soul. Let us think of the paradise lost and not desire the fruit of the tree of knowledge! If the irresistible attraction of mystery wins him over against the voice of the two towers, nothing then will stop this fated man. Summoned to submit to the fearful trials of initiation, he will go into the darkness of a thick forest where ghosts will brush past him; then with difficulty he will have to climb to a height from which his view will stretch far over the silver plain. But a precipice lies in wait for him, he slips on it and falls bruised into the bottom. The mud here deadens the fall of the climber, who gets up dirty, to limp to the running and purifying water. It is a fast-flowing river which he is forced to swim across, for he must get to the opposite bank which is arid and burnt. It is in these solitary parts that he must wander until dawn will allow him to get his bearings in the dunes behind which day will dawn.

Arcana 18 represents the Moon as a silver disc on which is outlined in profile a feminine face with puffy features. From the disc come long yellow rays between which appear short red glows. These colours attribute to the Moon a weak spiritual activity (red) but a great strength in the sphere of materiality (yellow). That signifies that the imagination, or lunar faculty, favours the visionary by giving objective form to his thought, but it scarcely helps to understand and to seize the real essence of things. Although Hecate is deceiving we must pass through her school in order to learn not to be the dupe of her phantasmagoria. The spilt drops, red, green and yellow which the Moon seems to attract correspond to the globes of the same colour in arcana 16, but the emanations from the earth go to the satellite which takes without giving anything in return. The cold light and the night star tend to reabsorb the vitality which the Sun gives off, hence the popular advice never to sleep exposed to the Moon's rays.

An ancient Tarot shows a harpist, who, in the moonlight sings to a half-naked young beauty leaning on the windowsill to let her hair fall loose; a strongly barricaded door protects the coquette from the advances of the wooer.

DIVINATORY INTERPRETATIONS

Objectivity. Outward appearance. Visible form. What comes within our senses. The contingent, the relative, the theatre where human existence is played out. Illusions of materiality. Maya.

Imagination, whims, fads, fantasies, extravagance, errors and prejudices, mental laziness, credulity, superstition. Indiscreet curiosity, false knowledge, the art of the visionary. Intellectual passivity, impressionability of the imagination, clairvoyance, lucidity when sleep-walking. Criticism of oneself, conversion.

Sea voyages, navigation, long and difficult research. Work exacted. Material slavery. Ambiguous situation. False security, perils, traps. Flattery, deception, vain threats. Red moon and its disastrous effects. Lymphatic temperament. Dropsy.

XIX

The Sun

The vicissitudes which the Moon affords us are the indispensable trials which lead us to the light of the Sun. We only reach the light after languishing in the darkness and going astray through error. We do perforce make mistakes in a painful way in order to learn at our own expense the art of discerning the false from the true and finding our bearings towards the point on the horizon from which the light will burst forth. The trials of earthly life have no other object but that of our instruction; let us learn how to take advantage of their lessons, and initiation will be our reward.

To reach this the traditional purifications are essential. They aim at making our opaque layers, which enclose us, transparent, so that the true light of our world, that of the Sun, may penetrate us. In its shedding of light this star has an unchanging fixity. Always self-identical, it shines impartially for us all. If some of us profit more than others by its benefits that is because you have learned how to push aside the obstacles which stand between them and the pure light which can illuminate our minds.

It is not a question now of a deceptive light like that of the Moon, which lends itself to errors and does not allow us to distinguish objects with complete certainty. The Sun reveals the reality of things and shows them as they really are without the veil of any illusion. The fog clears and the ghosts vanish in its presence. It is in this sense that the incarnated soul finds in the Sun its promised Redeemer. The soul is not condemned to struggle in the heart of matter except with a view of purifying itself in order to make possible the union of the spiritual, imprisoned in the flesh, with universal spirituality.

Now let us consider arcana 19 whose symbolism is clear. The young couple holding each other tenderly entwined in the centre of a circle of green dotted with flowers. They represent the individual soul in harmony with the spirit whose feelings are married to reason; that is to say agreement and harmony realized on a small scale within the sphere of human personality, straining to be realized on a large scale in humanity as a whole, universal regeneration.

When men become reasonable, when the redeeming light of the Sun has freed them from their errors, then they will find Paradise again, not the Paradise of man's early and innocent idleness, but the laborious Eden of civilization today, in which complete peace through mutual help will lighten all tasks.

This ideal will not be reached straight away, by virtue of a miracle or a proclamation. Its realization must be sought through individuals. Let each of us begin by self-regeneration before dreaming of a social and widely human one. While stones are cut without a set square, no solid wall could be constructed. Now, before building the great Temple in which all men will commune, we must erect ramparts against the remaining barbarity, which is brutal and opposed to man's brotherhood. The élite which the children of the Sun represent, can only agree with each other in the shelter of a stonework enclosure, made up, as in arcana 19 of two blue intermediary layers which entwine with those other layers, whose stones are alternating red and yellow. These colours give social cohesion to the emotional ideal (blue, water) to constructive religion which is revealed in practical morality, as applied to actions in our lives. It is for the feelings to reconcile the antagonism of red and yellow by pacifying the conflicts between active energy (work-red-fire) and acquired knowledge or accumulated wealth (capital-yellow aspect of fire). The spirit of brotherhood and sisterhood which is the binding cement of all human construction; these alone can prepare us for reciprocal compromise on which a lasting evolving civilization can be built. When left to their own devices strength and intelligence cannot reach this ideal.

May the Tarot enable the lost to return to wisdom, the lost who anticipate a golden age achieved through force. Blind hatred nurtured by the fanatics of class struggle can only increase human misery. Only the spirit of enlightened intelligence (by the Sun) will bring about earthly happiness by the harmonious working together of opposing social groups reconciled by reciprocal understanding. Arguments which are addressed only to the intelligence do not have the gift of moving men's hearts to bring them closely together. What binds is truly religious and proceeds by good feeling from the heart, much more than from the brain, hence the importance of the blue layers in the ramparts of civilization. Thus good feeling (water-blue) is the foundation of the religion of the Sun which the wise teach. These wise men not happy at being enlightened in a cold manner, are filled with a great warmth which inspires acts of constant moral beauty.

Tarot of the Magicians

The double action of the Sun's rays, that of giving light and heat, is shown by the alternating beams, straight or flamboyant, golden or red from the great life giving star. The number of these beams relates them to the number twelve of the zodiac, hence to the cyclical work which regulates the seasons and all earthly life.

The Sun is not content to enlighten minds and give life to bodies, while warming their souls, for it is in addition, the distributor of supreme wealth. A fine rain of gold falls continually over the loving couple in the peaceful garden. More favoured than Danaé, they receive the Sun's gifts freely, for gold, whose form Jupiter took to fertilize the mother of Perseus,[66] meets no obstacle as it rains freely in the Sun's paradise, whereas it was only able to penetrate into the cell of the mythological princess by infiltrating through the thickness of brass walls.

The Sun enriches its children spiritually. The gold which it lavishes upon them is not the metal which tempts the avaricious, it is the Philosopher's Gold of the true disciples of Hermes. The initiated create no illusion about the value of things and yet they possess all because they covet nothing. They desire only what they need with a view to accomplishing their task, and in this respect they receive more than they would think of asking for. Their greatest wealth moreover is that of the heart, loving all persons, they feel loved by what surrounds them. So for them everything is embellished and they are happy on earth.

The happiness which they enjoy could not be taken away from them, for it is they who create it. Far from any selfish bliss, as artists they admire the work of God and associate their whole being with it, vibrating with all that is within them. As appreciators of beauty they bear the redeeming light into the heart of the tumultuous confusion which is born out of the strife of blind human passions. As participants in the Great Work of universal Redemption, they help to raise man from his first fall (arcana 16) and they work to restore him to his dignity as a divine being.

The children, happy together beneath the Sun, correspond all the more to Gemini; seeing that this constellation affords us the longest days. It is true that Castor and Pollux were of the same sex, whereas a boy and a young girl replace them in the Tarot. The symbolism is not affected by this for the New Adam and the New Eve of arcana 19 could very well be in tune with the lyre which is the chief attribute of the sons of Leda, of the same issue as their sister Helen. One might wonder whether Helen, the queen of beauty, has not been put in the place of one of her brothers by the illustrators. The fact remains however that such a substitution is justified, as the Tarot is a teaching of how to completely unite maleness with femaleness.

As for the lyre, its absence is to be regretted, for it is through the harmonious chords that a powerful artist draws his inspiration, that stones take their form and come together of their own accord, as happened at the time of the construction of the ramparts of Thebes, the holy city, through the effect of the incantations of Amphion. The outer wall of the city of peace will be formed in the same way, with the help of animated materials obedient to the musical pleas of the Great Art, whose magic awakens man the constructor, dormant within the man of matter. Like living stones men comply with the chords of the lyre to unite in harmony; from their union is born the sacred building of the lasting civilization of the unity of humanity.

Working on the human substance, the first effective matter of the Great Work, the children of light transform the vile lead of base instincts into pure gold, both moral and intellectual. Out of a foolish, ignorant and selfish person, they strive to make a wise person whose desire is to enter into harmony with life in order to live in beauty. As artists in love with art, they labour joyously, happy to create. They seek to regain Paradise, for they love the Divine Work in which they freely participate to help to bring order into human chaos as befits their creative intentions. We will find lost Eden again as soon as we accept our tasks as creatures condemned to work, not through punishment, but by reason of progress for we cannot raise ourselves from our animal-like condition except by a complete willingness to work for the love of work, and pleasure in work. From being bound slaves of sharp mercenaries, we become Free Artists, Free Builders, or Freemasons, carrying out the plan of the Supreme Architect by virtue of our understanding of the ineluctable law of life which is that of creative work.

The Tarot of Charles VI and others after it, place beneath the Sun a graceful young girl, standing or sitting and holding a distaff, she seems to be weaving a happier destiny for men than the Parcae grant us. Other variations give the picture of an apocalyptic knight dashing through a shower of flames under the shelter of the unfurled standard of Solar faith.

DIVINATORY INTERPRETATIONS

The primordial light which puts order into chaos. The Word which enlightens all men that came into this world. Superhuman Reason which inspires all minds. Spiritual light which dissipates the darkness in the heart of which we struggle. Apollo victorious over the serpent. True knowledge in the face of which the fantastic notions of false prophecy vanish. Inspired enlightenment, poetry, fine arts.

Fraternity, harmony, peace, friendship, good understanding, judgement, Nobility, generosity, affection, greatness of spirit. Paradise regained, calm and lasting happiness, marriages, joy in marriage, clarity of judgement. Artistic tastes and talents.

Glory honours celebrity. Attachment to that which glitters, vanity, need to make oneself admired, desire to appear to be something, frivolity, affection, pose, lack of common sense. Painful idealism incompatible with the sense of harsh reality. Artist or poet, condemned to live in poverty, whose merit will not be recognized until after his death. Irritability, susceptibility.

XX

Judgement

However brilliant the light of the sun may be, it stops at the surface of things without being able to reveal to us the true essence which our senses cannot grasp. Now, works of pure beauty whether they are produced by Nature or by Art, show in their outward form an 'esotericism' or inner hidden spirit which the intelligence must discern. Judgement intervenes for the purpose of distinguishing the spiritual from the material, the deep significance from the expressive form, the living word from the dead letter. Everything is a symbol, for everything proceeds from a generating idea which is related to transcendent conceptions. Let us penetrate into the depths of things where a thought slumbers, waiting for our mind to waken and assimilate it. The charming story of the Sleeping Beauty develops this theme from which in its turn, the picture of the last Judgement, as drawn by the authors of the Tarot, took its inspiration.

Far from an idyll, here we are transported into the valley of Josophat, which an apocalyptic angel is making resound with a noise to awaken the dead. These dead are coming back to life, not in the body but in the spirit, for universal resurrection is not that of the flesh, unless the term is understood in an allegorical way to mean whatever is capable of being brought back to life. The past does not deserve to be relived except in its spiritual form, all the while this remains incomprehensible to present generations. Precious truths sleep in the tomb of oblivion: they are dead for the areas which do not know them. But nothing is lost in the realm of spirit; a faithful memory holds secretly what the wise ancients knew, so that all men may have their knowledge on the day of universal understanding.

Then humanity will experience the reign of the Holy Spirit which will bring about religious unity based on the esotericism which is common to all religions. These religions are not at variance with each other except through their exterior elements (forms of worship, dogmas), a dead letter whose abstractions we may make for the benefit of the life-giving spirit, the only universal spirit, hence catholic in the Greek sense of the word. Effective Catholicism is for the enlightened minds which are open to everything which is fundamentally religious. It is the religion of the Holy Family, who with hands joined in prayer, listen, without fear, to the final sentence which the angel of Judgement pronounces.

The human ternary which gives back life represents regenerated man. Father and mother face the son in whom the principle character of the Tarot is recognized . . . already met in the roles of the Magician (1), the Lover (6), the Charioteer (7) and the Hanged Man (12). It is the subject of the Great Work, the man to become initiated undergoing for the last time initiatory trials to gain Domination.

In order to reach in spirit and in truth, this final rank, one must die twice and be born three times. Then one enters upon the career of the Initiate as upon a new life, which one's second birth inaugurates. But while being superior to the life of the ordinary masses, lives of the Initiated of the first and second ranks do not yet realize the complete ideal. The good workman works with an intelligent docility under a direction which is beyond his reach, for he has not yet been admitted into the Council of Masters. He faithfully carries out instructions whose wisdom he appreciates, without deeming himself capable of formulating them himself.

The work of the construction of man's Temple is in effect carried on from one generation to another, following the light which is not simply that of the day in which we are living. The future does not improvize on it in an arbitrary fashion; it is strong only if it is built upon old aspirations, giving body to the fervent desires of those who in the course of centuries, without becoming discouraged have dreamed of the best.

The ancestral constructors of a better Humanity are depicted in the Tarot by the parents of the young resuscitated boy of arcana 20. Placed on the right, the father is the incarnation of all the constructive philosophy of the past, of every profound and wise thing that human reason has conceived concerning the Great Art which is that of life lived in full knowledge of its laws. On the left the mother corresponds to the heart, to religious feeling which truly pious souls have always had.

As the heir of his parents, the Son takes what comes from the right and the left, in order to act as a faithful executor, as a witness of the past still living. He is asserted as Master much as in the eternal Constructive Tradition, the legendary Hiram of the Freemasons who find in him their interpreter.

Is it possible that a body might change into spirit? Can we die to ourselves to the point of giving up our organism so that a more elevated spirit than ours may take possession of it? These questions pose the problem of spirit, the life-giving breath of an infinite plurality of manifestations, but single in its essence. By reuniting itself, our spirit, while remaining identical to itself, is transfigured to become god-like in proportion to the nobility which it reaches.

Such is the ideal put forward by initiation: to become divine by coming as close as human nature will allow to divine perfection. 'Be ye perfect as your Father who is in Heaven is perfect'. It can be expressed no better than this. The whole problem of initiation implies a growing spirituality, becoming more and more complete, but never aspiring to neglect the obligations of earthly work.

The Initiated die, not to desert the battlefield, but in order to be able to participate more efficaciously in the struggle for good. If he escapes from the harsh mêlée, to hover like a pilot, it is with the view to directing carefully those who risk fighting with too short a vision.

But initiation prefers peaceful images. The victory to be won is that of the spirit, which through intelligent work, and without cruel victory, overcomes the obstacles imposed by matter against him. This matter is not to be treated as an enemy which must be destroyed, but as a substance to be put to work. It imprisons the spirit, not to hold it indefinitely, but to force it into an effort to free itself.

As long as we remain inward upon ourselves, confined to the narrowness of our individual life, we do not participate in the great and true life, and we bear ourselves like isolated dead in their bodies' tombs. Let us awaken, and standing upright in our open sepulchres, let us breathe the breath of the universal spirit. Let us now in this life live by eternal life!

In the Tarot the Angel of the awakening of spirits unfolds her green wings, for her domain is that of the spiritual life. (In the church, green is the colour of the Holy Ghost.) Her blue tunic edged with white relates to the pure heavenly ideality. The inspiration of ceaseless action, as the red arms of the herald of Judgement indicate. Red is also the colour of the pennon on the golden trumpet that sounds the reveille. A cross of gold divides the space into four squares which attribute the active power of a quadruple Philosopher's Stone to the highest form of spirituality.

Alternating purple and gold, moreover, characterize the emanations of the Angel of Judgement, whose golden hair shines with a bright red in her round-shaped hair-style, similar to the wide-brimmed hat in whose shade the Magician (1) practises his ceaseless mental activity. Here it is a question of the heart in which inspiring thought is condensed which draws the gold out of unchanging truths, into a living state. The Angel's hair corresponds to the transcending principles from which flow notions which are inaccessible to human intelligence, notions which are depicted by the luminous glory enclosed in the circle of the clouds from which radiate red and gold beams. Our intellectual view is enclosed in the limits of this circular cloud, in which abstract becomes concrete in our favour, in order to become manifest in the form of inspiring beams. Some of these, for our intelligence, are revealed in brilliant ideas (golden rays), while the others (red rays) encourage us in great and noble actions.

Tongues of fire, like those of Pentecost, leap out from these permanently inspiring beams. These flames are red, green and yellow, for they grant, each one

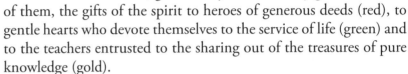

of them, the gifts of the spirit to heroes of generous deeds (red), to gentle hearts who devote themselves to the service of life (green) and to the teachers entrusted to the sharing out of the treasures of pure knowledge (gold).

On the Angel's forehead shines the sign of the sun ☉ a mark of discernment which we have already met as the emblem of illumination in Justice (8) and in Temperance (14). This triple appearance of the ideogram of the co-ordinating word is related in the first place to the co-ordination of physical chaos, in the midst of which the law of Balance (9) brings about relative stability which lends itself to the constitution of organisms. Constructive light is then inherent in the manifestation of life, for life is not spread blindly: it unfolds intentionally, with a fixed aim in view, hence the illumination of the spirit with two urns (14). But order and clarity are nonetheless present in the spiritual domain where full light is only brought about by virtue of the individual intellect entering into communion with the collective Intelligence of the human species (20).

To discover the constellation which presents the closest with arcana 20 we should picture the swan of Leda as being the Pagan equivalent of the Dove of the Holy Ghost. Superhuman spirituality, in the figure of the Ruler of Olympus, is changed into a great white bird in order to impregnate a mortal who will give birth to the twins and their sister Helen, otherwise known as Fraternity (19) and Beauty (17). Jupiter moreover, personifies the life-giving celestial fire which is related to the fertilizing rains which the Watercarrier pours out (Ea, Indra, Jupiter Pluvius), and with which the land is watered under the sign of Pisces (17). Now the celestial Swan heralds spring, the awakening of vegetation, hence the yearly rebirth, following the symbolism of arcana 20. It should be noted that the Swan unfolds her wings on the Milky Way, the path of souls which are drawn to the palace of Jupiter where they will enjoy immortality.

DIVINATORY INTERPRETATIONS

The Holy Ghost. The breath of inspiration which fertilizes intelligence to make it discover the truth. Spiritual penetration, understanding, assimilation of inner thoughts, esotericism, spiritualization of matter. Freeing from bodily ties.

Alchemic sublimation. Awakening to spiritual life and participation in this life which is that of the great collective and permanent human being.

Inspiration. Man in communication with divine spirit. Divination, prophecy, spiritual clairvoyance, seeing into the future, literary or artistic genius. Enthusiasm, piety, spiritual religion, elevation of the spirit and the soul. Evocative power which makes the spiritual past come alive again. Resurrection of the dead who are worthy of being called back to life. Return to forgotten traditions. The rebirth of Hiram, youthful again in the person of the new Master. Second death, the door to integral initiation.

Raising of healing powers and return to physical, moral and intellectual health. Liberation, freedom, separation from wrongs suffered. Wise judgement of posterity. Reputation, renown, echoing, noise, publicity, advertisement, bewildering noise.

Prediction, apostolate, propaganda. Exaltation, intoxication, over excitement both natural or artificial, lack of balance. Dionysian ecstasy.

XXI

The World

The construction of the Tarot in ternaries and septenaries gives to the number 21 supreme synthesizing value. It corresponds to the whole of anything which is made manifest, hence to the World, the result of permanent creative action. Reality which this action creates, is not limited to what comes within our senses. These senses are instruments adapted not to the real World, but only to the deceptive materialism of the poor sublunar world in the illusory dusk from which we struggle. Of what exists we see only the dying surface, made up of cinders about to harden and become relatively immobile in an apparent and illusory materialization. We are ignorant of the living essence of things and our conceptions suffer because of it.

If we were better instructed, we would envisage the Real in more refined terms. The World is swirling in a perpetual dance where nothing stops; everything turns ceaselessly in it, for movement is the generator of things. This concept which the most modern science does not reject, goes back to prehistoric times in as much as the veneration attached to the swastika will allow us to judge. For that is what this cross is known as, with its branches bent into right angles or curved into a hook 卐 卍 .

This emblem, taken over today by the advocates of pan-Germanism, is found everywhere on monuments and objects of wondrous antiquity. It is related to the movements of the sky, a movement which, in the eyes of our distant ancestors, was communicated to persons and things, animating some and moving others. From this movement flowed life, which in earlier times had been thought to be divine.

The Tarot was inspired by these ideas many thousands of years ago when it shows us the Goddess of Life running, enclosed within a garland of green, like a squirrel who makes his cage turn round. In this sweet divinity we recognize the young naked girl of arcana 17, but who this time is modestly veiled in a light drapery of red, the colour of activity. Because of her incessant running this indefatigable Atlanta remains fixed and still in the heart of this giddy giration which she keeps going. Hence her attitude reminds us less distinctly, it is true, than the Emperor's (4), of the sign of sulphur ♄, for her head and her arms outline a triangle, beneath which the left leg raised behind the right, indicates the cross. Thus the agile and animating Goddess of the World is related to the central fire which burns without respite in its fixed abode. Pluto (arcana 4) could be her father, although there is nothing infernal in her aspect. She is the corporal soul of the universe, the Vestal Virgin of the hearth of life whose fire burns in every person. This role explains the two wands which the sulphureous maiden holds in her left hand. They have round knobs at the end, of which one is red and the other blue. With the first, fiery energies are picked up, which will be associated with the life-giving fire which would die out if it were not constantly revived by the breath of air which the blue knob attracts. When the energies are picked up they are passed with the right hand to the red veil that she is holding.

The Italian Tarot prefers to place in each hand a wand similar to the Magician's (1); this Eliphas Lévi compares to magnetic action alternating in its polarization, whereas according to him the wands held in one hand would indicate a simultaneous action through opposition and transmission (*Rituel de la Haute Magie* p. 172).

The girl who uses the magic wands represents the 'Major Fortune' of the geomancers. In this respect she promises more than the small amounts of ephemeral success of 'Minor Fortune' whose wheel is that of arcana 10. Here the wheel is no longer the circuit of individual life dominated by the Sphinx; it is fused with the orb of the World, outside which the opposing and crossing of elementary attractions takes place, these being represented by the Kabbalistic ternary of which the Sphinx is the synthesis.

The life-giving circle which encloses all things is seen in arcana 21 as an oval garland with three rows of green leaves held together at the top and bottom by golden ribbons. The Italians adorn this crown with four roses arranged in the form of a cross. These flowers embellish and spiritualize life, thanks to the breath of the regenerating spirit (arcana 20) which becomes manifest in life itself (4 × 5 = 20).

Their sweet perfume charms souls and exalts their noble ardour, at the same time drawing them away from violence and ferocity. The rose befits the knights who put their strength and unshakable courage at the service of an ideal of pure love.

The cosmogonic quaternary of religious tradition in arcana 21 receives a holy representation. The ox of Saint Luke which represents Earth in the spring is black here, but its horns are red in accordance with fiery energies inherent in matter which appears to be passive. The impetuous Lion of Saint Mark follows this heavy and patient animal who ploughs the soil. The lion's yellow and red tinged mane flies out like devouring fire, symbolized by the wild animal who as much as the constellation of the zodiac gives us the torrid heat of summer, fatal to the green plants which it dries up, but at the same time is indispensable to the ripening cereals. Diagonally with the earthly Bull, the Eagle of Saint John gets ready to spread its wings which are gold outside, like its beak and its claws, whereas the rest of the bird is blue, the colour of air. Between the Eagle and the Ox, the constellation of autumn and spring is placed the Angel of Saint Matthew who, in astrology is the Watercarrier, the sign opposed to Leo; it is also the spirit of Temperance (arcana 14). Dressed in red, this angel is enveloped in clouds above which it spreads its golden wings. These wings carry the angel aloft to the most pure intellectuality of which the rising vapours are full. These condense around the angel, waiting to form into rain which will enrich spirituality.

The angel and the four sacred animals are represented in the sky by the brightest stars situated at the four cardinal points: *Adelbaran* or the Bull's eye, *Regulus* or the Lion's heart, *Altair*, the light of the Eagle, and *Fomalhaut* of the southern Fish which absorbs the water which the Watercarrier pours out. These stars mark the ends of a cross whose centre is the polar star, which, through its motionless state in the centre of heavenly movement, corresponds in arcana 21 to the young girl framed in an oval of green representing the zone of the ecliptic.

In the Tarot printed in Paris in 1500 the World is represented by a globe, similar to the one that the Emperor (arcana 4) holds in his left hand. The branches of the bent cross which surmounts this globe are as sceptres showing domination over the Quaternary of the Elements. The double opposition of the generating forces of matter is not depicted by the zodiac symbols of the equinoxes and solstices: Angel-Lion; Eagle-Bull, for the World is here supported by the breath of the four winds of the spirit as if it were the result of the clash of ethereal movements coming together from opposite directions. Above the sphere of the World stands a tall woman, completely naked who holds in her right hand an immense curtain whose ends she has caught up in her left hand.

She is truth displayed without reserve, drawing aside the veil of appearance to communicate the secret of the essence of things. To possess this secret is to have at one's disposal the universal knowledge and the unlimited power which it grants, it is the realization of the ideal of the skilled Adept.

What distinguishes the wise man is the fact that he has no illusion about the false reality to which our senses are prey. Everything becomes spirit in face of his spiritual view of life. The World appears to him like the miracle of the Single Thing of the Hermetists. By conceiving the radical Unity or oneness of what exists, we rise to Gnosis, the supreme reward given to efforts made in search of the true. This direct knowledge and understanding (Gnosis) is found in the intellectual ecstasy inspired by contemplation of the sanctuary of which the Priestess (2) holds the keys. No one enters the Temple where the pure light of the Spirit shines; but when matter dissolves in the face of our mental perception, then no obstacle stands in the way of our complete illumination. When we are penetrated with Divine Light, raised for ever from our fall, we become full of enlightenment and we thus complete the cycle of our regeneration.

The twenty-first letter of the Hebrew alphabet is the Shin and not the Tau. However it is the letter which fits the arcana marked number 21 for it corresponds to the complete whole to which logically the seven ternaries and the three septenaries lead. The early Tau is a simple venical cross + or oblique ×.

DIVINATORY INTERPRETATIONS

Cosmos. The ordered universe. Reign of God. The ideal Temple completed. Totality. Re-integration. Perfection.

Integral knowledge. Sovereign spiritual power. Ecstasy. Apotheosis. Reward. Incorruptibility. Absolute integrity.

Complete success. Achievement. Crowning of work undertaken. Atmosphere. Background favourable to decisive result: all or nothing, entourage. Benefit drawn from collectivity. Statesman, minister. Superior hostile functioning. Insurmountable outside obstacle.

XXII

The Fool

le fou ʍ

The order of the arcanas of the ancient Tarots is marked in numerals from 1 to 21; then comes the last composition which is different from the others in that it has no numerical mark. Its rank is the twenty-second, but its symbolic value is equivalent to nought, for the Fool is the person who does not count because of his lack of intellectual and moral existence. Insentient and irresponsible, he drags himself through life as a passive being who does not know where he is going and is led by irrational impulses. Not belonging to himself he is as a being possessed: he is alienated in the full sense of the word. His costume is many-coloured to show the multiple and incoherent influences which he constantly undergoes. The whimsically inflated turban is red, green, white and yellow, but the red is more like orange, the colour of destructive fire which suggests dangerous ideas. This is also the colour of the stick which the Fool holds in his right hand. It is a useless burden to him, for he uses it neither as a walking stick nor for support; in fact he uses it even less than the Hermit (9) does to sound the earth on which he is going forward. With his eyes lost in the emptiness of the clouds, the foolish man continues haphazardly on his way, following his impulses without wondering where he is going.

With his left hand the Fool holds on his shoulder a short, roughly hewn cudgel, from which hangs a bag, his treasure of odd and useless belongings. This sustains a wild idealism, hence the colour blue of the second stick.

The Fool's yellow stockings are slipping off and reveal what they should cover. This unseemly exhibition makes us think of what happened to Moses who wanted to look at Jehovah face to face. Just as the Ineffable escapes us, so the indiscreet person has to be content with the view of creation which corresponds to the reverse of divinity. We must be sufficiently reasonable not to step outside the sphere which is bound by reason. The Infinite is not yet within our powers of understanding, so that when we try to approach it, we are in danger of a fatal loss of reason. So let us be careful when following the Fool, who, bitten on his left calf by a white lynx, must perforce walk continuously, for the course of the wandering Jew has no aim or objective. It is pursued indefinitely and is a complete waste.

The lynx with piercing eyes, is pursuing the insentient Wanderer towards an upturned obelisque, behind which a crocodile lies in wait, ready to devour whatever is destined to return to chaos, that is to the primeval substance from which the ordered world was born. As a symbol of conscious lucidity and of remorse for faults committed, the lynx would restrain a person capable of discretion; but far from stopping the Fool, the bite hastens his course towards his inevitable destiny.

It is not stated, however, that the Fool cannot recover his senses, for a deep-red-coloured tulip suggesting active spirituality, whose petals are not withered, grows at his feet. If this flower is not dead, this means that the spirit does not entirely abandon the innocent but irresponsible people. The Fool moreover, is wearing a valuable gold belt which clashes with the poverty of the rest of his clothes.

This belt is made up of plates, probably twelve of them, by analogy with the zodiac, for it encircles the body of a cosmogonic person of extreme importance. In fact the Fool represents all that is beyond the sphere of the intelligible, hence the Infinite outside the finite, the absolute enclosing the relative. He is Apsu, the bottomless deep, the ancestor of the gods who were sent by these same gods outside the World when they resolved to create supreme power for themselves.

For Apsu was happy in his infinity and roamed there with delight, and refused to leave it. He would never have created anything if his union with the undifferentiated and primordial substance had not, unknown to him, made him father of the first divine couple. This first born pair holding each other, began to dance in a circle, that is they began to evolve in circular movements in the ether so creating in it the first generating movement of all things. But let us keep away from all anthropomorphism and picture the son and daughter of Apsu, for their nebulous form is related to that of ophidians,[67] and no doubt more especially to that of Ouroboros, the serpent who bites his own tail. The Fool's belt makes a very likely allusion to this. The circle formed by the belt may, moreover, be compared more simply to the Alchemists, Alum, whose sign is nought, an exact circle, O. Now Alum is the chief of all other salts, in other words, the immaterial substratum of all materiality. It is the so called nothingness which fills the primordial space from which all proceeds, a passive substance which the Fool personifies.

This foolish man puts us on our guard against digression which lies in wait for us as soon as we tend to pass the boundaries of what is real, which 1 and 21, Aleph and Tau, make the beginning and the end. The numberless arcana is related to what does not count, to the unreal phantom which we evoke in the name of nothingness, as opposed to the All in One, outside which no existence at all is conceivable. The wise man cannot be fooled by words. Far from an exterior objectifying of the verbal negation of Being, he seeks the Fool within himself, becoming conscious of the emptiness of the narrow human personality, which is so prominent in our poor concerns. Let us learn that we are nothing and the Tarot will have instructed us in its deepest secret.

The constellation which best fits the symbolism of the last arcana of the Tarot is that of Cepheus, king of Ethiopia, the husband of Cassiopeia (arcana 2 The Priestess) and father of Andromeda, the naked girl in arcana 17. This African monarch is black in colour, the colour which we give to the Fool, although the illustrators did not think of making him a negro, any more than they did not give a dark skin to the Priestess, who guards the dark shadows which hover over the abyss where intelligence is lost. As the daughter of a black father and a mother who could strictly be white, Andromeda of arcana 17 ought at least to be dark and not fair. But comparisons with astrology which are easy for us, were scarcely within the reach of the authors of the Tarot whose work remains to be perfected on certain points. In the sky Cepheus has his feet on the tip of the tail and the back part of the Little Bear, who therefore could not bite him unlike the persistent lynx biting the Fool's leg.

Divinatory Interpretations

Parabrahm, Apsou. The bottomless Abyss. The Absolute. Infinite. Ensoph. Whatever is beyond out understanding. The irrational, the absurd. Emptiness, Nothingness. Cosmogonic night. Primordial substance. Disintegration, spiritual annihilation. Nirvahna.

Passivity, impetuousness, giving way to blind instincts, to gross desires and passions. Irresponsibility, alienation, madness. Lack of self direction; incapable of resisting outside influences. Agency, subject to domination, loss of free will. Slavery.

Non-entity. The toy of occult powers. Unbalanced and easily influenced. A subject for hypnosis. Instrument of other people. Lack of consciousness. Unable to be initiated. Dragged blindly towards one's downfall. The foolish person prey to his own whims. Insensitivity, indifference. Nonchalance. Incapable of recognizing one's wrong doings and feeling remorse for them.

PART THREE

Résumé and Recapitulation

CHAPTER 7

Cosmogonic Outline

With the symbolism of each of the twenty-two compositions being justified even down to their smallest detail, we should now return to the complete work to reveal the spirit of it. What is the ideological inspiration of this symbolic work of the art of the illustrators of the Middle Ages? At a time when official doctrines alone held sway, the most daring intellects willingly moved in the direction of a secret philosophy which one had to learn how to divine. That was the origin of a mysterious wisdom hidden beneath the mask of the apparently incoherent dissertations of the Kabbala and of Hermetism; but the significant pictures of the Tarot throw light on this wisdom better than anything.

As nothing is ever destroyed in the sphere of ideas, it would be absurd to consider as dead the concepts to which deep thinkers were attached. What they brought back to life remains alive, although nothing of this is reflected in contemporary yet generally accepted ideas. Intellectual fashions hold sway, but they pass to be renewed sooner or later by whatever deserves to survive from the forgotten past.

Now let us see how, in the light of revived intellectual traditions, we can persuade the Tarot to tell us where we came from, what we are, and where we are going.

1. Everything goes back to creative activity, symbolized by the Magician, the personification of the thinking unity which suggests the idea before its conception. The god of the Tarot is the Magician, the father of all things, the eternal generator of the Word which takes form. As the primordial abstract cause, he is the mathematical point of no dimension, but whose movement brings about all geometric shapes. He is the subjective centre around which objectivity is conceived. Its simplest graphic symbol is the upright stroke 1 (number 1, the Aleph of the Hebrew alphabet, the initial of Allah) in place of

the dot which cannot be represented and must be conceived as the centre of the pupil of God's eye ☉.

2. Having an objective becomes prominent here, for activity operating in emptiness remains invalid. In the presence of Nothingness, God is nothing, without creation, no creator; without the child, no father. So we must attribute to the Eternal Father a wife who participates in his eternity in order to procreate eternally. Thus productive Nature is explained, the Mother of all things, which in the Tarot takes the form of the Priestess. In this feminine divinity the male creator god is in opposition to himself so as to escape from his sterile unity, for without any differentiation the Being within oneself would be content with one's original character of Being-non being, in the sense that while being, it would be as if not being.

   Strict self-identical unity escapes us. We say it is ineffable because it is beyond what we can conceive or imagine. In order to understand intellectually we must make distinctions through contrast, thus abandon integral unity in favour of the Binary. All knowledge proceeds from the splitting into two of what, within oneself, is one. Isis is the great revealer in as much as she is the mother of the multiplicity in which is reflected, in a way intelligible to us, the inconceivable and radical unity. —*Symbols*: the horizontal stroke—the black disc ●, or the two Binary Columns.

3. Distinction brings about conception of the idea. The Priestess has as her daughter the Empress, a winged virgin, the symbol of wisdom which brings conception. This queen of the heaven of ideality dominates creation. She places her foot on the moon, the maker of concrete images, for the conceptions of the immaculate sovereign woman are related to pure ideas, prototypes according to which creation is accomplished. She whom the builders of cathedrals called Our Lady was, in their eyes, the mediator, communicating to them the plan of the Great Architect of the Universe. This explains the professional devotion which is revealed in works of art that are destined to remain sacred. —*Symbols*: the receptive triangle ▽, as well as the set-square (Gimel ℷ or Gamma Γ).

4. For the world to be constructed, it is not sufficient for it to be conceived as an 'ideal'. Conceptive Wisdom would conceive and there would be sterility if she were not married to Executive Power, the power to bring about, of which the Emperor is the personification in the Tarot. The sombre monarch becomes the spouse of the Empress, not exactly like Pluto ravishing Prosperine, but in a mystically similar way. The essence of what is infinitely high, ethereal, dilated through sublimation, in order to create with some purpose, unites with what is related to oneself and concentrated to the highest degree. The Emperor condenses the creative activity in a multiplicity of opposing centres opposed to each other, but concordant within the collective work. He is the

creative god, the maker of the World. God in him descends into the depths of the beings to which he gives life, so that they shall act according to their destiny. —*Symbols*: Delta △, or better still the triangle with the eye in the centre; the sign of Sulphur ♧.

5. All is divine; since God is One, the living God resides in the multiplicity of what is. But divinity is not revealed straight away to living beings. We are born unconscious of the nature of our actions, in the state of automats reacting completely mechanically; then we gain awareness, in a confused way at first, while still not being in full possession of ourselves. Having to control our acts in order to have control over ourselves, we are led to distinguish between good and evil. We have a conception of duty which is the expression of the moral law to which all active beings must submit.

Obedience to this law draws together individual efforts which unite to bring about the Great Work of universal construction. When it is scattered and sown in the infinite multiplicity of its centres of action, then Divinity is reminded of itself. This memory is revealed in the feelings of piety which are at the base of every religion. It is for the Hierophant to listen to the divine inner voice, in order to make it heard by the active personality. If this personality refuses to be inspired by the divine, it would struggle in incoherence and disorder, without contributing to the work of creation—for which all beings exist. So we must live in a truly religious way to deserve existence and not to vanish into nothingness —*Symbol*: the pentagram ☆

6. God who is everywhere could not move away from himself. By penetrating into living beings, however, he seems to become obscure within them, as if he meant to spare their weakness by refusing to impose himself upon them.

   As soon as one reaches awareness, every person has the choice between two paths, of which only one leads to our becoming divine. The Lover stops hesitant at the fatal cross-roads. He feels free to make up his mind to take either the right or the left, to choose the strict path of duty, or a life of pleasure. Does he wish to live truly, or is it enough for him to vegetate? It is for him to reply and pronounce the sentence of his destiny. This is the great test of freedom: drawing back when faced with our divine task, we may prefer to give ourselves the least effort, like the schoolboy scornful of learning while he can enjoy himself. —*Symbols*: the letter Y, dear to the disciples of Pythagoras (the early Vav) and the hexagram ✡.

7. If we are resolved to take life seriously, the Chariot becomes our reward. This vehicle represents the organism to which everything is related. Let us learn how to steer our double harness well, and to stay in control of all the energies which are destined to obey us. Let us show ourselves to be like God in the sphere of our microcosm; let us practise divinity on a small scale, let us put order into chaos, so that perfect harmony reigns in us! We only make ourselves

divine by acting in a divine way. —*Symbols*: the cross of Lorraine ☨(the early Zain) and the square surmounted by a triangle △or ⧖.

8. In order to live according to the divine intention, we must take part in the creative work which is eternal. Everything is constructed and we are constructive workers. We each work in our own sphere, but not in isolation, for the stone which we are cutting to shape is destined for the Temple which we are building together. It is imperative therefore that we should all conform to the same rules of architecture, which have nothing arbitrary about them since they proceed from the logic of things. Strict observation of them results in the order, harmony and stability of every construction which is strong only by reason of the cohesion of its elements that have been arranged to form balance. Now, indispensable equilibrium is maintained in the world by Justice, the executive power of creative law.—*Symbols*: the double square ⊟ (the early Heth) from which the number 8 is taken, originally outlined as ⬦.

9. Before taking form, what is destined to come into being has potential existence. For a seed to develop, the active forces within it have had to coordinate. An invisible creation precedes that which we can perceive through our senses; the world is already organized potentially before it becomes so in fact. Everything is constructed according to an image, to an 'ideal' of the species. A prototype therefore, is evident as coming before the collection of imperfect reproductions which make up the physical universe. The mysterious artist who dreams the prototypes appears to us in the Tarot in the features of the Hermit, the experienced old man, evoking the future, according to the past. He is the weaver of the immaterial and permanent loom on which is embroidered the transitory pictures. —*Symbols*: the square divided into 9 ⊞, the figure became ✚, from which is taken ⌐9, the schematic form of the number 9 and ⊕, the early Teth.

10. Whatever has combined to take shape undergoes the attraction of the great whirling movement, represented by the Wheel of Fortune. This wheel is dominated by the motionless Sphinx which presides over the girations, and regulates their uninterrupted movement. An irresistible current draws the spirit into matter, which it drives down; it rises again as it accomplishes its evolutionary work. The descent implies forgetfulness of heaven and a selfish closing up of the personality, the individual then feeling cut off from the Great All. The being who has bodily form exists only for himself until he had entered into full possession of his earthly realm (Malcut). This phase of conquest corresponds to bodily growth which completes the construction of the instrument which the incarnate spirit must learn to use. —*Symbols*: the swastika 卐 and the diagram of the looped nought adding up to ten ◇ ◎ .

11. The personality blooms only to cease relating everything to itself. The objective in life is not the flower but the fruit; summer with its heat and storms fol-

lows gentle spring. What develops then in the individual, is Strength, known also as energy for work. Our personal development being complete, we must prepare ourselves for the task in hand. This is the point of gaining strength. From now on we must act by making ourselves obeyed by the creature with whom we are associated. What work could we produce if human animality, once tamed, were not constrained to laborious tasks? —*Symbol*: the pentagram inscribed within the hexagram ✡.

12. In order to work well we must abandon ourselves to work with abnegation, devoting ourselves to the task undertaken. To accomplish a task without enjoyment or love of it, is to labour like a slave and not as a free divine artisan, encouraged by creative inspiration. Lack of self interest makes the artist who is dedicated to the religion of Art. In his devotion this creative workman is quite the opposite of the practical man; he does not stand upright, with his feet firmly on the ground, for he hovers between sky and earth, hooked by his foot to the gallows of the Hanged Man. We must consent to torture in order to bring about the Great Work ☿. Forgetfulness of self allows us to live in a divine way, in the spirit of pure and creative mysticism. —*Symbol*: the sign of the completion of the Great Work ☿.

13. He who accepts suffering by devoting himself to the divine work does not fear death. Without waiting for his physical disintegration, he hastens to die in a mystic way by detaching himself from all that is corruptible. Thus he makes his regeneration possible, and this in turn makes him live again a more noble life. —*Symbols*: the early Mem ♓ and the sign of Saturn ♄.

14. To die means to free oneself from slavery. By dying of one's own free will to what is inferior, we raise ourselves to benefit from a fuller and higher life. This life is not limited like that of the physical organism; it is lasting and inexhaustible as the water of Temperance which flows perpetually from one vessel to another. Let us bathe in this water of youth and we shall be reborn. Then we shall participate in the eternal life by living a higher life, not limited as at present. —*Symbol*: the sign of the Watercarrier. ♒.

15. The earthly Agent of creative activity would get lost in a false mysticism if he lost sight of his material task. He has taken bodily form with a service in mind to which he must remain faithful. We have a mission to transform the lower forces at the command of higher ones. Baptism in magic waters (14) confers upon us the power to tame the Devil. Baser energies have to bring about the course work of creation. Without them the inert masses could not be raised. Let us scorn neither the unskilled work of steel like muscles, nor the humble beast of burden: let us use both of them equally for the benefit of the Great Work. — *Symbols*: the pentagram turned downwards and ✷ the early Samek ‡.

16. Using forces and materials that we have at our disposal, we construct our Tower according to our tastes. This is only a transitory building, but nothing

is lost and it is not in vain that we labour with honest intent. While aspiring towards an ideal we commit error; as imperfect architects we make many rough sketches which are destined for destruction. But no failure discourages the human spirit who unceasingly constructs and reconstructs in the midst of the ruins and collapse of his own works. Like Titan untamed, he does not cease to build the Tower which is to unite earth and heaven. —*Symbols*: the sign of Mars ♂ and that of Scorpio ♏.

17. Human work is not cursed. We work deep in the darkness of ignorance and incomprehension, giving ourselves more trouble than we need. But we are not forsaken. The Stars shine above us and teach us to find an ideal for our life. Our bravery has been rewarded by the affection of a goddess who embellishes our prison and adorns our laborious existence. She cultivates in us the sense of beauty and makes us love the task which is imposed upon us. Thanks to this magician, our earthly prison tends to become like paradise again. —*Symbol*: the Chaldean hierogram ✳ or the Star of Ishtar with eight beams.

18. From the dream to its realization there is the long rough path difficult to see and always perilous, which man takes. It winds through treacherous regions on which the Moon spreads only a deceptive light. It is the path of earthly life, with its trials, falls and bruises, the path which leads us to recognize error. As we go along it we lose our illusions and we make our way towards the dawn of full light. —*Symbols*: Moon and triangle ☿, the sign of Cancer ♋, the cosmic Egg fertilized by the Chinese.

19. The light we wait for is that of pure illumination. By turning away from error—which we must have recognized—we veer towards the truth; let us dispel the illusory and reality will be revealed to us. Deceptive appearances no longer have a hold on the Children of the Sun who live in the garden of delights, in the heart of their city of light. They represent humanity which has become reasonable and kind; having emerged from inept and ferocious barbarity. This humanity, enlightened both intellectually and emotionally, realizes the ideal of a complete civilization. It is blessed with earthly happiness, because it has been able to redeem itself from its original fall. —*Symbols*: the sign of the Sun and of Gold ☉ and that of the Gemini Twins ♊.

20. As soon as the spirit is open to enlightenment and the heart open to kindness, then living ceases to be imprisoned solely by the values of the flesh. The Trumpet of Judgement awakens the sleeping so that they shall come to life again and commune with the ancestors whose activity is never hindered. The dead are not those who have disappeared, but ourselves who move in the darkness of the fleshly tomb. —*Symbol*: The oblique cross with a vertical stroke through it ✳.

21. Order follows upon chaos, the Great Work is complete, the World brings the divine plan to reality, the Temple is constructed. At least we can perceive the

result of the creative activity in which we participate with our whole being. The heavens open before us and as prophets we contemplate the achievement of eternal creation. Our ecstasy is not in vain, for it proceeds from the supreme lucidity which rewards the faithful worker, who is allowed to enter the secret of the Great Architect of the Universe. —*Symbols*: the early $+$ or $\times$ and the swastika 卐.

22. More accurately 0. The image or multiplicity in which order has been put, brings us to the strict Unity which has no limits, whereas we are narrowly limited, so much so that what we can perceive remains pitifully childish. Beyond what we succeed in imagining stretches a bewildering immensity in which our spirit is lost. It is the bottomless abyss from which creation emerges and to which it perpetually returns. Reason gives up her rights here in favour of the Fool, a personification of the unintelligible Infinite, which placed between the beginning and the end (1 and 21), humiliates the thinker who is tempted to pride himself on the little that he understands in the heart of unyielding incomprehensibility. —*Symbol*: Alum $\bigcirc$, reminding us of the nought of our own numerical order.

CHAPTER 8

The Programme of Initiation as Revealed by the Tarot

1. The person to be initiated must depend on no one. He must have nothing to do with a borrowed knowledge, or with a poor schoolboy's knowledge. Without intellectual initiative, no one can approach the door of the Temple where one must *dare* to knock with the energy of a forceful will-power in order to *be silent* there.

2. Initiating knowledge is not that of objects which we can perceive with our senses. It is revealed to whoever is able to look into himself. Turn away from the glitter of objects; descend into the inner darkness where your spirit will be face to face with itself.

3. Now come up! Rise to the very height of the Heavens! Learn how to contemplate steadily the immensity of what is outside of yourself. Extend to its limits the scope of your views so as to escape from your narrow conceptions.

4. Put your mind to action! Avoid extremes and recognize the region where opposites clash (the plain of the clashing of swords in the second ritual journey of the Freemasons). Take possession of yourself, seize the sceptre which commands your personality; be your own Ruler!

5. Learn! Listen to others, but especially to what speaks within you. Meditate in order to understand. In your own way formulate your own knowledge and in your head conceive the religion which convinces you.

6. Decide freely upon your destiny. Do you feel that you have the courage to fight keenly, or do you fear effort? Choose between heroic action and the easy life of a weak mortal. Take this warning that nothing is obtained gratuitously; if you want to be strong, be willing to suffer; by escaping from suffering you become weak. Now whoever becomes weak also becomes diminished, but each one of us remains free to become diminished and to make his path towards nothingness.

7. Walk in the chosen direction and with a brave heart face the trials which await you. Show that you know how to direct your path, and you will take the direction of forces which will accompany you. Diverging forces becomes attached to your personality; be their conciliator and let yourself be carried forward on the triumphal path which lies open before you.

8. Only desire what is right for your career to be accomplished according to the Law. Live not just for the sake of living, but to fulfil the aim of life; in this way you will learn how to live and you will possess life in which everything is rigorously balanced. Bring about justice in yourself and you will be stabilized in the balance.

9. Keep within your limits! Concentrate your faculties, plunge into silence and isolation. Draw from within yourself the light which shows clearly the path that you must follow. Let your wisdom take inspiration from the tasks which burden you; advance cautiously so that you never have to retreat.

10. Now that your concentration is good, come out of your preliminary solitude to enter into the human round. Keep your place there and descend to weaknesses. Be a man in order to become a god; do not scorn the inferior which you must help to raise. Alone, you would remain what you are, without accomplishing any progress. You cannot live and progress except by involving yourself in the destiny of others.

11. Every involvement implies a common and concordant action which demands of each one involved an effort in discipline. An association benefits from the reserves and inner resources of each individual involved. By giving free rein to your vigorous impulses you give evidence of weakness and not of strength. The strong person is the one who tames himself by controlling the ardour of his passions without putting out their stimulating fires.

12. None can participate in the Great Work if he intends only to work for himself. Lack of blind self-interest creates the artist. Apply yourself to what brings you nothing and behave in the opposite fashion of the egoists. Give without thought of receiving.

13. When you have given everything, you will be reduced to the state of a walking skeleton. You will be as dead, and they will say: flesh has left the bones. Reaping the illusions of the past you will then prepare the land for the future harvests. In the heart of sepulchral darkness the Philosophical Child known as the Son of Putrefaction will take birth.

14. One must die in order to live again; by losing the earth you win the heavens whose waters wash and regenerate. The alliance with forces from above makes you live again, no longer as a recalcitrant serf, bound to the soil of the earth, but as a free plougher, ambitious to harvest for the benefit of all the hungry.

15. If the fire of hell did not heat the earth, the water from the sky would remain infertile. If it were not for the forces below, those from above would remain

unproductive. The Devil which is in you is only an enemy when you have not learnt how to reduce him to servitude. Your animal instincts are not cursed; they afford you unlimited powers, provided that you know how to dominate them. Magic is no bait for the person who can make himself be obeyed by instinct.

16. Art is difficult. In theory everything is simple, but beware of complications when it comes to putting things into practice! Be fearful of becoming the victim of the audacity of your enterprises. When applied your forces are limited; know how to handle them and never exhaust them. Moderation is important to those anxious to accomplish their task. It is important to assign oneself limits, even in the search for truth, for error lies in wait for whoever wants to know too much. Be moderate in your ambitions and discreet in your legitimate curiosity.

17. Live without feverish excitement, careful to give yourself the rest which repairs spent energy and accumulates further energies to be used. Sleep gives the dynamism necessary for work in the service of your actions. You are not wasting your time, either by sleeping or by enjoying the charm of the sweet pleasures of life. The master in the art of living is not a morose ascetic; he makes use of what is offered to him, and on earth appreciates the gifts of heaven, without taking advantage of anything. He admires beautiful things and falls in love with what is worthy of being loved.

18. To encourage you to fulfil your task faithfully which life has imposed on you, life itself grants you pleasures which it is wise not to scorn. You have a right to them in your fierce struggle against the obstacles which the material world puts in your way. Being forced to struggle in the half light of risky discretion, we must learn only at our own expense, and progress only at the price of painful experiences. As the victims of appearances we never cease to be deceived, falling from one gross error into a lesser one, without reaching real knowledge. While based on necessarily incomplete laws and verifications, human knowledge proceeds from likelihoods and remains until the end of time equivocal.

19. Light enters spirits when they go beyond the sphere of materiality. The Sun enlightens intelligences which rise above the mist of generally accepted ideas. True enlightenment is of a purely moral order. The universe does not unveil her secrets to you, but you can know for certain how to behave in this world. Have the wisdom to desire to see clearly only what concerns your conduct. Let us learn to understand each other, so that we can give mutual help as brothers. When aspiring to earthly happiness, never forget that it could only be collective. Make yourself worthy of what you will not obtain unless you deserve it.

20. The spirit of enlightened man is released from the bonds of his body. He communes with the life-giving breath which revives both the intellectually

and morally dead. Inspiration rewards the one who emerges from himself and participates in a higher and fuller life. Nothing is lost. The past remains alive in that it has import for the future and you can evoke it in order to find the 'lost world' of the ancient Wise Men.

21. The past reveals the future to us: we can conceive what you will be according to what was. By rising above the present you become initiated into the completed Great Works; you enter into the cosmos, that is to say, into the World of potential lasting order. It is a question of subjective realization which has no element of chimera about it. Man is the self-feeding furnace, the athanor in which the philosopher's pure gold is ripened. Bring about in yourself the ideal of creation to make your Microcosm conform to the harmony of the Macrocosm, for such is the final objective of the wise man.

22. When you have reached the summit from where all the kingdoms of the earth can be seen, your view will extend beyond what is conceivable and you will succumb to the giddy view of the Infinite. Ensoph, the bottomless abyss, will take hold of you and bring you into the motherly bosom of the Great Night, the giver of life to all beings and to all things. Here reason is silent before the ineffable Mystery of mysteries, fatally silent. Be conscious of your nothingness, for without pious humility there is no reintegration into the primordial ALL!

CHAPTER 9

The Tarot Seen in the Light of Hermetic Philosophy

1. (The Magician or Operator.) The Alchemist resolved to undertake the Great Work.
2. (The Priestess, the revealer of the mysteries, the holder of the keys of the Great Work.) The first matter of the wise; the initial enigma which is for the operator to solve before approaching the great master. This mysterious matter is everywhere, it can be obtained at a low price, but only the Children of the Art succeed in distinguishing it. Without it all chemical actions remain useless.
3. (The Empress, super-celestial Water, the mother of things.) In matter which is 'one' can be distinguished Salt ⊖, Sulphur 🜍 and Mercury ☿. This ternary is related, not to substances, but to principles of transubstantiation. Salt ⊖ shows the static state of first matter. It dissolves in Celestial Water ▽, the generator of forms.
4. (The Emperor, the universal power of realization.) Sulphur 🜍 is the principle of 'shaping fire' as its signs show (△ fire, + fertilizing union, action to be exerted). It burns in the centre of all beings and assures its fixity. Its beams give vital heat which disappears as soon as Sulphur is extinguished.
5. (The Pope, the teacher of the Children of the Art.) Mercury ☿ the universal fluid of an inconceivable subtlety, penetrates all things and undergoes the coagulating attraction of Sulphur, whose burning it sustains. He is the great animator, thanks to whom everything is drawn out of its potential state into reality. The Alchemist who has recognized Mercury is instructed in the theory of the Great Work and can risk its practice.
6. (The Lover, the two paths or the young Hercules choosing his career.) Two diverging paths lead to the dignity of the great master, one is dry, the other humid. The first is rational and the second is emotional, for the gold of the philosophers can be obtained either through the nature of the intelligence

and the acquisition of knowledge profoundly understood, or through the sincerity of a love confident, trusting, which follows completely the dictates of the heart. According to the natural aptitude of the operator, he goes boldly into the work either as a philosopher anxious to realize the ideal which he conceives, or as a mystic aspiring to conform to Divine intentions. The Philosopher's Stone is the attribute of both the successful Wise man and the true Saint.

7.   (The Chariot, the vehicle of the spiritual soul.) The Work is accomplished methodically, not following the whim of the operator. This operator must know how to direct operations, if he intends to reach his goal. As the driver of the Triumphal Chariot of Antimony, he must not deviate either to the right or the left of the route marked out. If incapable of controlling his double harness, he lets himself be drawn sideways, then his downfall will be complete. The Adept advances straight ahead.

8.   (Justice, the hand of the operations of nature.) Art puts itself in the service of nature, whose laws force the careful artist not to undertake anything which does not conform to the immovable order of things. In agreement as to intention with wisdom bringing order into the universe, the good Workman labours at carrying out a plan which has nothing arbitrary or fantastic about it.

9.   (The Hermit or experienced Adept.) The transforming work of the Wise man is applied to what is to be born, and not to already formed productions. In his ignorance the common Alchemist handles dead substances, whereas the worthy Son of Hermes influences life before it has come to be applied. To act in a useful way let us only wait until the dynamism which can be influenced has taken form. Over what has already taken shape materially our action remains weak, but it can become powerful over what is on the way to formation. The future is modelled on the image which the conspirer makes of it when he shuts himself from the present in order to create potential forms ready to become objectives.

10. (The Wheel of Fortune; permanent Genesis.) Although the sphere of objectivity is not his, the Hermetist is not uninterested in the whirling of earthly life, on the pretext that his kingdom (Malcut) is not of this world. In order to lie in wait for the opportunity to intervene usefully, he stands outside the current which draws the crowds. His initiative is produced when the hour chimes: he knows how to wait for the call or the sign summoning him to action.

11. (Strength or the Woman conquering the lion.) To be in the right stage of action at the opportune moment, one must have accumulated energies at one's disposal. Whoever expends himself thoughtlessly has nothing to give when an effort is needed. (The Parable of the Foolish Virgins.) Now it is important that the Adept should be strong. That is not possible unless he knows how

to control himself. Mysterious Power is the attribute of the person who has resisted the temptation of using his strength unwisely.

12. (The Hanged Man or the accomplishment within oneself of the Great Work.) The purifications undergone have prepared a strong spirit for the accomplishment of the Great Work ☿. This work demands from the operator a complete lack of self interest. If he possesses treasures, then he must scatter them for the benefit of those who will pick them up. Giving up common sense which is valued by the mass of people, he needs the courage of a noble unmindfulness of himself and the dedication of an irresistibly active love.

13. (Death, the constant source of renewal.) The Work done in darkness marks the success of the first operation, during which the subject dies and decomposes. Death separates the subtle from the dense; it sets the spirit free from matter. All the while we stay imprisoned in the body, we can only judge according to the nature of our senses. Now these sensations only reveal the outward cover of things, their dead bark which is of little interest to the Hermetic philosopher.

14. (Temperance or the Fountain of Youth.) Whatever rises from the dead body is condensed as it rises, and falls down again in the form of rain onto the decomposed corpse which is thus gradually washed and whitened. The waters of the soul purify and restore life to whatever submits passively to their action. Matter is recomposed into a new life, like the catechumen as he emerges from the waters of baptism.

15. (The Devil, the great magic agent.) Ablution is only carried out if the power of Fire is wisely controlled in phases of measured intensity, alternating with deliberate periods of moderation, allowing the steam to condense into rain water. The Fire which the Operator has at his disposal is not from the sky; it is an earthly heat which one could see as being diabolic, but without which the work would never enter into the practical sphere. The Artist uses the Devil without binding himself to him in any pact whatsoever.

16. (The Lightning Struck Tower; Alchemy of the Ignorant.) No one can claim certain success in what he undertakes. The practice of the Art includes unfortunate attempts which should not discourage us. Experience shows the faults to be avoided. Too much ambition leads to fatal catastrophe. If promoted unwisely Fire causes explosion.

17. (The Star; the influence of the stars, Astrology.) The Wise man does not burn with impatience; he observes the seasons and waits calmly for nature to accomplish her share in the Work which he watches over. If he counted only on himself, he would obtain only a poor result. Without the assistance of the star-filled sky man struggles blindly in the earthly darkness.

18. (The Moon; phenomena, observation of sense data; materialism and superstition.) The stars grow pale when the moon sheds its brightness. This planet

enlightens the struggling human spirit in the grip of matter and its deceptive appearances. As a good mother, Diana replies to all the questions put to her by childish curiosity. Her replies are truthful but are shrouded in a mystery which prevents precise understanding. The White Work corresponds in this way to the possession of a precious symbolic truth (silver) which however does not yet reveal the supreme ideal of the Philosopher's Gold.

19. (The Sun; discretion, enlightenment.) Gold symbolizes the Truth, as can be conceived by man who has abandoned deceptive illusions. To possess the Philosopher's Stone one must know how to change error into truth. Through lack of discernment men make mistakes; they create their unhappiness through lack of intelligence and comprehension. When the healthy reason of the sun enlightens them, they will be happy, for they will avoid hurting each other. The Golden Age is yet to be achieved.

20. (Judgement, understanding of the past tradition which has been understood and revived.) Intelligence and full comprehension of what is human engenders the Religion of the Spirit. Past but revived beliefs are reborn in this religion. Supreme Judgement justifies faith and re-establishes superstitions which have been scorned. Truth spreads abroad and unrecognized in its many and varied disguises, is revealed in all its light and is restored to its unity. Through the effect of projection everything that is transmutable becomes gold.

21. (The World; reality distinguished from deceptive appearances.) The Great Work is accomplished; the World is functioning according to Divine intention, for in it everything relates harmoniously. The reign of God is brought about by the fact of transmutation which has been made.

22. (The Fool and his domain; the inaccessible, that is beyond human understanding.) In the last analysis what is the purest gold in its unalterable fixity made of? The substance which is at the root of things, the chief Salt of all other Salts, has as its symbol any empty circle O and is called Alum. Everything is made out of nothing and returns to nothing. But the All-Nothing is the Great Mystery, the Arcana of Arcanas, in face of which reason confesses its powerlessness. The Fool humiliates the haughty who pride themselves on their 'wisdom'.

CHAPTER 10

The Masonic Harmonies in the Tarot

All symbolism is valid. That of the Freemasons puts into constructive allegories the facts of initiation as expressed in terms of metallurgy by the Alchemists. The Tarot relates the same ideological tradition to coloured pictures chosen from the selection of the popular artists of the Middle Ages. The community of the Esoterics authorizes us to read the Tarot in the Masonic way. So let us now be allowed to test ourselves in it.

1. (The Magician, juggler or mountebank.) Postulant seen as a future Initiate because of his aptitudes and his good characteristics.
2. (The Priestess, Isis Mother of the Initiated.) The knowledge of initiation which one must be able to find for oneself. Isis only entrusts the key to mysteries to her sons, to the 'Children of the Wisdom' worthy of knowing her secrets.
3. (The Empress, Lady of supreme Ideality.) Wisdom which has conception. After turning inwards into himself (chamber of reflection) the apprentice rises from the dark depths to the high ideal of Freemasonry. If he did not assimilate the pure idea which must be realized, he could not be initiated.
4. (The Emperor, the centre which provides initiating power.) From the ethereal heights of the ideal, the constructive aspirant is thrown headlong into the land of action. (The test of the first symbolic journey.) It is the battlefield of life. Here swords cross. But the aspiring Initiate does not involve himself in the pointless battles of opinions and sides: he reserves his energy in order to be able to apply it in the shaping of the 'Cubic Stone'.
5. (The Pope, the supreme holder of the knowledge of the Initiated.) Without complete theoretical instruction no one can tackle the effective practice of the 'Royal Art'. To pass a 'Brother' one must be practised in the handling of tools and be ignorant of nothing in the rules of architecture. The 'workman' who

has reached the light perceives the Brilliant Star and knows the significance of the letter G, for geometry must be familiar to him.

6. (The Lover, or the Initiate of the first degree undergoing the trial on which his increase in salary depends.) Intellectual initiation confers Freedom. The learned man does what he wants, he chooses the direction which it suits him to follow. If in the full knowledge of the facts, he decides to dedicate himself to the Work of the Constructors, he will not be able to go back on his undertaking. The oath which he pronounces determines his future.

7. (The Chariot occupied by the Master assuming the direction of collective work.) The Initiate submits to the 'Set Square' which points to the master chosen to direct the work. The elected chief shows himself to be conciliating, sociable, always concerned with maintaining harmony. Out of the clash of warring opinions he can draw the conclusion which reveals impartially that part of truth which is implicit in these opinions.

8. (Justice, the same law for everyone.) The 'Spirit Level' assures Equality before the Law of the work. Everything exists with the view only of performing a function. In the order of the universe everyone is bound to fulfil his task. We live in order to work, not to enjoy life without paying. Increases in salary reward the good 'workman' who by aiming at living better, benefits from the superior way of life to which he has risen.

9. (The Hermit, Wise man whose influence works discreetly and irresistibly. The Master who has reached complete mastership.) As he works the Initiate reflects. He refuses to act like a machine. The artist is interested in his work, which he loves and understands because he feels it. Rules are not imposed upon him superficially, for he has assimilated them by the process of thoughtful and logical justification. The 'Plumb Line' has directed his mind into the inner area of things, towards Esotericism which escapes the uninitiated.

10. (The Wheel of Fortune; the Apprentice displaying his initiative.) In the centre of himself, the Initiate perceives the Warm Hearth which corresponds to the column of J: his wages as Apprentice are expressed in an energy of which he has an inner source, that makes him undertake tasks with daring, but never without regard to fitness. For the Mason sets to his task when the time has come for the work to be started.

11. (The Strength; the brother who has become strong through mastering his own person.) Trial by Fire exteriorizes inner heat. The Initiate who undergoes the test feels within him a vacuum which attracts the exterior dynamic agent. Because of this he comes close to the column of B from which executive strength is drawn.

12. (The Hanged Man or self abnegation.) Initiating influence is worked mysteriously without recourse to profane means. It goes by unnoticed, for it is expressed neither in resounding speeches nor in actions which attract attention.

Of his own free will the Initiate condemns himself to an apparent impotence which allows him to act as he wishes and with efficacy. The plan which develops in reserve and silence, removed from all useless agitation, gains the strength to be put into practice. The dreamer who has no self-interest and works for his dream with self-denial is preparing the future by forgetting the present.

13. (Initiating Death leading to Mastership.) Whatever is dreamed to some purpose is set out on the 'Drawing Board' which no one approaches before he has entered the Middle Chamber. In the darkness where the whiteness of skulls and bones stands out, there all illusion vanishes and judgement is moulded. The Initiate dies to all that is factitious and prepares himself to receive Mastership.

14. (Temperance, or the bath in life-giving water.) According to the oldest concept known to us, the fountain of life wells up from beneath the slab of the central sanctuary of the city of the dead.[68] We must die in order to live again. By depriving us of whatever keeps us in a state of inferiority, death elevates us and makes us participate in a less narrow life. To live only for oneself restricts life, while on the other hand life is broadened for the altruistic person whose aim is to live for others. The 'Lodge' gives its wages to the Brother who knows how to work and proves himself worthy of becoming master.

15. (The Devil, instrument of the Art of Initiation.) All energy is sacred: none should be cursed, even if it proves harmful in its application. The Initiate should know how to tap all currents and channel their uncontrolled movement. The Devil is at his service, if by reaching the order of the second degree he does not take up an attitude of showy vanity. Let us work fervently towards the realization of the Great Work and we will draw together a collection of everything that can help us.

16. (The Lightning Struck Tower; the work of the poor workman.) Hiram falls beneath the blows of the 'three bad brethren'. The first personifies Ignorance, which is incapable of seizing the mind, makes teaching impossible and spreads the errors which every half understood truth engenders. The second denotes Fanaticism, which reduces the Temple to the proportions of an exclusive and isolated tower. The third resembles Ambition which is incapable of moderating itself in the erection of the Tower of Babel destined to crumble into ruins.

17. (The Star which shines in the night: Ideality aspiring to truth.) The murder of Hiram interrupts all work. All becomes dark for the bewildered constructors, deprived of any direction. In their distress they disperse to look for the dead body of the Master who has disappeared: an acacia branch suddenly gives them hope for they see in it a token and sign of the perenniality of life and of resurrection. The desolate countryside where we wander is not arid; it is covered with consoling vegetation on which the eye rests and lets itself be charmed. 'Adoring Beauty' does her work and the Artist joins her school.

18. (The Moon; journeying into the heart of the mirages of error.) The Masters travel no longer in isolation like the Apprentices and the Brethren, but in groups, giving each other mutual support. They explore the sublunar world in search of the material remains of Hiram. As worthy 'Children of the Widow' they are inspired by the example of Isis travelling throughout the world to gather together the scattered remains of the body of Osiris. To revive the tradition, let us carefully gather what remains of it in the form of legends, misunderstood rites and superstitions.

19. (The Sun; the conquest of initiating light.) When light dawns in the spirit Hiram is found again, deep in a sleep from which the Masters must wake him. They assemble for this purpose in order to pool their intelligence and affection. Hiram is revived because his thought finds a new expression (his lost power of speech returned to him) and because his constructive aspirations animate all hearts.

20 (Judgement; the resurrection of the Master.) The rejuvenated dead person lives again in the Son of Putrefaction. Everything which possesses life within itself emerges from the tomb of oblivion when the trumpet of the great Judgement sounds. The experience of centuries gives to men wisdom and understanding. Hiram resumes the directing of work which will never again be interrupted.

21. (The World; complete Initiation.) The Temple is constructed, it is complete and nothing is missing. The building is perfect in its design and in its execution. The ideal is attained, the Great Work accomplished, the Divine rule of Love and intelligence is established in the regenerated World.

22. (The Fool; the Initiate has no illusion about the relativity of his knowledge.) Completion could only be relative for work is continued indefinitely. If it ceased everything would vanish into Nothingness. What is, is the result of a necessary activity which an inconceivable passivity could neither follow nor precede. By opposing Infinite and Finite we come into the fool's domain. The compass outlines the limits of reason: let us learn how to keep ourselves within it, respecting the 'Ineffable Mystery' which we are forbidden to penetrate.

CHAPTER 11

The Arcana Interpreted in Terms of Good and Bad

1. The Magician
The beginning, the first cause, Mercurial influence.

Good
Dexterity, ability, diplomacy, eloquence, convincing ways, an alert mind, a quick mind, business acumen.

Bad
A persuasive boaster, an illusionist, intrigue, careerist, politician, charlatan, imposter, liar, a crook, an exploiter. An agitator, a lack of scruples.

2. The Priestess
Mystery, intuition, devotion, passive Saturnian influence.

Good
Reserved, discreet, quiet. meditation, faith, patient, religious feelings, resignation, modesty. Necessary inaction.

Bad
Hidden intentions, dissimulation, hypocrisy, inaction, laziness. Sanctimonious, holds a grudge, an indifferent disposition, interest in the mystical.

3. The Empress
Prudence, discretion, idealism and intellectual solar influence.

Good
Understanding, intelligence, instruction, calm, courteous, sociable, elegance, politeness. Domination by the mind, abundance, riches. Servility.

Bad
Affectation, poseur, stylish, vanity, pretentious, distain, frivolity, idleness, luxury, extravagant. Sensitivity to flattery, lack of refinement, ways of *nouveaux riche*.

4. The Emperor
Firm, positivism, executive power, Saturnian-Martial influence.

Good
Right, rigid, certitude, fixed ideas, realization, perseverance, strong will-power, acts on decisions. Powerful protector.

Bad
Tenuous opposition, stubborn, hostile, prejudice, opinionated, bad government, big risks of failure. Tyranny, absolutism.

5. The Pope
Duty, morality, conscience, Jupiterian influence.

Good
Moral authority, respectability, teaching, good advice, goodwill, indulgent generosity, forgiveness. Meekness.

Bad
Papal sentence, strict moralist, strict teacher, small-minded theorist, bombastic preacher. An adviser with a lack of practical sense.

6. The Lovers
Feelings, freewilled, testing, double influence of Venus or more exactly of Ishtar the warlike star of the morning, then amorous as the stars go down.

Good
Voluntary determinism, choice, wishes, aspirations, desires. Examinations, deliberations, responsibility. Affections.

Bad
To go through doubts and indecision. Dangerous temptation, the risk of being seduced, misconduct, liberty, weakness, lack of heroism.

7. The Chariot
Triumph, command, superiority, Martian-solar influence.

Good
Legitimate success, deserved advancement, talent, health, aptitudes put to good effect. Governmental tact, diplomacy, efficient direction, appeasement. Progress, mobility, journeys on land.

Bad

Unjustified ambition, lack of talent, usurped situation, illegitimate government, dictatorship, harmful concessions, dangerous opportunism, worrying about which way to go, preoccupations, overworked, feverish activity without rest.

8. Justice

Order, regularity, method, equilibrium, placid lunar influences.

Good

Stability, conservatism, organization, normal functioning. Law, discipline, logic, co-ordination, adapting to necessities, moderate opinions, practical sense, reason, administration, economy, obedience.

Bad

Bourgeoisism, submission to users, lack of initiative, slaving over books, functionalism, papers. Police station. Legal dispute, law suit, quarrel, exploitation by the legal system.

9. The Hermit

Prudence, reserve, restriction, Saturnian influence.

Good

Isolation, concentration, silence, profoundness, meditation, study. Austerity, continence, sobriety, discretion. Doctor, discreet occultist.

Bad

Timid, misanthrope, mute, exaggerated circumspection, lack of sociability, sullen character. Avarice, poverty, celibacy, chaste. Conspirator.

10. The Wheel of Fortune

Destiny, instability, lunar-Mercurial influence.

Good

Sagacity, an opportunist, luck in all undertakings, luck, fortuitous success. Spontaneity, an inventive disposition, liveliness, good humour.

Bad

Carelessness, speculation, game, insecurity, unserious, the unexpected, gypsy character. Unstable situation, sudden change, winnings and losses. Adventures, risks, minor fortune.

11. Strength

Virtue, courage, Jupiter-Mars influence.

Good

Moral energy, calm, intrepid. Mind over matter. Intelligence conquering brutality. Subjugation of passions. Success in industry.

Bad

Anger, impatience, immoderate enthusiasm, insensibility, cruelty, fighting, war, conquering with violence, a surgical operation, vehemence, discord, fire.

12. The Hanged Man

Self-sacrifice, approved sacrifice, lunar-Venus influence.

Good

Disinterest, unselfish, devotion, submission to duty, patriotism, generosity, apostolate, philanthropic, gifted. Dispersal of ideas.

Bad

Good ideas not executed, projects not realized, good plans remain as theory. Promises not kept, love not shared, exploitation of good feelings. Powerless achievement. Losses.

13. Death

Inescapable fate, necessary end, disenchantment, active Saturnian influence.

Good

Profound, intellectual penetration, metaphysics, disillusionment, severe discretion, disillusioned wisdom, detachment, resignation, stoicism.

Bad

Inevitable failure. Discouragement, pessimism, absolute change, starting again in a diametrically opposed fashion.

14. Temperance

Serenity, coldness, adaptation, Mercurial-lunar influence.

Good

Accommodating character, practical philosophy, happy, carelessness, accepting the inevitable, bending to circumstance, sociability, educability, adaptive transformation.

Bad

Indifference, lack of personality, passive change, changing moods. Tendency to change with the environment, submission to fashion. Results do not come up to aspirations, inability to influence the flow of life.

15. The Devil

Disorder, passion, sexual excitement, conjunction of Mars and Venus.

Good

Sexual attraction, passionate desires, magical action, magnetism, occult power, practising mystical influence. Active protection against bewitchment. Protection against sorcerers.

Bad
Trouble, over-excitement, amorous, lust, complication, stupidity, intrigue, use of illicit means, bewitchment, fascination, enslavement of the senses, weakness resulting in an awkward situation, selfishness.

16. The Tower

Explosion, destruction, fall, lunar-Mars influence.

Good
Delivery, salutary crisis, defiance, fear resulting from reckless enterprises. Benefit from other people's errors. Good sense, detention, genuine timidity. Attachment to the observance of piety, religious materialism.

Bad
Illness, punishment, catastrophe provoked by imprudence, clandestine childbirth, scandal, discovered hypocrisy. Excess, abuse, monopolizing, presumption, pride. Fanciful enterprises, misleading alchemy.

17. The Star

Practical idealism, hope, beauty, solar-Venus influence.

Good
Candour, abandonment to sensible influences, naturism, confidence in destiny, aesthetics, poetical sensibility, presentiment. Kindness, compassion.

Bad
Wild, imprudence, frivolity, lack of spontaneity, unhealthy artificial constraint. Romanticism, one who turns away from the practical life.

18. The Moon

Imagination, appearances, illusions, active lunar influence.

Good
Objectivity, the sensitive world, experimentation, work, the difficult conquest of reality. Instruction by pain, imposed task, fastidious labour which is necessary. A passive view, lucidity. Navigation.

Bad
Errors of sense, false suppositions, ambushes, traps, deceptions, deceptive theories, fantastic knowledge, visionaryism, flattery, menaces, blackmail, loss, journey, whim, lunacy.

19. The Sun

Light, reason, harmony, solar influence.

Good
Limpid discernment, clarity of judgement and expression, literary or

artistic talent. Pacification, harmony, good relationship, conjugal felicity. Fraternity, reign of the intelligence and good sentiments. Reputation, glory, celebrity.

Bad
Glaring, vanity, poseur, show-off, pride, susceptibility. Misunderstood artist. Hidden misery, bluff, false appearance, assimilated façade, prestigious decor.

20. Judgement
Inspiration, redemptive blow, a lunar-Mercurial influence.

Good
Enthusiasm, exhaltation, spirituality. Prophecy, sanctity, theurgy, miraculous medicine. Past resurrection, renovation, birth. Propaganda, apostolate.

Bad
Spiritual and mental intoxication, illumination. Reclaim, noise, agitation for no reason.

21. The World
Completion, recompense, deification, Jupiter-solar influence.

Good
Major fortune, complete success, completion, achievement. Decisive intervention. Very favourable circumstances, propitious atmosphere. Absolute integrity. Contemplative absorption. Ecstasy.

Bad
Tremendous obstacle, hostile atmosphere, self pity. Distraction, lack of attention and concentration. Large setback of fortune, ruin, social disregard.

0. The Fool
Impulsive, alienation, passive lunar influence.

Good
Passive, absolute abandon, renouncement of all resistance, carelessness, innocence, irresponsibility. Instinctiveness. Abstemtion.

Bad
Nullity, incapable of reason. Abandonment to blind impulse, unconsciously unruly. Extravagance, punishment, foolish acts, vain remorse, annihilation.

PART FOUR

The Tarot as Applied to Divination

CHAPTER 12

Imagination

When legend represents humanity as having fallen from an original state of spontaneous enlightenment, it seems to be alluding to the instinct which helps animals. Nature takes care of living creatures who obey her passively and she enables them to accomplish, without error, the actions which the programme of their life demands. As long as it remains obedient to its impulses, animality enjoys privileges lost to the creature who aims at directing his life according to his own judgements. As soon as reason, while still weak, assumes the directing of the individual, then there is revolt against the natural and primordial order of things. Reason disturbs the lucidity of the instinct, hence the state of fall of the creature who has but imperfect reason.

A difficult apprenticeship is imposed upon us, for reason develops only to the detriment of instinct, and this instinct loses its clarity when faced with the triumph of complete clarity of reason within us. A period of distress comes between the reigns of instinct and pure reason. The transition would be painful were it not for a faculty which is neither instinct nor reason, but seems to fall between the two. It appears with the dawn of intelligence; its diffuse light gives diversion before instruction. The pictures it shows are incoherent, but they fascinate and give birth to ideas. This faculty is imagination.

Let us be careful not to spurn it. It was held in honour thousands of years before the Greek civilization. To it we owe all fundamental human knowledge, the original concept of religions and sciences, for all glimmerings of light which brought a seed of clarity into the human brain were received by the intuition of primitive and humble men.

On leaving the realm of instinct we certainly do not think of asking ourselves philosophical questions; when faced with the spectacle of nature we undergo and give in to impressions without reasoning about them. So objects exert a power of suggestion on our imagination of which nothing stands in the way.

From this we have an extraordinary 'faculty of imagination' which surprises us when we observe it in children or in 'subjects' who have been able to retain something of the child in them. This type of consciousness was that which belonged to humanity in earlier times, as it remains still with less civilized peoples today.

It was characterized by its lack of power to formulate clear and precise ideas. Properly speaking primitive man does not speak; he dreams. Rebellious of any intellectual effort, he is a receptive, passive agent in relation to what comes to his mind. His mind is open and he takes as true anything that comes into it. Imagination is led to extravagances; therefore it would not be wise to set the imagination up as the arbiter of our decisions.

Some countries whose civilization makes us marvel, however, have listened to the imagination when consulting the oracles and paying due reverence to the colleges of soothsayers who were entrusted to interpret these oracles. In the very beginning of social groups we find, not philosophers, but very humble priest-sorcerers, the ancestors of the fetish worshippers of our savage tribes. With instinctive faith being absolute, the authority of clear-minded subjects becomes dominant; they became quite naturally priest-kings, like the first sovereigns in the history of Egypt and Mesopotamia.

Their power was exercised in the name of the divinity which manifested its will through the intercession of diviners. To judge by its duration, this regime gave cause for no more misuse than others which have succeeded it. The Celts had no complaint against the Druids and more than one lay monarchy has made us regret the loss of earlier theocratic government.

It is quite likely that all went well as long as the soothsayers were sincere and the people believed. When there were doubts on both sides things grew worse. Reason appeared in the guise of craftiness; soothsayers became the accomplices of the powerful to the detriment of the believers. The art of divination was lost, and fell under the shadow of disrespect. It is dead in so far as official and public practice are concerned. Richelieu, however, had recourse to the enlightenment of an astrologer, and divination in private has never been so flourishing as it is today.

For the modern mind would this be a sign of decrepitude? Are we slipping back into childhood after swearing in the eighteenth century that we would sacrifice everything to the cult of reason? This is not the case at all: we are progressing intellectually since we are discovering that Reason ☉ has as her sister Imagination ☽.

We intend to continue reasoning, but while allowing ourselves at the same time to cultivate our faculties of imagination.

Having been brought up as they were in the school of imagination, the ancients divined things which escape us. Why should we not try to find their 'Lost World' again? If such is our ambition, let us learn to divine. How?

By teaching ourselves the rules of the art of divination to put them into practice in an experimental way.

CHAPTER 13

The Art of Divination

In spite of the positivism on which they pride themselves, our contemporaries are often diviners without realizing it. Such and such a person succeeds in life thanks to his flair, because he guesses at what is favourable and acts accordingly. Another becomes rich because of a certain lucidity which guides him towards lucky speculation and away from unlucky. Certain financiers have established their fortunes on the intuition of their wives. And as for our soldiers; have they not talked of bombs exploding on the very spot they had just left on a sudden impulse?

In the above mentioned cases there was a spontaneous divination, escaping the rules of a conscious art of divining, to which one could have recourse in case of perplexity. But does there exist an art of this kind, based on the development of the intuition and on the rational study of clairvoyance which is normally manifest outside any preparatory education?

History and archaeology dispel all doubt about the existence of such an art in the distant past. Is it possible for us today to have a fair idea of this and go back to its principles? There is nothing fanciful about this enterprise. Let us try to demonstrate it in the light of our personal experience.

The theory is simple. If you have a vivid but wild imagination, then try to discipline it. To this effect teach it to be at repose and restrain itself, at the same time purify it of anything that might disturb it, then leave whatever interests you to reflect within it. It is easily said, but there are great difficulties in practising it.

For the anxious-minded of the twentieth century, the hardest thing of all is imposing silence upon themselves. How can we silence our thoughts and make ourselves intellectually passive? Our distant ancestors only had to shut the eyes of the body in order to open almost instantaneously those of the soul. They were more disposed than we are to a loneliness which detaches us from the world of the senses and is favourable to inner imaginative reflection. Let us practice forgetting what surrounds us in order to become attentive to the subtle manifestations which echo within us.

If it were possible to realize the ideal of receptive neutrality, then our impressions would correspond exactly to the object in cause. From this object proceed waves similar to those of light, but perceptible only through the imagination, which for them performs the job of a photographic plate.

For the soothsayer it is a question of tapping the images that vibrate around him faithfully . . . a difficult operation for the mirror-image is very easily distorted. Emotions, desires, affections, the nature of any individual, and anxiety are elements of disturbance and deformation. The mere fact of being interested in the oracle's reply makes conditions unfavourable for the diviner who is usually more lucid for others than for himself.

If the imagination of a soothsayer functions like that of a registering device then it is clear that divination can only satisfy the consultant's curiosity within narrow limits. If nothing vibrates in the person concerned then no message can be communicated to him. Insisting is of little use, because it provokes a reply that runs risks of not being genuine divination. Generally speaking whatever is announced spontaneously is more worthy of attention than revelations that are more or less extorted by the soothsayer.

The lucidity of the same diviner moreover varies according to the person who consults him. There are some people who hold up the functioning of the divinatory mechanism either because their vibrations neutralize the waves that the diviner must pick up, or for some other reason. In such a case the soothsayer is ill at ease and soon irritated, all of which finally makes him incapable of officiating to any purpose.

Conversely, the person consulting can bring a psychic atmosphere which is propitious to divination. The diviner then becomes the interpreter of telepathic messages which the addressee communicates to him like unopened letters or those whose significance is unintelligible. Thus the most sensational revelations are often made, like going through occult correspondence which has been left in abeyance. The revelations are produced when one least expects it and could not be conjured away in current divinatory practice any more than the prediction of the future.

Let us ask of divination only what it can give. A firm intention, a well-drawn-up plan can herald an act which is not yet accomplished; hence a conjecture that the event will or will not confirm, for in the last instance the execution can be hampered for a motive not explicit at the time of the prediction. Therefore it is wise to hold back on the future and only seek to divine the present in its unknown aspects and in what it is useful to elucidate.

The soothsayer who stretches out his receptive antennae can only tap what vibrates; he is not responsible for the absence of messages destined for the consultant. So his pride must not come into it if nothing appears in his field of vision.

Let him be careful above all not to insist on converting sceptics. No one is forced to believe that soothsayers can speak the truth. It is not the aim of divination to provide proof through experiment.

Be that as it may, divination turns towards real priesthood. To dazzle the person who consults him, is not the objective of the diviner who is possessed of the sacred fire; to be useful, to help one to move out of perplexity, to give good advice, these are the motives of this confessor who sometimes divines faults without their having been confessed to him.

CHAPTER 14

The Instruments of Divination

The interpretation of dreams seems to have been the oldest form of divination. The fact remains that the 'Keys to Dreams' are found in abundance among the bricks covered in cuneiform letters.

But the ordinary dream which is not our concern here, does not lend itself to the practice of divination unless the dreamer has the faculty of falling asleep at will, then of dreaming aloud for the benefit of listeners. The Pythanisses carried out this programme.

Without having recourse to sleep other people show a predisposition for dreaming in the state of wakefulness, using a simple and spell-like fixation of their imagination. In this way a great variety of 'mancies' were born (from μαντεια divination).

Each mancy draws its name from the instrument which lends to the diviner's imagination the material support which allows him to become fixed and apply himself, instead of losing his way in vagueness.

In this connection the every-day coffee ground has nothing grotesque about it, in as much as it is an instrument of divination. When scattered out on a plate the particles do indeed outline shapes and make up geometrical patterns that are extremely suggestive to a mind sensitive to the language of shapes.

Similar but predicted combinations are found in 'geomancy' an extremely old method of divination based on the interpretation of the sixteen figures made by dots taken separately or in pairs and superimposed four times.

The geomancers designate each of these figures by a name which directs them into their divinatory perplexity. Eight figures are positive (those of the first row); they were baptised:

Path, Conjunction, Major Fortune, Acquisition, Joy, Girl, White, Head.

By opposition they are related to the negative figures (second row):

People, Prison, Minor Fortune, Loss, Sadness, Boy, Red, Tail.

These are examples of some of the many titles of a classification in which the diviner must try to fit all that he is capable of conceiving. If he succeeds in this, the figures of geomancy will help him to sort out the chaos of his impressions and will fulfil the function of an instrument of divination used with skill.[69]

The Chinese instrument of divination also proceeds from odd and even elements, depicted not by dots but by strokes: ▬▬ ▬ ▬ . Superimposed in threes these elements engender the eight Trigrams of Fô-Hi, set out thus:

Sky	Vapours	Fire	Thunder
▤	▤	▤	▤

Wind	Water	Mountain	Earth
▤	▤	▤	▤

Two trigrams one on top of the other make up one of the 64 mutations commented upon by the *I Ching* (the Book of Changes), which is the classical treatise on learned divination in all the Far East.

If these numerical tables, these varied and complex associations of the single and the double, could suffice to stimulate and direct our imagination, then we would have nothing to do with even crude illustrations like those of the Tarot.

But we must make a decision; being less metaphysical than the Orientals; we are inclined to anthropomorphism and familiar pictures are more suitable for inspiring us than too subtle abstract combinations.

Marvellously adapted as it is to our mentality, the Tarot prepares us for divination in a methodical and sure way if we take the trouble to study it conscientiously and with all the perseverance required. A superficial knowledge of the symbolism of its 22 keys would not be sufficient, for the diviner must 'possess his instrument' if he wishes to distinguish himself in the art of divination. He

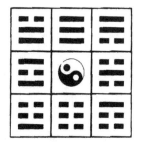

must work following the example of a musician who goes over and over the demanding exercises, hence the gymnastics of the imagination which we advise in the first part of this work. The arcanas become clear through comparisons; compared two at a time and four by four, in threes, fours and sevens, they finally reveal an inexhaustible eloquence. But by themselves they remain silent; while our imagination sleeps it understands nothing about pictures which can instruct it as soon as it awakens. The awakening is sometimes slow; so let us learn how to be laborious and patient.

Tarot of the Magicians

CHAPTER 15

Consulting the Tarot

When the instrument is known it becomes possible to make use of it. One is tempted to treat the Tarot like an ordinary game of cards and to spread out the cards as fortune-tellers do after shuffling them and having them cut by the person consulting. No rule stands, but from Stanislas de Guaita we have a method which Joséphin Péladan pointed out to him and which is distinguished both by its logic and its extreme simplicity; here is the principle of it.

When a question has been asked the answer is provided by four arcanas drawn in succession from the Tarot, as will be seen below.

The first arcana drawn is seen as affirmative; it pleads in favour of the cause and in a general manner indicates what is 'for'.

On the other hand, the second arcana is negative and represents what is 'against'.

The third arcana drawn depicts the judge who discusses the cause and determines the sentence. This sentence is pronounced by the arcana drawn last of all.

A fifth arcana completes the throwing of light upon the oracle which it synthesizes, for it depends upon the four arcanas drawn. Each of these bears the number which marks its rank in the series of the Tarot (the Fool, who is not numbered, counts for 22). When these numbers are picked out, it is enough to add them together to obtain, either directly or by theosophic reduction,[70] the number of the fifth arcana (22 indicates the Fool, 4 the Emperor, 12 The Hanged Man etc).

Now let us go into how it works in detail. Before anything else we should guard against frequent use of hasty consultations, reiterated at every turn, at the slightest whim and without any real need. Those people who once consulted the oracles did not come forward with empty hands. The rule is restraint, but the strictest requirement is that there should be no self-interest on the part of the diviner. The consultant therefore, will impose upon himself the sacrifice of a modest offering, but not entirely insignificant as far as he is concerned. A collecting box whose contents will go to the poor will make the divination less frivolous.

This preliminary ritual gives the consultant the right to a serious reply. It is equivalent to the conclusion of the classic pact of divination, a pact concluded under the auspices of good deeds.

But what does he want to know? It is of capital importance to pose the question when divination is to be made on a definite object, rather than to leap into the vague spheres of fortune telling. 'Tell me what is going to happen' is not an acceptable formula. The consultant must always relate his question as much as possible to the present. Does he wish to be guided towards a decision that is to be taken? Is he right or wrong to persevere with such a plan? Can he hope to succeed in what he has just undertaken? Should he fear a failure and take steps accordingly? Does such a person deserve his confidence?

The consultant is not obliged to explain himself exactly on what he asks and the diviner will not demand to be initiated more than is useful into the secrets of the consultation. The request can therefore be made in general terms, not revealing its precise object; however the diviner must know enough about it so as not to go astray in his interpretations. Therefore it is in the interest of the consultant to speak without reticence and make the diviner's task easier limiting his effort in divination. When the fixed question is agreed upon with the diviner he then shuffles the cards composed only of the 22 arcanas, and invites the consultant to tell him the first number which comes into his head equal to or below the number 22.

The number called intuitively by the consultant is used for cutting the pack, showing the number of cards which are to be taken out of the shuffled pack. The last one is put back: this is the affirmative arcana. The number which it bears in the order of the Tarot is noted; then all the cards are put back and shuffled a second time.

The consultant then says another number, which is indicative, by the same procedure, of the negative arcana whose number in turn is written down. Then the reassembled pack is shuffled for a third time, the consultant states a third number which reveals the reply of the oracle. Finally a fourth and last turn is made determining the statement.

The numbers of the drawn cards (which must not be confused with the numbers which occurred to the consultant) are added up. If the total equals, or is below 22 the synthesis is the Fool or the arcana to which the sum total corresponds in the numerical order of the Tarot. If the total is more than 22 then its two numbers added together indicate the synthesizing arcana (23 = 2 + 3 = 5) (57 = 5 + 7 = 12 etc).

The four cards drawn and their synthesis make up the silent reply of the Tarot. When set out before the consultant, it takes the form of a cross.

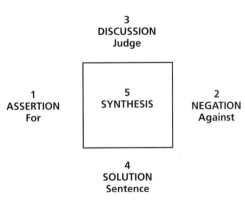

3
DISCUSSION
Judge

1
ASSERTION
For

5
SYNTHESIS

2
NEGATION
Against

4
SOLUTION
Sentence

Tarot of the Magicians

CHAPTER 16

Interpretation of the Oracle

Before speaking the diviner must try to resolve a sort of equation. He must try to fathom in what respect Negation is opposed to Affirmation, and to justify the Discussion which comes out of this opposition to provide the solution; then the Synthesis in his eyes must be reflected in the other elements of the reply. If he sees clearly into the whole, then he is enabled to speak rightly even if he remains diffuse in his interpretation. It can happen that he is not able to express a thought clearly around which he is turning in a multiplicity of images without finding the one which satisfies him. Sometimes the consultant benefits from this apparently digressing chaos by grasping wonderfully a language which is unintelligible to the diviner himself.

After a moment of silent reflection it is good to approach the interpretation through whatever strikes one or appears to be clearest.

'Affirmation' puts one on the track of what is favourable and points out what it is wise to do, the quality, the virtue, friend or protector on whom one can depend.

Conversely 'Negation' indicates what is hostile or unfavourable, what should be avoided or feared, the fault, enemy, danger, the pernicious temptation.

'Discussion' throws light on the decision to be made, on the kind of resolution one should adopt and the intervention which will be decisive.

'Solution' allows one to foresee a result taking into account the 'for' and the 'against' but especially the Synthesis.

This synthesis in fact relates to what is of prime importance and on which everything depends.

The replies from the Tarot are far from being always clear; there are some discouraging ones which resist every effort at sensible interpretation. These occasions need not discourage the reader, because the good answers can be distinguished by logic and by the reduction to the minimum of ambiguity inherent in the oracles.

The imprecision of the oracle is in fact opposed to categorical replies.

Divination is happy with the vagueness of indications which are just sufficient to enable the beneficiary to take advantage of them by adding his own to them.

Readings seldom give direct commands; suggestions are more common. Veiled advice, warnings to make one think, to put one on guard against avoidable errors. Readings seldom announce a fatal event. They indicate trends beforehand rather than give certain results, as if events are not quite definite before they happen.

There is no need to linger over an indecipherable reply; it is better to repeat the question by trying to put it more precisely, or by changing the viewpoint. In this case it means proceeding with a new consultation, the result of which might be more satisfactory.

The second reply often throws light on the first. It happens that the cards drawn are partly the same or they offer a striking likeness in their significance, as if the cards were not drawn out by chance. The practice of divination, moreover, leads one to doubt the fortuity of sometimes exceptionally intelligible discoveries in the cards.

The skill of the diviner develops with practice. By dint of struggling with symbolic enigmas, the imagination becomes more supple. It finally acquires lucidity in interpretation. In a general way this lucidity initiates one into the subtleties of symbolism allowing one to penetrate into the esotericism of works of art, of mythological poems and of religions.

CHAPTER 17

An Example of Interpretation

How should one advise a would-be diviner? This is the question we have asked of the Tarot, proceeding then as related above.

The cards drawn were 4, 18, 2, and 14. These numbers when added together give 38, so 3 + 8 = 11. The oracle is set out thus:

II
The Priestess

IV	**XI**	**XVIII**
The Emperor	**Strength**	**The Moon**

XIV
Temperance

Surprised by the Synthesis 11, let us try to orient ourselves. The woman who overcomes the lion seems to make the divination depend upon courage, moral energy, virtue. Must we attack our study of the Tarot with heroism by conquering a treasure similar to the legendary Golden Fleece?

While asking ourselves the question, let us glance at the arcanas which frame Strength.

Being 'for' the Emperor puts himself at the service of Strength to whom the Moon is detrimental, being against. The Priestess on the other hand intervenes to bring about Temperance. Without losing sight of the whole, let us now go into a detailed examination of the oracle.

The Emperor who is in conjunction with the Enchantress puts his rigorous positivism in opposition to the Moon. His fixity conglomerates and solidifies the fluidity of the Moon. Dominating whatever is interior and of innate need he makes success in divination depend upon special talents which the future diviner should possess, potentially. Right and natural inclinations are indispensable; but they must be cultivated with perseverance, hence the necessity of the sacred fire represented by the Emperor (the Alchemist's Sulphur). The necessary apprenticeship demands individual initiative (arcana 4) for knowledge of divination is not assimilated as borrowed learning is. The diviner is called upon to create ideas which are his own; what he has found himself will be more precious than others gifts. One thing he must gain: that is the power to create thoughts drawn from within himself. A schoolboy reciting a lesson he has learnt would be no more than a parrot playing at being a diviner. In order to unveil, one must discover, and to make discoveries, perspicacity in divinatory matters is necessary.

In short, in order to practise divination, it is good to be a born diviner, but the necessary and appropriate inclinations must be developed methodically and with will-power.

The opposition of the Moon confuses us, since the imagination to which this planet alludes is the divining agent we imagine what we divine. The Moon should therefore be 'for' and not against. Yet the Tarot is right, for the imagination is dangerous if it is not held in check and disciplined; left to itself it gives into whims and wanders as it pleases. To prove itself wise this wild element must be tamed like the lion of Strength, by a positive tamer, allowing only measured and firm concepts like the cubic stone, the Emperor's throne. We tend to imagine rightly as soon as our fantasy is reined. Whims and wrong suggestions form an obstacle in divination, hence that which is 'against'. To conquer this enemy the Emperor is indispensable, for he personifies the deductive and mathematical spirit.

The diviner who remains intellectually active and masters his own imagination, however exuberant it may be, is distinguishable from the visionary who is beyond exerting any control. Fickle, capricious and rebellious when performing steady tasks, the moon must be reduced to slavery by Strength for the benefit of the Emperor. Such is the evident meaning of arcanas 4, 11, and 18.

The two others confirm the lesson, for the intervention of 2 as judge, who formulates her statement through the voice of 14, completes the instruction given to the aspiring diviner. Urged as he is by a wild imagination, and at the same time held back by wise and realistic ponderings, he would run the risk of being made motionless if it were not for the help of the Priestess. The High Priestess's arbitration reconciles the flight of the imagination and the demands of calm and methodical reasoning. If he reasons as a philosopher, the poet who rhymes directs the Pegasus of divination in the way it pleases him. But whoever becomes a diviner cannot remain uninitiated: he becomes initiated into the mysteries by penetrating into the Temple of the Priestess.

He does not step over the threshold of this Temple without being convinced of the sacred nature of divination. We do not divine as we calculate or speculate in a worldly way. When the spirit is asking for enlightenment which the first one to come along can make no claim to, then he enters into prayer. The call is only answered if the diviner is worthy of the priestly function that he is carrying out. The practice of the art of divination develops a special religious feeling. The disciple of Isis is conscious of the fact that he knows nothing through himself and that he only succeeds in speaking with truth by becoming the pious interpreter of a very mysterious divinity.

As the holder of the secrets of destiny, this divinity keeps her confidences for the wise person who embodies the ideal of serenity as is shown by arcana 14. The gift of lucidity is only conferred upon the calm spirit who is neither stirred nor troubled by any over-exhilaration. In the presence of feelings, passions, fears and dramas of life the diviner needs the heart of a sympathetic doctor whose calmness remains intact. If the anxiety of the consultant took hold of him, how could he decipher correctly the language of the symbols? Desires which he shared too ardently would influence his interpretations which must only be inspired by a kindly neutrality. The difficulty of remaining clearly indifferent makes the divination more hazardous for oneself or for relatives, than for friends whose destiny is not linked to ours.

The indifference which becomes a virtue in divination is that which the angel in Temperance teaches. It is a detachment which rises above the human misery and overcomes contingencies; it is a way of seeing things in a broad and kindly way. He who understands never condemns; he bends over our moral wounds and tends them with affection. He does not lament over past error, but uses it as an example to teach us not to fall into the same error again. His mission is not to preach an abstract morality, but to give practical advice, adapted to make it possible to put it into practice. To demand the impractical by appealing to abstract morality would be a mistake from which tact must preserve the diviner. Useful advice is not that which in theory would be the best but the one which the interested party will follow to bring about just the relative good of which he is capable. This efficacious task is proportionate to the degree of evolution in each one of us.

Temperance at which the diviner must aim forbids him all artificial excitement for his imagination would not be properly impressed if stimulants or narcotics influenced him in a morbid way. Coffee is not to be recommended and even less the tyrannical use of tobacco; on the other hand ordinary wine could not do any harm provided that it were taken in moderation. One light drink after a frugal meal may even be advantageous in preparing one for the holy duty of divination which is helped by sensitivity in meditation. It could not be a question of Dionysiac ecstasy in spite of the saying 'In vino veritas', for Temperance is opposed to incipient drunkenness as it is to all intoxication however light.

In the case of a passing mental torpor, of fatigue or poor state of health, it is wise not to try anything, but to wait for a better opportunity. Let us never force our talent in divination even when tempted to do so. Let us not be stubborn as if nothing showed; the diviner who sees nothing, must make his decision quite serenely. He will see all the better for it when elements of vision really exist.

CHAPTER 18

The Reality of the Art of Divination

The reader has the right to wonder whether our example of interpretation takes its texts from arcanas *really* drawn from a pack which has been shuffled and cut according to the number which came to mind. These arcanas answer the question (posed) so well that one would swear that they had been deliberately chosen to suit the case.

This is not so; the Tarot has really spoken through itself and better than we could have done it if we chose the arcanas. This choice would have left us perplexed, and we have relied on divination which has not betrayed our confidence in it.

We were prejudiced against it when, being solely interested in deciphering symbols, our first Tarot was published in 1889.[71] We could not refuse giving satisfaction to friends who asked us to tell their fortune by showing them how it is possible to consult the Tarot.

The idea did not come to us of adding faith to the replies serving as examples, so we felt some pity for our first consultants when they assured us that the Tarot was speaking truthfully; their belief in cartomancy influenced their judgement. But what could we think of sceptics who expressed their amazement!

We had no choice but to state findings that were disconcerting, particularly because of the amount of repetition in them which was outside the laws of probability.

Moreover, the oracle showed a predilection for certain people by answering them with a clarity which it denied others. The way the question was framed counted for much in these differences. To a frivolous or vague question came usually an ironic or vague answer; to an indiscreet question no reply; to a serious and precise question an adequate answer.

It was becoming impossible to deny psychology to the divinatory Tarot; an enigmatic person was being revealed. Was it not a question of just the splitting in two of our own personality? Was our super-consciousness becoming evident in combination with that of the consultant? The field must remain open to hypotheses.

In what concerns us personally, the objective observation of facts has converted us to divination. Putting aside all near or distant sorcery, we recognize in it the normal effect made by our faculties of imagination going into action. To divine is to imagine rightly. The whole secret of the art of divination consists in the education of the imagination which must be disciplined with a view to its being put to some rational work.

Let us restore this art and cultivate it with discretion, instead of leaving it to the powers of simple people or to the cunning of those who exploit human weakness.

Moreover there are limits to the exploitation of credulity, for everything has its limits, even human stupidity. If our professional clairvoyants get themselves a clientele which they keep, then it is because they give them satisfaction. Therefore they have to give proof of a certain lucidity in spite of the unfavourable conditions in which their work takes place. Let us remove all commercialism from an art which being on a par with other art and with even better reason than them should be considered as sacred. We do not do anything really well except what we accomplish in a religious spirit, conscientiously and activated by the sincere wish to render service. The diviner has a priestly function which is the venerable ancestor of all the others. Let us have the feeling of this when we undertake to make the Tarot speak.

Let us not treat divination as if it were a childish intellectual game nor as a pleasing and inconsequential art, for divinatory talent can lead us very far. How far will the divining thinker go in the philosophical sphere? Freeing himself from a too narrow rationalism, he will not allow Voltaire to bar his way into the past. Going back through the centuries he will understand the ancient wise men and will bring new life into their ideas.

One must divine in order to understand and acquire the clairvoyance of which the narrow rationalist in his blindness, deprives himself. This rationalist runs the risk of assuming the heavy gait of a learned beast.

CHAPTER 19

Conclusion

After paying homage at the beginning of the book to the memory of Stanislas de Guaita and his source of inspiration, we cannot close without expressing our gratitude to Eliphas Lévi who first showed us the importance of the Tarot. In his most important work this author comments upon the twenty-two arcanas from the point of view of traditions in magic. The two volumes concerned with *Dogme* and the *Rituel de la Haute Magie* in this respect are full of original surveys and they are distinguished on account of their eloquent and spirited style.

We would reproach ourselves if we did not now quote the passages which relate directly to our subject. Here they are in the order that we find them in the 5th edition (1910) of *Dogme*:

> What a strange phenomenen! Among the holy books of the Christians exist two works which the infallible church makes no claim at understanding and never tries to explain: the prophecy of Ezekiel and the Apocalypse, two Kabbalistic key works, kept no doubt in heaven for the commentaries of the three wise men; books closed with seven seals against the faithful believers, and perfectly clear for the unbeliever who is initiated into the occult Sciences.

> Another book still exists; but that one, although it is in some way popular and can be found anywhere, is the most occult and the least known of all because it contains the key to all the others; it is generally on show without being known by the public; one does not think of finding it where it is, and if one suspected its existence one would be for ever wasting time in looking for it in a place where it is not to be found. This book, older perhaps than that of Enoch, has never been translated and is written

completely in primitive characters and on separate pages like the tablets of the Ancients. Without it having been noticed a distinguished scholar has revealed not exactly its secret, but its antiquity and its unusual state of preservation; another scholar, with a fanciful rather than a judicious approach, spent thirty years studying this book and has only guessed at its vital importance. It is in fact a monumental and remarkable work, simple and strong like the architecture of the pyramids, and therefore lasting like them; it is a book which sums up all kinds of knowledge and the infinite combinations of these can solve all problems; a book which speaks by making us think, it inspires and regulates all possible concepts; the masterpiece perhaps of the human spirit and surely one of the finest things that antiquity has left to us; a universal key work whose name has been understood and explained only by the enlightened scholar Guillaume Postel; there is but one text, whose first letters alone transported the religious spirit of Saint Martin into ecstasy, and would have given back the sublime and unfortunate Swedenborg his reason. We shall speak of this book further on and its rigorous and mathematical explanation will be the complement and crown of our thorough work. (*Dogme*, page 71.)

The key to all allegories in magic is found in the pages which we have pointed out, and which we believe to be the work of Hermes. Around this book which may be called the keystone to every building in occult science, gather innumerable legends which are either the partial translation of it or else the commentary which is continually renewed in a thousand different forms. (Page 89.)

The secret of ancient initiaton was not unknown to Homer who traces its plan and its principle diagrams with minute precision on Achilles' shield. (Page 92.)

The Bible, with all the allegories that it contains, expresses only in an incomplete and veiled manner the religious knowledge of the Hebrew people. The book that we spoke of and whose hieratic characters we shall explain, this book which Guillaume Postel calls the Genesis of Enoch, certainly existed before Moses and the prophets. Their dogma which is basically identical to that of the ancient Egyptians, also has its esotericism and its veils. (Page 97.)

We must however go on as far as chapter 10, dealing with the Kabbala, to find actual mention of the Tarot. Reticence can be seen again on page 236 where it is said:

All religions have preserved the memory of an early book written in diagrams by the wise men of the earliest ages, and whose symbols, later popularized and simplified, provided the scripture with its letters, the Word with its characters and the occult philosophy with its mysterious signs and pantacles.

The book, attributed to ENOCH, the seventh master of the world after Adam by the Hebrew people; to Hermes Trismegist by the Egyptians; to Cadmus, the mysterious founder of the Holy City, by the Greeks, this book was the symbolic résumé of the early tradition since known as Kabbal or Cabbal, from a Hebrew word which is the equivalent of tradition.

But on page 243 the word is released:

Now we have to speak of the Tarots from the Kabbalistic point of view. We have already pointed out the occult source of their name. This hieroglyphic book is made up of a Kabbalistic alphabet and of a wheel or circle of four decades, specified by four symbolic and typical figures each one possessing as its spoke a ladder of four progressive figures representing humanity; man, woman, young man, and child; master, mistress, warrior and servant.

The 22 figures of the alphabet represent first of all the thirteen dogmas, then the 9 beliefs authorized by the Hebrew religion, a strong religion based on highest reason.

Here is the religious and Kabbalistic key to the Tarot expressed in technical verse like that of the ancient legislators.

1. א All announces an active intelligent cause.

2. ב The number serves as proof to the living unit.

3. ג Nothing can limit he who holds all.

4. ד Alone, before all principles, he is present everywhere.

5. ה He is the only master, he alone is to be adored.

6. ו He reveals his true dogma to the pure in heart.

7. ז But one single leader is needed for works of faith.

8. ח That is why we have but one altar, but one law.

9. ט And never will the Eternal change its foundation.

10. י He rules over each phase of the heavens and our days.

11. כ Rich in pity and powerful to punish.

12. ל He promises his people a king in the future.

13. מ The Tomb is the way to the new earth, death alone has an end. Life is immortal. Such are the pure dogmas, unchanging, holy. Let us now complete the reverend numbers.

14. נ The good angel is he who calms and tempers.

15. ס The bad angel is the spirit of pride and anger.

16. ע God commands the thunder and rules over fire.

17. פ Vesper and her dew obey God.

18. צ He places the Moon as sentry at our towers.

19. ק His Sun is the source from which all is renewed.

20. ר His breath puts life into the dust of the tombs.

0 or 21. ש Where mortals unhindered descend in flocks.

21 or 22. ת His crown has covered the propitiatory. And on the cherubims his glory hovers.

With the help of this explanation, purely dogmatic, one can already understand the figures of the Kabbalistic alphabet of the Tarot. Thus the figure No.1 called the Magician, represents the active principle in the unity of divine and human self construction. No. 2 commonly known as the Priestess depicts the dogmatic unity based upon numbers; it is the Kabbal or gnosis personified. No. 3 represents divine spirituality in the guise of a winged woman holding in one hand the apocalyptic eagle and in the other the world suspended at the end of her sceptre. The other figures are just as clear and easily explained as the first ones.

Eliphas Lévi explains again in the same chapter how, according to him, the ancient priests of Israel 'read the replies of Providence in the oracles of the Tarot which amongst the Hebrew people was called Seraph or Seraphim, as the first Kabbalistic scholar perceived. This was Gaffarel, one of the titled Magicians of Cardinal Richelieu'. Other details and complete documents on the wonderful book of the Tarot are announced by the author who, at the end of *Rituel* proposes to prove that the Tarot 'is the original book, the key to all prophecies and dogmas; in short the book which inspires all inspired books, which neither Court de Gebelin in his knowledge nor Alleitte or Eteilla with their remarkable intuition have perceived. . .'

Then mention is made of two ways of interpreting the Kabbalistic alphabets from which the Rabbis 'form two sciences called Gematria and the temurah and by inventing the notorious art which basically is none other than the complete knowledge of the signs of the Tarot and their complex and diverse application to divination of all secrets either of philosophy, of nature or even of the future'.

In what concerns divination Eliphas writes quite fully for he devotes to this subject the 21st chapter of *Dogme*. Let us be content to note the following passages:

> Taking the popular meaning of the word, to divine[72] means to conjecture on what one does not know; but the true sense of the word is inexplicable because of its being sublime. To divine (divinarir) is to practice divinity. The word divinus in Latin means more and something else besides the word 'divus' whose meaning is equivalent to Man-God.

> To be a diviner taking the full sense of the word, therefore means to be divine, and something even more mysterious. (*Dogme* pp. 371 & 372.)

> The Tarot, this marvellous book, the inspirer of all the sacred books of the ancient nations, is because of the provision of comparisons in its figures and numbers, the most perfect instrument of divination that can be used with complete confidence. Indeed the oracles of this book are always rigorously true, at least in one sense, and even when it predicts nothing, it always reveals hidden things and gives the consultants the most sound advice. (*Dogme* page 378.)

'Rituel', in chapter 21, dealing with the science of prophets, talks about the different ways of divining. We read this on page 344:

> Of all the oracles the Tarot is the most surprising in its replies, because all possible combinations of the universal key of the Kabbal give as solutions, oracles of knowledge and truth. The Tarot was the only book of the ancient wise men, it is the earliest Bible. . .

But it is when dealing with the book of Hermes in the last chapter of *Rituel* that Eliphas gives the most copious details concerning the Tarot. We find there on pages 368 onward the description of the 22 arcanas whose meaning is summed up as follows:

1. א Being, spirit, man or god; the comprehensible spirit, unity mother of numbers, first substance.

2. ב The house of god and of man, sanctuary, law, gnosis, Kabbal, occult church, the binary, woman, mother.

3. ג The word, ternary, fullness, fertility, nature, generation in the three worlds.

4. ד The gate or government among Eastern people, initiation, power, the tetragram, the quartet, the cubic stone or its base.

5. ה Indication, demonstration, teaching, law, symbolism, philosophy, religion.

6. ו Linking, crochet, phallus, tangle, union, embrace, struggle, antagonism, combination, balance.

7. ז Arm, blade, the flashing sword of the cherub, sacred septenary, triumph, royalty, priesthood.

8. ח Balance scales, attraction and repulsion, life, fear, promise and threat.

9. ט Goodness, horror of evil, morality, wisdom.

10. י Principle, manifestation, praise, manly honour, phallus, male fertility, paternal sceptre.

11. כ The hand in the act of taking and holding.

12. ל Example, teaching, public lesson.

13. מ The sky of Jupiter and Mars, domination and force, rebirth, creation and destruction.

14. נ The sky of the Sun, temperatures, seasons, movement, changes in a life for ever new and always the same.

15. ס The sky of Mercury, occult science, magic, commerce, eloquence, mystery, moral strength.

16. ע The sky of the Moon, alterations, subversions, changes, weakness.

17. פ The sky of the soul, thoughts overflowing, the moral influence of the idea over forms, immortality.

18. צ The elements, the visible world, the Moon reflected, material forms. Symbolism.

19. ק Compounds, the head, summit, prince of the sky.

20. ר Vegetative life, the life giving force of the earth, eternal life.

21. ש Sensitive elements, flesh, transitory life.

22. ת Microcosm, the resume of all in all.

On page 378 it is said of the Tarot:

It is a real philosophic machine which prevents the mind from wandering, yet leaving it with its initiative and freedom, it is mathematics as applied to the absolute, the union of positive with the ideal, a lottery of thoughts all rigorously exact as are the numbers. In short this contains perhaps all that the human mind has ever conceived both in simplicity and greatness.

The manner of reading the hieroglyphics of the Tarot is by arranging them either in a square or a triangle placing the even numbers in opposition and reconciling them with the uneven numbers. Four signs always express the absolute in any order and they are expressed by a fifth one. Thus the solution of all questions of magic is that of the pentagram, and all antimonies are explained by a harmonious unity.

Arranged like this, the Tarot is a true oracle and it answers all possible questions with more precision and infallibility than the Android of Albert the Great: in this way a prisoner deprived of books, but having just the Tarot that he knew how to use, could have acquired a universal knowledge in a few years. He would also speak about everything with unequalled learning and inexhaustible eloquence. This wheel in fact, is the true key to the art of oratory and the great art of Raymond Lulle; it is the secret of the changing of darkness into light; it is the first and the most important of all the stages of the Great Work.

We shall not undertake to point out what is debatable in the appreciations of Eliphas Lévi, whose lyricism knows no scientific restraint. The reader will wish to do this where necessary.

If we formulate a criticism it will not attack the untempered enthusiasm of the original thinker to whom we remain the grateful debtors. The master appears to be respectable even in his effusions, but those who call themselves his disciples have not the right to expect indulgence from us.

Those adepts of the so-called occult science shock us immediately by the scorn with which they regard a pure simple science because of its modesty which prevents it from claiming to decipher all enigmas. Having an answer to everything, in our eyes, this proves not initiation, but a stupid and pretentious ignorance showing lack of initiation. Did this occultist bow before the Priestess for whom nothing occult exists any more? These impatient novices, assimilating once and for all a synthesis, the key to universal knowledge, neglect the effort of slow methodical study, and preach dogmatically and with unshakable confidence in the infallibility of their intuitive mental penetration. Alas they are but victims of an unbridled imagination which they are careful not to discipline; so this imagination makes them see as true every weird fantasy which suits their school of thought. Lured by their faith in doctrines which have the gift of winning them, they swear in the name of Masters whose profound thought they have not understood and they erect in Perez their occultist church.

The traditional masters of the science of the occult enjoy such a prestige that no one dares to attack their dogma. Believed in by what they say, they are not understood because of having been 'killed' by the disciples who claim to succeed them. It is not a question of committing a murder even on a ritualistic effigy, but of killing an accepted doctrine in order to make it live again, entirely renewed. Every true master aspires to be 'killed' in this way for the benefit of a science which can only remain living by self renewal. Stagnation means death. Whatever is repeated without being profoundly understood to the point of being dissociated, is never put back into a state of revival. Error is to be found in whatever is human; if we do not correct what we receive, then the false very rapidly supplants the truth.

So it is with books that succeed each other and are copied, and each time with their fantasies embroidered still further. These assertions could have been risked once, but now being better informed we are obliged to put them right in the light of our positive knowledge.

In order to renew Occultism let us not be afraid of 'killing' the old masters. We will be paying service to Fabre d'Olivet by purifying his metaphysics of all the false 'science' which distorts it. The same understanding and affectionate devotion will allow us to take permanent possession of many another precious heritage which we must accept only without liability to doubts beyond the assets handed down to us. In drafting this present work, the fruit of nearly forty years research and meditation, what is our highest ambition, if it is not to be justly 'killed' in turn? Whoever shows us where we have been wrong and tells us what we omitted to explain, he will be our true disciple. What he confirms to us after reviewing everything severely to us will be worth the lasting monument of glory for which we are grateful in advance.

We dream also of contributing to the revival of an occultism which knows how to divine methodically by disciplining the imagination. It would be fitting to make a real Book of Old Wisdom of it, teaching the wisdom of the Ancients, for the essential source of this wisdom was divination.

Let us learn how to divine! If we were incapable of it we would for ever have to submit to the sectarian tyranny of weak pseudo-rationalism. In the interest of human progress the time has come to unite Imagination and Reason. The female and male must support each other in order to give the great redeeming light to the world. One last word: We have only been reasoning since a relatively recent date although this is difficult to determine. Before the reign of logic we were under the rule of the imagination, the first born in the sphere of our intellectual faculties. Being passive, impressionable and completely credulous primitive man accepts the ideas which come to him spontaneously. His mentality can be observed in uncivilized countries and is found also in the 'subjects' who talk in their sleep, just as mediums would when absorbed in the practice of passive receptivity. Would not a state similar to that of the medium characterize man emerging from a purely instinctive animality?

What is certain is that by claiming only to take reasoning into account, we are reducing our spirit's field of action. There is some obscurantism in the philosophy of the rationalists who do not dare to imagine. These are the shy navigators who in the ignorance of the laws of navigation are terrified by the Ocean. Shall we stay on the ground when the future of our minds is on the water?

Let us brave the treacherous element, but let us learn to navigate. Sailors can guide themselves on the sea and come back to port after perilous crossings. It is the same with the diviner, the explorer of the unknown. Let us instruct ourselves in the art of divination, which when taken seriously, will be linked with the methodical work of reason.

Let us learn from the Tarot. This book above all books is the ideal Bible for the diviner. The ordered collection of its symbols instructs us in forgotten ideas, the indispensable heritage to be held in the interest of human progress. Let us continue to reason, but let us learn how to discipline our faculty of imagination in order to walk intellectually on the two legs that are given to us to make our way towards the truth.

If you stop reading then meditate! Turn inwards, following the precept of the Wise man who urges you to search for the Stone hidden in the inmost depths of self.

SOME INDICATIONS ON THE SYMBOLISM OF THE PANTACLES WHICH ACCOMPANY THE TEXT OF THE PRESENT WORK

THE PANTACLES

A diagram whatever it is, is significant, but it only becomes a pantacle provided that it puts the mind on the path of thoughts which tend to thrust it into an incipient intellectual ecstasy.

At the sign of a pantacle we ought to enter meditation and through ourselves find the all (pan), the world of thoughts to which it is related. In the state of nature man is open to the suggestion of forms and the ideograms become quite naturally his form of writing: he can read and write without going to school. The combination of lines which used to instruct our distant ancestors unfortunately now mean nothing to the modern scholar who only knows his ABC to which the formation of words is due. Words alone are admitted to hold sway, to the exclusion of symbols which are considered as being obscure and nebulous.

As our practical education makes us deaf to everything which does not strike our eardrums, we need some preparation for understanding pantacles. The reader who has followed us up to now surely guesses at the sense of those figures which we have not had the opportunity of commenting upon. We think however, that we owe him a quick glance over the symbolism which we attribute to them, hence the appendix offered here to those who wish to invigorate the mysterious realm of speaking pictures.

Circle   Hexagram   Swastika

The Illustrators' tarot is placed under the protection of a wheel and the six points of two triangles joined by a bent cross called the swastika, extended beyond the rim of this circle.

This cross is related to the cosmic movement, revealed to prehistoric observers in the giration of the stars around the pole. Seeing the sky turn, they set it up as the universal motor the source of all life; but as heat accompanies life they had the ideal of a life-giving fire which was sent out by the turning cross, marked out on the sky by the four particularly brilliant stars:

Aldebaran — Bulls Eye — Spring
Regulus — Lions Heart — Summer
Antans — Scorpions Heart — Autumn
Fomalhaut — Southern Fishes Head — Winter

This quartet of stars gives the cross its earliest meaning which justifies the attachment of the Swastika, a religious emblem among the most ancient peoples of Europe, Asia and America. It was brought to light by archaeologists.

This sacred sign until now has never been found made into one stroke with the double triangle of the seal of Solomon 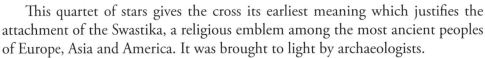. At the time of the founding of the revue *Le Symbolisme* we allowed ourselves in 1912, an anachronism in the mar-

riage of two symbols, one of high antiquity and the other only going back to Judaism and the Kabbal. Our intention was to bring the binary of the triangles Spirit-Fire △ and Soul-Water ▽ into unity. The result of their unifying combination is universal life, a life eternal which holds the existing being.

The circle which is added to form the wheel, ROTA or TARO, was not indispensable. It is justified however, as being a symbol of the circular ocean like river which bears the forms Python of the Soothsayers, the orb of the astral light from which the diviners draw their illumination.

The little which has just been shown makes the *Clef du Grand Arcane* less abstruse a work on which Eliphas is too sparing in his commentaries. Keeping well behind Guillaume Postel he leaves us perplexed when faced with the beautiful pantacle which we have borrowed from *La Clef des Grande Mystères* (page 316).

S	A	T	O	R
A	R	E	P	O
T	E	N	E	T
O	P	E	R	A
R	O	T	A	S

We give up trying to decipher the enigma of the central square in which we read:

The set of words perhaps hides an unfathomable Kabbalistic depth, but we prefer to confine ourselves to whatever tortures our brain less. So let us stop at relatively modest pictures of the fertile union of Father God and Mother Nature

Tarot of the Magicians

which takes place 'in aeternam' on the cosmic turning wheel kept in rotation by the four animals of Ezekiel.

These animals which are attributed to the Evangelist correspond in Hindu symbolism to the four Vedas. The Eagle whose eyes penetrate all things, confers the knowledge from which nothing escapes. The Bull links the animal to the supreme life giving force just as the Lion makes it participate in the limitless power of the Universe. As for the Angel who holds open the book from which the Initiated read, he is the Instructor from whom the serpent Amanta unwinds itself. This serpent holds the beautiful tempting apple which we bite into when we wish to raise ourselves above instinctive animality where we are incapable of distinguishing good and evil. Our power to discern makes us like gods, sentient and responsible.

Without formulating the principle of the conservation of energy with modern precision, the Ancients understood it intuitively when identifying 'movement' and 'life'; they realized that nothing stops or dies in the All, the eternal round which they represented by the tail biting serpent known as Ouroboros. In Hermetism a simple circle has taken the same significance, as the ideogram of Alum O proves the salt of Salts or Substance of Substances. It is not just a vacuum but a space full of life though dark and chaotic in its nature.

However, this is not chaos itself whose hieroglyph would be a black disc ● represented not by a properly so-called Serpent, but by a 'crocodile' or a 'dragon', hence the four-legged Ouroboros of the Greek manuscripts, quoted by Berthelst in his *Origines de 1'Alchimie*.

The four limbs correspond to the Elements like the quadruple horn which crowns the reptile. His legs are green as well as his belly and the part of his body which comes into contact with materiality. Now this colour is 'saline' compared with the 'mercurial' yellow and the 'sulphurous' red of its middle part and the back of the monster. Normally internal, sulphur ⚶ has become exteriorized to be put at the disposal of the Alchemist who sets the Fire of Nature to work, drawn from the first matter as symbolized by the Ouroboros.

This Old Serpent in which the primordial living substance eddies impulsively is the support of the world to which it supplies both the materials for its construction and the constructive energy from which the Co-ordinating Intelligence draws benefit. This Intelligence is two fold in Mind-Reason ⊙ and Soul-Imagination ☾, and they combine their action to clean off the Tartar ♁, as substance which appears in the cycle of mutations provoked by Hermetic Art. This is how the signs traced in the cosmic globe are explained. This globe is rightly

dominated by the cross outlined by four sceptres, allowing it to command the Elements to realize the ideal; Order out of Chaos.

The crocodile receives a human head and winds itself around the terrestrial globe which bears the Immaculate Virgin. We give a sketch of this copying the Spanish Madonna kept in Paris in the sacristy of the church of St Thomas d'Aquinas. From the esoteric point of view here it is a question of the demon of selfishness which sublime womanhood must conquer.

Our monogram of the planets is related to the Devil who exploits our baser instincts which are however indispensable to the functioning of the world which has fallen from its state of pure spirituality. The amalgam of Sun ☉, the Moon ☽, and Mercury ☿ surmount the cross made by Jupiter ♃ and Saturn ♄, while Mars ♂ is hooked on the right with a goad at the tail. Horns and claw-like hooks finally give the whole thing a threatening aspect, justified seeing that the seven cardinal sins are its subject. The Soul is called to triumph over them, according to the promise made to Eve whose posterity must finally trample on the head of the enemy creature.

The adversary (Satan in Hebrew) who hinders the divine work has been represented in most extraordinary forms. A Tarot of the *Cabinet des estampes* (Kh 34d) has made an Argus of him, having eyes scattered haphazardly over various parts of his body, in addition to those in his faces on the belly and on the knees. Nothing escapes the devil who sees all, but whose hands are rudimentary paws incapable of holding anything. His feet are not made for walking either, for they have just shoots at the end. As for the bats wings, their decoration reminds us of the eyes on the peacock's tail; the horns are like those of a deer, but they grow upward like the winged bat of Mercury. What does all this allude to? The fluid of the magnetizer, the agent of the hypnotic lucidity?

HERMETISM

The winged dragon is no longer the simple amphibian delighting in the mire of the geological period preceding the dry era. This flying reptile spits out fire in such a way that he appears to us like the synthesis of the four Elements that find in him an initial organic co-ordination. Let us not be surprised to find this monster weighing heavily upon the winged globe of the ethereal substance from which the initial Matter of the Great Work is drawn, this strange substance being at the same time single, double, triple and quadruple. This is indicated by the figures inscribed in the flying circle which highlight the importance of the fundamental quartet of the Hermetic ideogram forms: ○ ✝ △ □

The pantacle which we are analysing is extremely old, very likely dating from before the time of wood engraving, although it has been preserved in the treatise of *L'Azoth, ou le moyen de faire l'or caché des Philosophes* which was printed in 1659, following *Les Douze Clefs de la Philosophie traictant de la vraye médicine métallique*. Basile Valentin who is the author of this work, scarcely comments upon the engravings which the editor seems to have added by borrowing them from old manuscripts on alchemy. Any interpretation moreover, was superfluous for the adepts of Hermetic Philosophy. They knew the REBIS, the double thing depicted, in the form of an androgyne, with two heads that stands aloft of the defeated dragon. This is male and female Humanity entrusted with the accomplishment of the Great Work of putting the planets in order in the centre of the egg of the World. Being called to sort out the chaos on earth by following the programme of creation in the moral sphere, the bisexual Artist controls his work with the set-square and the compass in order to bring about the perfect cube of the Philosopher's Stone. The septenary of the planets whose signs surround him, guides the master who is attacking the coarse and heavy weight of Saturn-Lead in order to lighten the depreciated metal which, by washing and sublimations is raised gradually to the dignity of Jupiter-Bronze ♃, a stage in the path towards Humidity leading to the Work in white of the Moon-Silver ⊌ through the intermediary of Mercury-Quicksilver, an indispensable agent in all transmutations. Soft metals, lead and bronze are placed on the left of the personification of REBIS whereas the hard metals, Venus-Bronze ♀ and Mars-Iron ♂ take their place on the right where they signify the path to dryness of which Sun-Gold is the aim ☉ the crowning glory of the Hermetic art.

The planets differ from the metals because of their heavenly nature. Being outside the living whom they influence, they act by affecting the septenary of metals in the microcosm whose traditional homes place Reason-Gold ☉, Imagination-Silver ☾ and Discernment-Mercury ☿ on the right, on the left and on the top of the head. Propulsion-Iron ♂ and Sensitivity-Bronze (which determine reaction) ♀ reside in the Sun and the right side, whereas organic Tonality-Bronze ♃ and stabilizing Embodiment-Lead ♄ are relegated to the left.

Basile Valentin gives us a popular copy of a more complicated arcana on which he comments too briefly to enable us to decipher it. Eliphas Lévi reproduces it on page 408 of his *Histoire de la Magie* without deigning to offer a single line on what he calls the 'Grand Arcane Hermetique'. Let us try to spare ourselves the same reproach.

A frame forming a true square, the sign of what is perfect in the material order of things, holds up in the centre of its base the point of a large equilateral triangle. A vast circle divides this into three small triangles in which the words ANIMA, SPIRITUS, CORPUS are inscribed, accompanied by the image of the Sun, the Moon and a cube. Above the Sun burns a brasier containing a salamander (difficult to see and often omitted by the copyists). The Moon and the word

Spiritus, on the other hand attract the Dove of the Holy Ghost. These are the emblems of fire △ and of air ⏃, Sulphur 🜍 and Mercury ☿, each maintaining the combustion of the other. The opposite angles must logically give hospitality to the Earth and Water. It is indeed the case, for the fiery side shows us a mountain, the realm of a sun king sitting on a lion by way of a throne, while at his feet crawls an animal (not very clear), emerging from the bowels of the earth to spit out flames. The aquatic figure makes us admire Diana, seated on the back of a sea monster which she is guiding across the waves. The four elements are thus set out in places between a masculine right (Jachin) and a feminine left (Boaz) and similarly between a low bodily part and a high spiritual part.

The circle which lets only the three corners of the great triangle overlap it, is divided into seven equal parts by a star of which every point bears a number and the sign of a planet. The middle point at the bottom is black, so the number 1, the sign of Saturn ♄, and the perfect square of salt □ stand out as being white. The other six points are white; the second corresponds to Jupiter ♃, the third to Mars ♂ and to Sulphur 🜍, the fourth to the Sun ☉, the fifth to Venus ♀, the sixth to Mercury ☿ in so far as it is a planet metal and ternary principle of the Tri-unity 🜍 🜔 and ☿; in the last place comes the Moon ☾.

Between the points of the star, seven medallions relate to the operations of the Great Work. Saturn's cross is the insignium of the colour black which one must obtain at the very beginning of the enterprise if this is to give any hope of success. Between ♃ and ♂ a merciless battle takes place between two birds, the black devouring the white, hence the resulting grey which approaches whiteness. But the two birds, one white and the other red intervene between ♂ and ☉, fighting desperately against the satiate conqueror which they 'exterminate spiritually' according to Basile Valentin, 'so that all colours may appear'. The triumph grants a crown to the avengers, which they hold aloft in the sky, between ☉ and ♀. Then they rest on a tree, no doubt an olive tree between ♀ and ☿ as if the Work now had only to bring itself to fruition. Between ☿ and ☾ the tree is in flower and shelters the unicorn resting peacefully in the grass, while preparing the path for the king. The cycle is completed by a child who comes to life and will reign alone red and very pure.

The circle which holds the medallions bears these words:

VISITA   INTERIORA   TERRAE   RECTIFICANDO
INVENIES   OCCULTUM   LAPIDEM

The first letters of which spell Vitriol, the mysterious septenary, envisaged as revealing the secret of the Great Work. Let us add that the Stone is within us, in the centre of our personality. He who can descend onto himself by reforming (rectificando = straightening) discovers the supreme treasure of human wisdom. He learns to know Man whose face is seen as in a skylight in the centre of the start of the seven transformations. He is the Great Hermes whom the adept must make live within himself, as the true Master Builder ought to bring back to life within himself the architect Hiram. This is like the Christian who emerging from the waters of baptism once aspired to make the Spirit of Christ be reborn in him. We cannot doubt that this man is Mercury, since the wings of the god surmount the circle beyond which the right hand holds out the torch which enlightens spirits, while the left holds the seeds of life. At this point the reader will wish to refer to arcana 15 and compare the devil of the Tarot with the alchemic personification of the mercurial fluid, the universal agent of intellectual stimulation and renewal of life.

The mystery of the Philosopher's Stone can be summed up graphically in a square enclosing the ternary Sulphur ⚏, Salt ⊖ and Mercury ☿, with a cross which reminds us of Antimony ♁, but also the hieroglyph of a winged woman, victorious over all that is inferior. Let us assure the victory of the soul in our personality, let us no longer be slaves of anything and we shall possess wealth besides which material possessions have no value at all.

The Sulphur which burns in them maintains the life of individuals who would live indefinitely if their reserve of sulphur did not tend to run out. It is renewed thanks to alternating periods of rest and activity which nature imposes upon us, for we possess within ourselves a Phoenix which is continually reborn from its ashes; otherwise all fatigue would crush us permanently. Now we are reborn in a dynamic way after each of those partial deaths which we call sleep. If the organism did not wear itself out, nothing would indue us to part with it, but it deteriorates irremediably and we have to learn to come to terms with destiny. We will live better, if, unmindful of the narrowness of our own self we strive to live a more impersonal life. In the place of the impure sulphurs which burn within us, let us substitute little by little a pure 'philosophical sulphur'. In realizing this ideal the individual becomes stabilized, for a constant heat makes him rise above all that is mean, low or 'infernal' in the Latin sense of the word. He no longer lives as an egoist acquiring a vitality which is not his own, but as the legitimate owner of universal life. To find this life and to assimilate it, is the supreme ambition of the truly wise.

In the cube whose three visible surfaces bear the signs of Salt ⊖, Sulphur ⚏ and Mercury ☿ Hermetism sees the mysterious Stone, the creator of harmony through its rectangular shape. Its angles have taken from the planets the virtues which are opposed to the cardinal sins. Jupiter ♃ inspires a generous pride, which Saturn ♄, positive and careful, prevents from degenerating into prodigality. The Sun ☉ gives light economically having regard to Venus ♀ who judges by the heart and shows enthusiasm for serious motives, although reason does not always manage to discern them. Lastly the Moon ☾, the inspirer of dreams tempers Mars ♂ who is impatient to act, or else awakens him when he forgets himself in inaction. The Planets

each have their role; if not one of them fails in its role then everything functions harmoniously for the general welfare: peace and happiness are achieved.

It remains to mention the winged globe of the Egyptians which, in the eyes of the Hermetists represents their Matter in the state of sublimation. The two serpents are those of the Caduceus; they manifest the opposing polarizations of the great Mercurial agent.

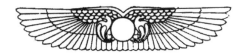

ROSICRUCIANISM

When seen in its entirety, the emblem of the Pelican which adorns the Rosy Cross of the Freemasons, reminds us of the ideogram of the accomplishment of the Great Work ☿, and for the soul implies the completion of its sublimating purifications. It is white and its self denial is complete like the bird who feeds her young on her own blood.

The Rose joined to the Cross gives life to the dead wood of generally accepted ideas by giving them the life of comprehension and discernment. The Rosicrucian is not a faithful follower, blindly subject to the tradition of dogma; he is an independent searcher instructed in the mysteries of the religion through his studies and reflections. In his way he interprets the sacred symbols and proposes various formulae to apply to the initials I.N.R.I. such as Igne Natura Renovatur Integra. Through Fire integral (uncorrupted) Nature is renewed. Restoring fire here is the fire which is shared out among all beings. They also say: Ignem Natura Regenerando Integret. Nature purifies fire by renewing it. This time the Fire is represented as prone to corruption if it is not perpetually reborn like the Phoenix.

More mysteriously it has been suggested: Igne Natrum Roris Invenitur. Through fire the Nitre of the Dew is found. The celestial water which is condensed in the night contains an active salt which the fire of the Philosophers take into their possession. Of what importance is it to him to tap energies unless it be the diffuse energy which, when condensed by the Adept, will allow him to accomplish marvels?

The students of Hebrew finally thought of Iam, Nun, Ronad, Inbashah. Water, Fire, Air, Earth, or more exactly Sea, Lamp, Breath, Salt.

Placed in the centre of the Greek Cross made up of five squares, the Rose with five petals doubly affirms the quinary which brings the quartet of objectivity back to subjective unity. The human mind conceives of 'one' which is shown by the aspect of 'four' hence the idea of quintessence, the basis of all things abstractly intelligible, like the Soul in relation to the Body.

Tarot of the Magicians

The Rose, a flower with a subtle perfume, is the symbol of this mysterious entity. Just like the Pentagram which it outlines in its centre, it alludes to all that is most highly human in man. As the emblem of chivalry and mysticism of the emotions, it suits the Initiated of Love, the fervent adept of the pure Great Work of supreme self denial.

When Stanislas de Guaita decided in 1888, to reform the order of the Rosy Cross, he made a new Rosicrucian emblem. Marking the branches of the cross with the four letters of the divine tetragram יהוה, in the centre he drew a pentagram whose points in turn are marked with the name of Jehoushah יהושה, Man-god, Divine Adam, synthesized by the letter א surmounted by three dots. Squeezed between the angles of the cross are four roses with rays beaming from them. This quartet can send us to the number 20 and to the corresponding arcana in the Tarot.

The flaming star of the Freemason is related in symbolic terms to the Rose. In its centre, a letter G in silver stands out against a purple background. G signifies Geometry and Gnose, that is to say knowledge of initiation. The star appears in the evening when the glow of the setting sun has darkened; it replaces the vanished sun while waiting for the Moon to rise. Its light is discreet but penetrating for it lights up the inner aspect of things as befits the rays of the Philosopher's Star.

The letter G fits into the style of the pantacle only by its relation to the ideogram of Salt ⊖, the symbol of wisdom and discernment. Like the Gamma Γ which is a set-square, as well as the Phoenician Gimmel ד.

The Star which guides the Brother on his journeys shines no longer in the Middle Chamber, the sanctuary of disillusion where the thinker falls into absolute darkness. Set-square and compass now only reveal the measure of all vanity; everything is dead for him and in him. In the aridity of the desert, however, he comes across a branch of green which makes him discover the body of a glorious past. The wise man will give back life to the dead by gathering the spirit which animates the Master who is mysteriously resuscitated. The Master Worker of the fifteenth century whose picture we reproduce here, taken from the *Jeanne d'Arc* of Gabriel Hanotaux (page 324) represents Berneval to whom we owe the stained glass window of Saint-Owen at Rouen.

ASTROLOGY

Astrological symbolism is based on the twelve signs of the zodiac, the seven planets and the four Elements. The divisions of the Zodiac are made in threes allotted to each of the Elements.

Fire ♈ ♌ ♐   Earth ♉ ♍ ♑
Air ♊ ♎ ♒   Water ♋ ♏ ♓

The distribution of the planets is made according to the home and place of exaltation. That is why the Sun is at home in Leo and the Moon is the mistress of Cancer. The other planets enjoy two homes, a main one and a secondary one. Mars has ♈ and ♏, Venus ♉ and ♎, Mercury ♋ and ♍, Jupiter ♐ and ♌, Saturn ♑ and ♒. The signs diametrically opposed to those of the homes for the same planets mark their places of exile.

On the other hand each planet is exalted in a sign whose master welcomes him with honour. So Mars welcomes the Sun in the Ram ♈, and Venus the Moon in Taurus ♉. Mercury extols himself in Virgo ♍ which is his home, whereas Venus is extolled by Jupiter in Pisces ♓, as Jupiter is himself by the Moon in Cancer ♋; as for Mars he is happy in Capricorn ♑ in the home of Saturn, who in turn finds favour with Venus in the scales of Libra ♎.

The signs that are in opposition with those of power and joy imply downfall and sadness for the planets in question. Just as Libra ♎ precipitates the declining sun into autumn, so Scorpio ♏ is seen as being hostile to the Moon. Pisces ♓ does not suit Mercury, and Venus does not agree with Virgo ♍. The warmth of Mars is extinguished in the waters of Cancer ♋, and Jupiter does not shine in Capricorn ♑; finally Saturn suffers in the Ram where Mars is too restless and gives it no repose.

These distinctions allows us to assign a meaning to each of the signs of the zodiac. The reader will benefit from practising to do this if he is aspiring to prepare himself for divination.

The seasons and all that accompanies them are at the base of the macrocosmic symbolism of the divisions of the zodiac. On the other hand, man, the microcosm determines the meanings which are attached to the homes of the horoscope. The number 12 is applied here, not to the cycle of the year, but to the 24 hour cycle of the earth's rotation. These hours are taken in twos according to the custom of the Chaldeans who counted in double hours in their sacred poems. The sky of the nativity is divided in 12 houses the first of which starts at the exact point of the ecliptic coinciding with the Eastern horizon. The child is born under the influence of the sign of the zodiac which rises at the breaking of the cord that attached him physically to his mother.

This sign, it is true, only directs home, the other eleven coming under the rule of the rest of the divisions in the zodiac.

The twelve houses moreover each relate very ingeniously to everything that concerns the individual, hence the following attributions:

1. Life, temperament, innate tendencies. What the individual brings into the world when he is born. Vita.
2. What he has the power of making for himself by feeding himself, then by acquiring goods, wealth. Lucrum.
3. Adaptation to his environment. Formative influences. Education in the family. Brothers and sisters. Fratres.
4. The mysterious and deep intervention of atavism. Relations, Father, Genitor.
5. Products, what the individual exteriorizes. Works, speculation, children. Filii.
6. Task, materials to be put into operation. Difficulties to be overcome. Inferiors to be ruled. Attention and care required by the body. Hygiene, health. Valetudo.
7. Attention to the individuality through combining with others. Associations, struggles, arrangements. Marriage. Uxor.
8. Dematerialization, detachment, spiritualization. Decrepitude. Death. Mors.
9. Intellectuality. Study. Exploring the unknown. Search for the truth. Religion. Spiritual undertakings. Journeys. Peregrinatio.
10. Vital objective. Ambitions, career, honours, dignities. Regnum.
11. Sympathetic attachments. Friends. Amici.
12. Whatever escapes the individual and transcends him. Fatality, illness, enemies, Inimici.

The Ancient astrologers represented the twelve houses with twelve triangles framing a square. This arrangement highlights the main houses which correspond to the Ascendant 1, in the depth of the night sky 4, to the setting sun 7 and to the centre of the day sky 10. The cardinal signs of the zodiac ♈, ♋, ♎ and ♑ correspond to these houses. There is moreover analogy between the houses of the Microcosm and the relative signs of the Macrocosm. In the sketch opposite, the twelve astrological figures surround the pantacle of the accomplishment of the Great Work, following the symbolism of arcana 12.

Libra is the sign of the autumn equinox which brings the Sun into the scheme of the earth's equator, from which is shared out an equal amount of light between the two hemispheres, North and South. But the balance is achieved only to be broken; the Sun continues its descent, and the days shorten rapidly to the benefit of longer and longer nights. The constructive energies which in youth bear it triumphant over the forces of destruction, they too become stabilized only for a short period in the age of maturity which precedes decline. Great things, however, are accomplished when the organism has stopped developing and when it gives as much as it receives. To establish a balance between inner life and its exterioration, this means being certain of the harmony in the rhythm of life. Hêt, especially in its earliest form, is the letter of the life consolidated by a wise use. Two set-squares form a rectangle whose lines not meeting leave an opening for an influx of life

which circulates freely around a fixed central point. Such is the scheme of the just man whose equity gives strength even from the physiological point of view.

MYTHOLOGY

For the Initiate Isis becomes the revealer of hidden things. She waits for the disciple in front of the sanctuary where a veil masks its entrance. With both hands the Goddess makes the sign of esotericism, showing by the two fingers held down that all cannot be explained in words. What is explicable only translates the vulgar aspect of things, whose subtle beauty remains hidden. The gesture of Isis however informs us that a secret analogy allows conjecture about things on high through what we have here below, and about the invisible through the visible. What is shown can teach us about all things if we know how to understand. Giving understanding to those whose minds you nourish for comprehension is synonymous with Gnosis. Great Isis, give to your sons the light of deep discernment!

Cybele the wife of Saturn, personifies the life-giving force of our planetary globe. Thanks to her, events follow on from each other intelligently and lead towards the accomplishment of a co-ordinating and constructive work. The Goddess's crown is made up of mason-like towers which appear under a full veil, an allusion to the mysteries of the production work of things. Cybele engenders forms as indicated by the crescent Moon which seems to follow her sceptre of fertility. This insignia of command stretches above a star whose seven beams are reflected in the wheel of the cube-shaped chariot which is drawn by two tame lions. Seven is the number of harmony which is realized ideally in the fixity of the star before it is reflected in the spokes of the turning wheel, the support of materiality. The tamed lions are related to the vehemence of the energies which Nature disciplines in order to force them into a consolidated effort from which progress results.

The Elomitie goddess wearing the royal tiara corresponds to Ishtar, the great Babylonian princess the giver of vital energy. It is she who makes mortals drink of the life-giving liquid which she draws from the spring which is restrained by the slab of the sacred threshold. Only the Anounnaki, the spirits of the depths and judges of the dead who are called back to life, ever cross this threshold. In her left hand this divinity holds the ring symbolizing the uninterrupted circle of life. Nothing dies, for nothing stops, nothing ceases, everything gravitates eternally.

Ishtar is not a mother who is moved to pity by her children and avoids all trouble on their behalf; she is an educator who has, as her ideal, generations of children hardened, brave and capable of enduring the hardships of life. She is a warrior, for battle is the law of objective existence. To live, let us consent to suffer. Did not Ishtar undergo all tortures when she descended voluntarily into Hell, in order to deserve to rise again in glory among the living? Would not the soul have to show proof of endurance before being allowed to reincarnate? The Chaldeans thought that the pleasures of life are enjoyed on earth, and that nothing pleasurable awaits us after death. But the pleasures of this world are the reward of our courageous efforts in the fulfilment of our life task. Ishtar loves us in as much as we pay her honour; she cherishes the hero, but scorns the coward.

Life has charms for those who are deprived of it. Why does not the other world permanently hold back the spiritual entities which feel the need for reincarnation? Would it be forbidding in the long run? The daughters of man with their beauty entice the sons of Heaven who descend, drawn irresistibly. The magic used is attributed to the siren whose singing bewilders the listener to cause his fall into the ocean of the life of the swarming multitudes. This seductress owes her power to the changing and renewing forms like the Moon whose crescent shines on the forehead of the Goddess . . . of great ancestry and great beauty. This is the Goddess which Basile Valentin shows as she is born from the Philosopher's Sea.

Tradition gives the unicorn a white body, a red head and blue eyes. Being agile, indefatigable and proud, it escapes from the hunter who pursues it in vain, whereas a pure and spotless virgin tames the wild animal who is very willing to stretch itself out obediently at her feet.

With a unicorn at each side the Siren is no longer the seductress who causes a downfall. She is a musician who charms with her music, but her arms raised towards the sky in a gesture of adoration make of her a priestess of the art which seduces spiritually by praying the religious feeling to contribute to the expression of Beauty.

Our pantacle shows the religion which will win over a humanity which is weary of dogmatism and false revelations. Nature in the form of Isis-Ishtar, the Siren will speak again to teach us the faith that is within us, the faith which comes from the heart and from sensitivity to which all simple hearts, accessible to the qualities of aesthetics, return.

The god with the double face symbolizes the principle of performance, for whom future and past are but one. This one is stable only in the instability of perpetual changes over which the crescent Moon presides. Everything is maintained purely by ceaseless change. Things are born and reborn all the time; creation is continuous, eternal, unceasing. We participate in it by using our labour and activity. What distinguishes the Initiated person is that he takes part in the Great Work fully conscious of his actions, knowing what he is doing when he works at the execution of the unchanging Architect's plan.

Northern races are not contented by a Janus looking both forward and behind. They have represented their trinity with a revolving triangle made up of three faces. In reality their symbolism is that of Intelligence which sees in a three-fold way, discerning the 'agent' at the same time as the 'act' which it is performing and the action which it accomplishes. The agent is only such because it acts, and could not act if there were no action, but the distinction is subjective, for in reality there is tri-unity. The terms of the ternary may be seen separately for the convenience of our verbal analysis, but they are nothing without each other. The creator creating and the creation created make but one with the creative activity which is perforce permanent. This theology was that of the Druids who on this three-fold basis formed more searching concepts than those of the dogmatism belonging to our contemporary seminaries.

TAROT

When they are translated into plain ideograms, the 22 arcanas can form a symbolic alphabet which it is easy to trace onto numbered cards which the diviner manipulates by preference with a coloured and illustrated Tarot.

It is right that the instrument of divination should be as personal as possible, hence the attachment of the clairvoyants to used packs, or better still to cards which they have drawn themselves and coloured to their liking.

To the earliest 22 arcanas there have been added 56 playing cards, divided into 4 series of 14, each one distinguished by a very significative emblem. Wand, Cup, Sword and Coin do in fact make up a magic quartet in which the Wand (stick) or Sceptre corresponds to the power of command, Cup to the Dionisic ecstasy, the source of divinatory inspiration, the Sword to discernment which banishes error, and the Coin to the support which magic symbols offer to the thinker who is not unlearned in their respect.

The Sceptre has the flower of ideality at its head; as its base the Cup has a macrocosmic hexagon; the Sword leaps like a beam from its sun-like pommel which overlooks the crescent Moon on its guard; as for the Coin, it puts into a fourfold shape the ideal of the Sceptre. The possession of the four instruments confers the occult Mastery and Expertise of the Adept.

When the four letters of TARO are arranged in an oblique cross they can be read as ROTA or ATOR and can lend themselves to other Kabbalistic combinations over which there is no need to linger. We have inscribed these letters between the branches of an upright cross formed by four pentagons attached to a central octagon which contains the key of Isis, in outline close to the sign of

Tarot of the Magicians

Venus. The hook of the Taw by its shape reminds us of the up-turned triangle of receptive intellectuality, the cup which receives the water from the sky; it can also make us think of the heart which is sensitive to the truths which are felt, but could not be expressed in words.

The octagonal frame holds the faculties of divination within the wise limits of balance and logical order, by reconciling the legitimate demands of Sun-Reason with the fantastic suggestions of the Moon-Imagination. But the pentagons on the right and on the left overlap in their opposition with that of the two other pentagons. The one at the bottom is a heraldic shield with the arms of the 'fleur de lys'. As the emblem of grace, nobility and purity, this ideogram requires of the diviner a soul free from all baseness. His lack of self interest, combined with a desire to be of use to the consultant, contributes in giving lucidity to the person who in good faith, is trying to shed light into the depths of the mysterious darkness that envelops us. He will succeed in this if the Virgo of the zodiac in the upper pentagram protects him. This winged maiden grants victory to those who deserve it. She rises above the earth, but is never lost in the clouds. Overlooking reality to perceive it at its full extent, this queen of spiritual harvests is objective in her inspirations. She prevents the diviner from aiming too high and keeps him in the sphere of a wise positivism. If divination remained wise by restraining its field of operation, it would be less exposed to error and would prove itself more worthy of being taken seriously

The diviner must not profess to have an answer to everything. What discredits divination is that far more is asked of it than it can give. Let us be reasonable in our questions and its answers will not deceive us. The cross of the pentagons is the sign in which the Tarot is called to conquest. Would that we could help the subtleties of divination to defeat the dull-witted mind which can attain no higher than calculation. Calculation can be taught, so why should we not learn to divine again.

REFERENCES

1. At the moment of prediction, Guaita knew nothing of my existence. So it was not his conscious thought that could have been transmitted to the sleeping woman. The way predictions work remains a mystery. The happiest are usually only realized in part, and the most exact err on the question of time. This element escapes clairvoyants who think that what they see clearly, they judge to be near in time.

2. *Le Symbolisme Hermatique dans ses rapports avec L'Alchemie et la Franc-Maçonnerie,* a work which appeared in 1910.

3. A symbolic study by Gothe, translated and commented upon in its esotericism, a work which appeared in the editions of *Le Monde Nouveau* in 1922.

4. Out of respect for the Church the Priestess and the Pope were replaced by Juno and Jupiter in the Tarot of Besançon.

5. Eliphas Lévi, *Dogme de la Haute Magie*, page 68.

6. Eliphas Lévi, *Rituel*, page 337.

7. *Précis historique et explicatif sur les cartes à jouer,* par une Société de Bibliophiles français, Paris Crapelet 1846, page 11.

8. Paris, Georges Carré, 1889.

9. Among similar productions of collective inspiration, the Catholic liturgy and the rituals of the three fundamental ranks of Freemasonry should be mentioned.

10. Through Germa Baillière he published *Dogme et Ritual de la Haute Magie* 1st edition 1856, 2nd edition 1861.

    Histoire de la Magie with a clear analysis of its procedures, rites and mysteries, 1860.

    La Clef des Grand Mystéres, following Henoch, Abraham, Hermes Trismègiste and Salomon, 1861.

    La Science des Esprits 1865. Chamel, moreover, published two posthumous works of Eliphas Lévi: *Le Livre des Splendeurs*, 1894 and *Le Grand Arcane* or *L'Occultisme Dévoilé*, which appeared in its second edition with Chacornac in 1921.

    Emile Nourri also had published in 1920 *Les Mystères de la Kabbale* or *L'Harmonie occulte des deux Testaments*.

11. Guillaume Postel (1510–1581) made two voyages in the East and brought back from there a sort of universal knowledge. In the *Clef des choses cachées* (Clavis absonditorum, 1546, in-16), he relates, TARO, ROTA, or ATOR of the Tetragram

12. The Marquis Claude de Saint-Martin known as the 'Unknown Philosopher' (1743–1803), the author of many works relating on one hand to the teaching of Martinez Pasqulis, his initiator, and on the other to the principles developed by Jacob Boehmr (1575–1625).

13. Swedenborg (1688–1772) a Swedish Mystic had great visions whose importance he himself exaggerated.

14. The reader is asked to place in front of him in the order indicated the series of the twenty-two arcanas taken from the Tarot pack or separately like the plates which accompany this work.

15. *Les Harmonies de l'Etre révélées par les nombres.* Page 223.

16. This exercise makes the imagination supple and prepares it for grasping the relationships between the pictures which it comes across. It is impossible to make the Tarot speak as long as the diviner has not assimilated the language of symbols. These symbols do not speak of their own accord, hence the necessity of interrogating them methodically. In this respect there is nothing more rewarding than the discipline of the tetrads as set out here.

17. These indications, like those that follow, are addressed to the reader who *wants to work*. They will spare him fumbling, if he meditates and searches by comparing the pictures, so that their aspect, together with the evocative power of the words should stimulate his thought. It is a question here of mental activity similar to that which the study of algebra or geometry requires. To read out of simple curiosity, without putting anything of oneself into it will not suffice here.

18. See the reproduction in Camille Flammarion, *Les Etoiles*, page 310.

19. Jenson, *Kosmologie der Babylonier,* pages 310 to 320.

20. The 22 letters are divided into 'mothers' (three of the four Elements), 7 doubles (7 planets) and twelve singles (signs of the Zodiac).

Mothers	א Air (Mercury of the Alchemists ☿)	
	מ Water (Salt ⊖)	
	ש Fire (Sulphur 🜍)	
Doubles	ב Sun ☉	ר Mercury ☿
	פ Saturn ♄	ג Mars ♂
	ד Venus ♀	כ Moon ☽
	ר Jupiter ♃	
Singles	ה Ram ♈	ח Crab ♋
	ל Scales ♎	ע Goat ♑
	ו Bull ♉	ט Lion ♌
	ז Scorpion ♏	צ Watercarrier ♒
	י Twins ♊	י Virgin ♍
	ס Arrow-Bearer ♐	ק Fish ♐

21. The crayfish of the 18th key is red, precisely to indicate its effrey colour.

22. The *Geometry* of Baldini's cards (see farther back, pages 24 & 25) trace the 3 fundamental figures of hermetic ideography as our copy shows, taken from the original in the Bibliothèque Nationale.

23. In the pictures of Alchemist signs, one finds, however, as a symbol of vinegar: nothing justifies this derogation to the logic of ideography.
24. Dom Antoine-Joseph Pernety, a Benedictine monk of the congregation of Saint-Maur, 'Dictionaaire Mytho-Hermetique', Paris 1785, on the word Alun, page 27.
25. Paul Dhorme. — Choix de textes religieux assyre-babyloniens, Paris. J. Galbalda. 1917.
26. *Histoire de l'Art Egyptien* p. 99 printed by Maspero. *Histoire Ancienne des Peuples de l'Orient Classique.*
27. This 'light' through which the occultists swear is comparable to the phosphorescent mist which would envelope the planet and stir the imagination of lucid subjects. It has been symbolized by the serpent Python whom Apollo (Reason) transfixes with his arrows. If he shows himself worthy, the great priestess will draw aside for him a second veil, to allow him to read in her face and especially in her eyes. The one in whom the goddess confides will not be dupe of any mirage, for he will possess the secret of things, by the fact that he will have practised 'imagining correctly'.
28. The oblique cross ✕ (crossing of swords) symbolizes a hostile encounter, a shock which can result in sparks; in opposition to this is the straight cross ✚ , indicative of fertile union, marriage or connection.
29. See the collections in the Bibliothèque Nationale. This same pack puts a sphinx next to the Pope (arcana 5).
30. According to the Chaldeans, this ethereal ocean enveloped the Universe and the faithful of Ea, the god of life-giving Waters, drew their inspiration from it, like Utnapishtim, the hero of the flood, the Babylonian Noah.
31. See above pages 76–78, the interpretation of the Alchemist signs Rock Salt ♃ and Antimony ♁.
32. The Anounnaki, the infernal spirits who judge the dead and shape the destiny of the living, sit too on cubes of gold in the centre of the Chaldean hell.
33. See page 28.
34. Esotericism explodes all familiar ideas. The one god is both the father, the husband and the son of the great Goddess. One must accept the strangeness of the symbols which express themselves in their own way and which constantly appeal to our penetration of mind. Their contradictions pose enigmas to which one has to find the clue. If we let ourselves become discouraged then we will never be initiated.
35. ☉ Pride, Vanity, ♓ Sloth, ☿ Envy, ♂ Anger, ♀ Lust, ♃ Greed, ♄ Avarice.
36. The Freemasons called themselves 'free and good living' because they claim that by controlling their passions they are free from being dominated by them. Their liberty results in the moral discipline which they have imposed upon themselves. They obey the Pope of the Tarot in as much as the latter represents in each of us the enlightened conscience.
37. Just by considering the somewhat frightening face of the Emperor and the open expression of the Pope, one might think that the Tarot has inverted the order of the Sephiroth, the fourth Grace, Pity seeming to be more in harmony with the character in arcana 5 than with arcana 4, destined to inspire fear through its severity. In reality the doctrine of the Sephiroth intends 'kindness which spreads life' (C'hesed) 'severity which rules given life' (Geburah) has a reciprocal moderating influence upon each other, hence the deliberate contrast of expressions between the two sovereigns, one temporal, the other spiritual, and the general import of arcanas 4 and 5.
38. See page 46.
39. In his *Dogme et Rituel de la Haute Magie* Eliphas Lévi says about arcana 7 'This hieroglyph is the most beautiful, perhaps, and the most complete of all those that make up the key of the Tarot.' On the triumphant driver's shoulders the famous occultist sees 'Urim and Thumin of the sovereign sacrificial rites depicted by two crescents of the moon in Gedulah and in Geburah'.
40. The double Sphinx has been replaced by horses by Eliphas Lévi. The ancient Tarots seem to be inspired by the Platonic harness, in which the wild horse is trying to drag along the reasonable horse.
41. *L'Azoth ou le moyen de faire l'or caché des Philosophes* by Brother Basile Valentin, Paris, 1660, 2nd part.
42. See the theory of the Septenary as set out in page 32.
43. Arcana 8 relates to perpetual motion, such as the functioning of the Universe brings about; in which all forces act with alternating and compensatory movements, as if it were a game of double springs of equal strength—one is stretched while the other is relaxed, and this will become taut again when the other is relaxed. What is enigmatic in the human mechanism is accomplished in the work of the cosmos in which nothing is lost, thanks to the principle of the conservation of energy.
44. See page 15.
45. Emile Burnouf, *Le Vase Sacré et ce qu'il contient dans 'Inde, la Perse, la Grèce et dans l'Eglise chrétienne*, page 14.
46. One can see the red outer rim as engendering compressing vibration which the expansive vibrations of the blue inner rim resist. (See the two agents described under the names of Hereb and Ionah in *La clef de la magie noire* by Stanislas Guaita, in the chapter entitled 'L'équilibre et son agent'.
47. The yellow of the head and the clothes of Hermanubis is related to the materialized light, otherwise called condensed or fixed.
48. See page 13.
49. Agni, the fire of Vedic sacrifice is kept burning thanks to the branches cut from the tree of universal life. (See Emile Burnouf, *Le Vase Sacré et ce qu'il contient dans l'Inde, la Perse, la Grèce et dans l'Eglise Chrétienne*, page 15.)

50. See above, Chapter 3, page 29.

51. The nourishing reserves of vital fire correspond to the Radical Damp of the Hermetists.

52. See arcana 13.

53. The Emperor (4) has already been called Prince of the World (see page 75) but he is distinguishable from the Devil because of the legitimacy of his position. He reigns through Divine will, over all that has bodily form, whereas the Devil figures as the usurper, he is a potentate whose joke we should throw off.

54. See O. Wirth *Le Poeme d'Ishtar, mythe babylonien interprété dans son ésotérisme,* Collection due Symbolisme.

55. See A. Siouville *Le Prince de ce Monde et le Péché Originel Introduction*, page IX, Collection du Symbolisme.

56. The sign ☿ unites the masculine sun ☉ with the feminine moon ☽.

57. See the table of the evolution of the forms of the Hebrew alphabet page 54.

58. The symbolism of Jachin and Boaz is indicated above pages 12, 44, 51. The Tower struck by lightning (16) is related to Jachin when seen by itself, thus to the energies which the individual draws from himself. Now, nothing durable is founded without the consolidating and preserving Force whose reservoir is in Boaz. The two pillars stand before the Temple, a permanent edifice which is not a temporary shelter like the Tower inspired by male egotism disregarding the needs of feminity.

59. The Tower of Babylon was made up of seven superimposed cubes, for creation is subject to the law of the septenary. There are seven notes in the scale of universal harmony, a harmony which is reflected in man, in the microcosmic world. The holy building of Babylon paid homage to the macrocosm, whereas the microcosm alone is concerned in the trembling building of arcana 16.

60. See page 54 the table of the successive changes in the Hebrew alphabet.

61. See our *Poem d'Ishtar.*

62. The Rosicrucian symbolism could not be set out here with the developments it includes. There is material there for a whole treatise.

63. Venus was not seen by the Greeks as the goddess of Life who starts with the awakening. They have entrusted to Mercury the task of stimulating our activity by assigning to him the cock, the announcer of dawn.

64. See *Epopée de Guilgamès* a Chaldean poem, more than five thousand years old, chant X. In this story of the 'Serpent Vert' which we have translated and edited, (Editions du Mond, 1923) Goethe imagines a park of sterile tree with lush foliage, but deprived of flowers and fruit. There stands the beautiful Lilia, a perfect beauty whose touch is fatal.

65. See Isaac Myer *Scarabs* New York 1894.

66. See page 104 where the son of the spirit of Jove, which is considered to be the highest, is likened to the active principle of the soul, which is exteriorized to accomplish the heights of psychic power.

67. The first Chaldean divinities are born of double nature, half male, half female. Two serpent shaped entities therefore give first life to the universal substance; these are the two serpents of Hermetism, the generators of life. They figure in the Caduceus as well as in the ideogram of the Cancer of the zodiac. The cult of the serpent, so widespread in very early times is explained by the cosmogonic role in primitive times attributed to gods who had the form of this animal.

68. Poem of Ishtar.

69. The number 16 seems to have been that of the letters of a very early alphabet. One may wonder whether the figures in geomancy are foreign to the development of the characters of our writing.

70. See page 27.

71. Through the help and care of the initiated printer George Poirel.

72. In French, *diviner* popularly means 'to guess'.

WIRTH AND WIRTH-INSPIRED DECKS

Many deck creators have either recreated the Wirth deck or included "touches of Wirth" in their own creations. Wirth himself drew from three of Eliphas Lévi's four surviving Tarot illustrations (the Chariot, Wheel of Fortune and Devil, but not the World). He also took several elements that Paul Christian (Jean Baptiste Pitois) described in *The History and Practice of Magic* (1870). In turn, the Waite-Smith deck utilizes some of these occult symbols.

In determining whether a deck has traces of Wirth, here are the most obvious characteristics (in addition to the Lévi designs) to look for:

- A red tulip in various states of bloom appears prominently on the following cards: the Magician, the Emperor, Temperance, and the Fool. Additionally, a butterfly lights on a red rose in the Star, and there's a white lily on the Empress.

- The objects on the Magician's table are a large-sized coin (or three coins), sword and chalice. In his left hand he holds a double-headed wand that has red and blue tips; he touches the coin with his right hand.

- The Priestess holds two keys and a partly opened book (sometimes with a yin-yang symbol on the cover); a crescent tops her papal crown.

- The Hermit holds a bamboo-like staff with seven nodal bands along it. An erect serpent with a forked tongue is coiled on the path in front of him.

- A lynx bites the leg of a bearded Fool, who sports a bulbous, multi-colored turban, while a crocodile lurks behind a fallen column.

While Wirth never created a Minor Arcana, others, in some cases, have added suit cards.

By Wirth:

Les 22 Arcanes du Tarot Kabbalistique (Paris: G. Poirel, 1889). B&W with stencilled color in 350 copies.

Le Tarot: Des Imagiers du Moyen-Age: Restitvé dans l'esprit de son symbolisme par Oswald Wirth (Paris: Le Symbolisme, 1926). Art Nouveau style cards in color with metallic gold ink in a portfolio of 11 plates.

Close Replicas:

Cards to accompany Oswald Wirth's *Le Tarot des Imagiers du Moyen Age* (new, revised edition: Paris: Claude Tchou, 1966, 1978). 22 cards in color with metallic copper ink, redrawn by Michel Simeon.

Cards to accompany Elisabeth Haich's book *Tarot*; English translation: *The Wisdom of the Tarot* (Stuttgart: J. Fink Verlag, 1969 and London: George Allen and Unwin, 1975). 22 cards in color, redrawn.

Oswald Wirth Tarot Deck (New York: USGames, 1976). 78-card color deck based on the new pictures by Michel Simeon (see above).

Wirth Tarot (Munich: Drei Eichen Verlag, 1986). 22-card replica of the 1926 art nouveau edition in color with metallic gold on cream card stock.

Le Tarot de Oswald Wirth (Québec: Editions de L'Aigle, Sherbrooke, 1997, 1998, 2001). 22-card replica of the 1926 art nouveau edition in color with metallic gold.

Adaptations:

Knapp-Hall Tarot (Los Angeles: Philosophical Research Society, 1929, 1934, 1981 and Stamford CT: US Games, 1985). 78-card deck by J. Augustus Knapp.

Lasenic Tarot; Lasenikuv Tarot (1938; republished Prague: Trigon, 1995, 2002). 78-card deck by Pierre de Lasenic (aka, Petr Kouhout), illustrated by Vladislav Kuzel.

Tarot Ideographic du Kebek (Ottowa: Editions de Mortagne, 1979). 22-card deck by Yves Paquin.

Le Tarot d'Argolance (France: Atelier d'Art, 1983, 1984). 22-card deck by Pierrick Pinot.

Les 22 Lames du Tarot (Paris: Editions Justine, 1986). 22-card deck by Marguerite de Surany & Elisabeth de Ribes-Van der Kemp.

Tarocchi Ermetici (Torino: Lo Scarabeo, 1989, 1995). 22-card deck by Sergio Toppi.

Radical Wirth (Woodstock: soul-guidance.com, c. 1990). 22-card deck by Carol Herzer with an imaginative recoloring of Simeon/Tchou version.

Kazanlár Tarot (Budapest, 1992; reprinted Stamford: USGames, 1996). 78-card deck by Kazanlár Ámin Emil and Kassák Kiadó.

Zanoni Tarot (Ojai: Runinga Press, 1993). 22-card deck by Roger Zanoni.

Universal Wirth (Torino: Lo Scarabeo, 2007). 78-card deck by Stefano Palumbo & Giordano Berti.

TO OUR READERS

The 1889 Wirth Deck

1 | LE BATELEUR | א

2 | LA PAPESSE | ב

3 | L'IMPERATRICE | ג

4 · L'EMPEREUR

5 · LE PAPE

6 · L'AMOUREUX

7 — LE CHARIOT

8 — LA JUSTICE

9 — L'ERMITE

10 — LA ROUE DE FORTUNE

11 — LA FORCE

12 — LE PENDU

13 LA MORT

14 LA TEMPERANCE

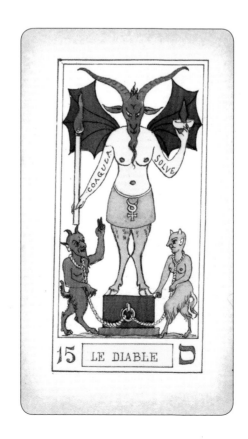

15 LE DIABLE

16 · LE FEU DU CIEL.

17 · LES ETOILES

18 · LA LUNE.

19 | LE SOLEIL | ק

20 | LE JUGEMENT | ר

21 | LE MONDE | ת

LE FOU